# Questions and Answers 1953

"Wednesday Class"

# The Mother

# Questions and Answers 1953

Sri Aurobindo Ashram, Pondicherry

First edition 1976
Second edition 1998

© Sri Aurobindo Ashram Trust 1998
Published by Sri Aurobindo Ashram Publication Department
Printed at Sri Aurobindo Ashram Press, Pondicherry-2, India
**PRINTED IN INDIA**

# *Publisher's Note*

This volume contains the Mother's talks to the students, teachers and sadhaks of the Sri Aurobindo Ashram in her Wednesday classes of 1953. They were held in the early evening at the Ashram Playground. The Mother began each class by reading out to the group a passage from one of her works — most are from her 1929 conversations — and then commenting or answering questions on it.

All these talks were in French and appear here in translation. The first eight talks were noted down by disciples, the rest were tape-recorded. They were first serialised in the quarterly *Bulletin of Sri Aurobindo International Centre of Education* from August 1967 to February 1973, then published in 1976 as Volume 5 of the Collected Works of the Mother. The present text is identical to that of 1976, except for a few minor corrections.

# Contents

| | | |
|---|---|---|
| 18 March | Rare significant moments: contact with the psychic | 1 |
| | "Families of beings": why people meet to collaborate | 2 |
| | Lady visitor to the Ashram: external motives are pretexts for the psychic | 3 |
| 25 March | Using the Divine as a cloak to hide desires | 5 |
| | Sincerity: difficult but effective | 5 |
| | The true flame | 7 |
| 1 April | Ambition: a canker | 8 |
| | "Homogeneity in our being" and different personalities | 8 |
| | Signpost or psychic mirror | 9 |
| 8 April | Service to humanity and giving to the Divine | 12 |
| | What do I call 'myself'? | 17 |
| | Desires and their formations | 18 |
| | The power of thought, of prayer | 19 |
| | "The victory you win" a gain for the whole world | 20 |
| 15 April | Pulling the divine forces | 21 |
| | Insincerity, its own punishment | 21 |
| | "Basis of equanimity" | 22 |
| 22 April | Sleep and dreams: quietening the mind | 24 |
| 29 April | Organising one's dream | 26 |
| | Wounds in the vital being and illness | 27 |
| | Symbolism of dreams | 27 |
| | Personal dream-imagery | 28 |
| | Foolishness and vanity | 29 |
| | Religions, truth, consciousness | 30 |
| 6 May | Psychic memory | 32 |
| | Rebirth: stories | 34 |
| | Automatic-writing, spirit-communication | 35 |

# Contents

|  |  |  |
|---|---|---|
|  | Dreams | 36 |
|  | Contact with the Divine: the key to everything | 39 |
| 13 May | Pseudo-Meditation | 41 |
|  | Escapism and changing the nature | 43 |
|  | True meditation, true humility | 44 |
|  | Will, concentration, effort: active surrender | 46 |
|  | Being perfect instruments; progress | 47 |
|  | Boredom | 50 |
| 20 May | Offering and surrender | 52 |
|  | Mistakes and insincerity | 54 |
|  | The flame of aspiration, self-giving | 55 |
|  | The physical being as a tool of another Power | 55 |
|  | Story of a Sufi mystic, a musician | 57 |
|  | Transformation of the body: three hundred years | 58 |
|  | Replacing body-organs by centres of energy | 59 |
|  | Collaboration in the Divine's work | 62 |
|  | Living in the true consciousness; stepping back | 64 |
|  | Appendix |  |
|  | Sri Aurobindo's talk with a French scientist disciple | 66 |
| 27 May | Music: its origin and type | 68 |
|  | Inspiration and technique | 69 |
|  | Individualisation, separation, inconscience | 70 |
|  | The remedy: to become conscious again | 72 |
|  | All touch the same Thing | 72 |
|  | Understanding others: (beyond words) | 73 |
|  | Sources of music; genius | 74 |
|  | Indian and European music | 76 |
|  | Pure perception of the Divine and mental formations | 78 |
|  | Explaining things: the entire universe needed | 80 |
|  | The Divine is the only existence | 81 |
|  | Value of Art | 82 |
|  | Work and realisation | 83 |
| 3 June | Determinism and freedom | 85 |
|  | Formations from different planes | 86 |
|  | Prayer changes the determined course of things | 88 |
|  | Nature devises sense of freedom to make us act | 89 |

# Contents

| | | |
|---|---|---|
| | The Divine Grace and Karma | 90 |
| | Aspiration and prayer have a magical power | 92 |
| 10 June | Attacks of adverse forces and man's response | 93 |
| | Cases of possession; refusal to change | 96 |
| | The asura of falsehood: "Lord of the Nations" | 97 |
| | Beings of the vital plane | 98 |
| | Man will transform his earth | 99 |
| | True function of the mind and vital | 100 |
| | Discerning hostile attacks: sincerity, self-observation | 101 |
| | On learning: understanding | 103 |
| | On teaching: preparing courses, method of education | 105 |
| 17 June | Function of the intellect: ideas and thought-forms | 107 |
| | Cause of death | 111 |
| | Growth in perfection | 111 |
| 24 June | Power of the vital | 116 |
| | Cause and cure of fear | 117 |
| | Body's instinct | 118 |
| | On laziness and work | 119 |
| | Illness, its causes and cure | 121 |
| | Concentrating to gain time | 124 |
| | Work at school: organising the mind | 126 |
| | Science and art | 127 |
| 1 July | Paradise, purgatory, eternal hell | 129 |
| | Imagination, a form-maker | 131 |
| | Power of good formations; healing | 132 |
| | After death, where? Unifying the being | 133 |
| | "Spirits" of death and of fire | 135 |
| | "Consenting" to die | 137 |
| 8 July | Prayer and aspiration | 139 |
| | Ill-will: a bad thought is a bad act | 143 |
| | Cause and remedy of evil | 145 |
| | Animals; vital origin of the insect species | 147 |
| | Desire to devour, an expression of "love" | 149 |
| | Instinct; the consciousness in Nature | 150 |
| | Widening the consciousness | 151 |

# Contents

| | | |
|---|---|---|
| 15 July | Superstitions | 153 |
| | Religious rules and hygiene | 154 |
| | Discerning the adverse forces; their attacks | 155 |
| | Sincere aspiration and trials | 157 |
| | Mental conceptions imposed on the Divine | 158 |
| | The hold of the hostile forces upon money-power | 158 |
| | Giving money for the Divine's work | 159 |
| | God and His creation | 161 |
| 22 July | Protection prevents adverse forces, accidents, etc. | 165 |
| | Fear brings illness, accidents | 166 |
| | Mental, vital, physical fear | 167 |
| | Taking every trial as a proof of the Grace | 168 |
| | Illness: moral condition more important | 170 |
| | Illness: causes: disequilibrium | 171 |
| | Organic and functional imbalance | 171 |
| | Equilibrium in all parts of the being necessary | 175 |
| | Lack of receptivity — "the grain of sand" | 175 |
| | Finding the inner causes of illness, not its microbe | 177 |
| | External causes of illness: contagious vibrations, etc. | 177 |
| | Attacks; black magic | 178 |
| | Small vital entities in the earth-atmosphere | 179 |
| | Origin of microbes: forces of disintegration | 180 |
| | Epidemic in Japan | 180 |
| | Vampires | 182 |
| | Curing illness | 183 |
| | Spiritual purification | 185 |
| | Trust in life: children | 186 |
| 29 July | Events on different planes | 187 |
| | "India is free": Mother's pre-vision | 188 |
| | Possibilities; changing events; story of premonitory dream | 189 |
| | Degrees of change possible; intervention | 191 |
| | To understand truly needs a universal consciousness | 192 |
| | "Individual initiative" | 194 |
| | Projecting yourself on a screen and observing, organising | 197 |
| | "Know thyself"; learning, self-discovery | 199 |

## Contents

|  |  |  |
|---|---|---|
| | The reason for existence; being master of one's destiny | 201 |
| 5 August | Progress of the psychic being; rebirth | 203 |
| | Progress of those not conscious of their psychic | 204 |
| | Manifestation and progress | 205 |
| | Inspiration; receptivity; exchange | 206 |
| | Progress of mind, vital, physical | 208 |
| | Mind justifies everything; the psychic knows | 210 |
| | Will and impulse "The last time I am doing it" | 211 |
| | Impulse and its expression in action | 212 |
| | Incarnation of the psychic being | 213 |
| | Psychic growth; Karma | 215 |
| 12 August | Knowing people through self-identification | 217 |
| | Methods of knowledge; concentration; passing through | 218 |
| | Widening the consciousness; progress | 219 |
| | Phenomena of self-identification; Paris theatre story | 221 |
| | Knowing the Divine: identification, the only way | 223 |
| | Concentration, one-pointedness | 224 |
| | In Nature all possibilities exist; no two things alike | 224 |
| 19 August | Aspiration in trees and animals | 227 |
| | The Presence in all things | 228 |
| | Stones can accumulate forces; their use | 228 |
| | Exchange: wish to get, acquire, due to limitation | 231 |
| | The more one gives, the more one grows | 232 |
| | Instinct to destroy and spoil due to influence of adverse forces | 232 |
| | Being a true hero | 233 |
| | Faith in the Grace makes the return to Light easy | 234 |
| 26 August | Source of Love | 235 |
| | True love and its deformations | 237 |
| | Love of animals for men | 238 |
| | Psychic consciousness; intelligence and calculation | 240 |
| | "Love" in flowers, crystals, animals | 241 |
| 2 September | Religion and the spiritual life | 244 |
| | Castes | 245 |

## Contents

|  |  |  |
|---|---|---|
|  | Evolutionary movement; history of civilisations | 247 |
|  | Nature's play; her collaboration required | 248 |
| 9 September | Divine Force chooses its instrument | 251 |
|  | Progress of the mind and vital | 252 |
|  | Converting the vital | 253 |
|  | Contact with the psychic; heroes | 254 |
|  | The vital, an all-powerful instrument | 255 |
|  | Depression; the vital as source of most wrong movements | 256 |
|  | The vital's power | 257 |
| 16 September | Receptivity of the body | 259 |
|  | Fixity in physical world | 259 |
|  | After death certain developed faculties remain in the earth-atmosphere | 260 |
|  | The psychic's new birth; fusing with Overmind being | 263 |
|  | Progress and battle; Titanic forces | 265 |
|  | Yogic force prevents rigidity of the body | 266 |
|  | Growth of consciousness: rebirth | 267 |
|  | Consciousness and memory | 268 |
|  | Resistance and receptivity | 269 |
|  | You are all in a sea of tremendous vibrations | 269 |
| 23 September | The physical world, a symbol of universal movements | 271 |
|  | Illness in animals | 272 |
|  | The universe: a serpent biting its tail | 274 |
|  | The earth, the concentrated symbol of the universe | 274 |
|  | "Evil Persona" | 275 |
|  | Mother's experience of the luminous earth | 276 |
| 30 September | Earth-memory | 277 |
|  | The rule of the Overmind and the Supermind | 282 |
|  | Sri Aurobindo's yoga begins where others end | 283 |
|  | Men with realisation often fixed and unplastic | 284 |
|  | Children as malleable stuff for transformation | 286 |
|  | To be a child all one's life | 287 |
|  | Children and other people in the Ashram | 287 |
|  | Remembrance and memory | 289 |

# Contents

| | | |
|---|---|---|
| 7 October | Consciousness of a complete cure | 291 |
| | Mental, vital, physical, spiritual aspiration | 292 |
| | Body-consciousness | 293 |
| | Body's sure instinct | 294 |
| | Trust in life | 296 |
| | Dynamic faith | 297 |
| | Why are some children here in the Ashram | 298 |
| | Learning to know others by identity | 299 |
| | Responsible people: governments, teachers | 299 |
| | Supermind's action: transformation | 300 |
| | To know oneself: one's field of work | 302 |
| | Solidarity; individual and collective progress | 303 |
| | Descent of hostile vital forces and its effect | 305 |
| 14 October | "Formateurs" taking part in creation of the world | 307 |
| | Evil as a disorder; division from the Divine; free choice | 308 |
| | Understanding the universe "All is He" God and creation | 310 |
| | Identification with the Divine: problems disappear | 311 |
| | Refusing collective suggestions; the fear of death | 312 |
| | Remedies for the fear of death | 314 |
| | Psychic being's sense of immortality; conquering death | 316 |
| | Fear attracts the thing feared | 317 |
| | Fear contagious; the mystic's remedy | 318 |
| 21 October | "Artists": stained-glass windows | 320 |
| | Expressing the Divine in art and other activities | 321 |
| | Relation with the Divine | 322 |
| | On the Ramayana and Mahabharata | 323 |
| | Japanese gardens | 324 |
| | Buddhism of the South and the North | 325 |
| | Ravana and Sita; the Asura's choice | 327 |
| | Sense of beauty, artistic taste varies | 329 |
| | To know true beauty rise above all form | 330 |
| 28 October | True art; realisation of divine beauty | 331 |
| | Evolution moves in spirals; modern art | 332 |
| | Universal progress; spherical spirals; Nature's "plan" | 333 |

## Contents

|  |  |  |
|---|---|---|
| | Art and commercialism; fatuity | 336 |
| | The "mushroom species" and true art | 338 |
| | Art in India | 340 |
| | Nature's huge cauldron | 343 |
| 4 November | On the "sphere with spirals" | 344 |
| | Sacrifice | 346 |
| | Feeling the Divine Presence; man a moralist, not the Divine | 347 |
| | Sincere aspiration for the divine life and moral merit | 348 |
| | Bargaining and "sacrifice" | 349 |
| | True *raison d'être* of life: to become aware of the Divine | 350 |
| 11 November | Readings from *Quelques Paroles*: the aim to be achieved | 351 |
| | The seventh creation: "of Equilibrium" | 352 |
| | "The eternal word": the spiritual programme worked out by Mother | 353 |
| | The deformations of truth in human expression (generosity and avarice) | 356 |
| | Money: a force; "the middle path" | 357 |
| 18 November | The mind or vital, if organised around the psychic, continue in the next life | 358 |
| | Nature's progress: constant and slow changes | 359 |
| | Justice (determinism) and Divine Grace | 360 |
| | Man learns through past experiments | 363 |
| | The intervention of the Grace | 366 |
| | Faith | 366 |
| | The idea of indispensable needs | 367 |
| 25 November | Smiling at an enemy | 369 |
| | Trust in the Divine and receptivity; "bargaining" | 370 |
| | Sincerity and the Divine's help | 371 |
| | Story of Creation (old tradition) | 371 |
| | The first four emanations, their opposites, and the gods | 371 |
| | World of freedom of choice | 373 |
| | The Asuras; their conversion | 374 |

# Contents

|  |  |  |
|---|---|---|
|  | Stalin and Hitler | 376 |
|  | Ravana; dissolution of the Asuras | 378 |
| 9 December | Spiritual ego | 382 |
|  | Entities behind the forces of Nature | 383 |
|  | Radha's Prayer; all is divine | 384 |
|  | Suffering and bliss; vibrations and reactions | 385 |
|  | "One is surrounded by what one thinks about" | 385 |
|  | The sacrifice of the Divine Mother; of incarnations | 387 |
|  | Questions on *Savitri* | 388 |
| 16 December | Methods of identification and self-finding | 391 |
|  | Aim of life | 391 |
|  | Psychic guides, organises circumstances | 393 |
|  | "Rest in action"; quiet faith; knowing how to wait | 395 |
| 23 December | Knowledge and the mind | 397 |
|  | Concentration: its power | 398 |
|  | Conscious contact between different parts of the being | 398 |
|  | Uneducated people with gift of vision | 400 |
|  | Illness: disequilibrium | 401 |
|  | Mind and body; mental formations that cure | 402 |
|  | Accidents: moment of choice | 402 |
|  | Character, awakened consciousness, and averting danger | 404 |
|  | Collective accidents: mixed atmosphere | 405 |
|  | Bringers of bad luck | 407 |
| 30 December | Children: inner sensitivity; influenced by forces | 409 |
|  | Psychic being choosing its next birth | 411 |
|  | Wickedness in children; its causes | 411 |
|  | Consciousness of parents at the moment of conception | 412 |
|  | Tamas and need of excitement | 413 |
|  | Education in the Ashram School | 414 |
|  | Ashram children | 416 |
|  | "let your acts speak for you" | 417 |

# 18 March 1953

> *"We are conscious of only an insignificant portion of our being."*
>
> Questions and Answers 1929 (7 April)

*What are these insignificant parts of our being?*

Almost all of them.

There are very few things which are not insignificant; all your ordinary reactions, ordinary thoughts, sensations, actions, movements, — all this is very insignificant. It is only at times, when there is a flash of the higher consciousness through the psychic, an opening into something else, a contact with the psychic being (which may last for a second), at that moment, it is not insignificant. Otherwise, all the rest is repeated in millions and millions of copies. Your way of seeing, acting, all your reactions, thoughts, feelings, all that is ordinary. And you believe you are extraordinary, particularly when you are seized by extraordinary sensations and feelings, those that you consider extraordinary — you believe you are lifted higher, nearing something superhuman; but you are quite mistaken. It is nothing but an ordinary state, deplorably ordinary. You must enter deeper, try to see within yourself if you want to find something which is not insignificant.

*You have said that in a previous life we were together; but if we had not done Yoga, couldn't we have met all the same?*

Not necessarily.

I remember the circumstances in which I said that; it was to a lady who had come here and asked me how it was that she had come here.... This is true in a general way; when those born scattered over the world at great distances from one another are driven by circumstances or by an impulsion to come and gather here, it is almost always because they have met in one life or another (not all in the same life) and because their psychic being has felt that they belonged to the same family; so they have taken an inner vow to continue to act together and collaborate. That is why even though they are born far from one another, there is something which compels them to come together; it is the psychic being, the psychic consciousness that is behind. And only to the extent the psychic consciousness is strong enough to order and organise the circumstances or the life, that is, strong enough not to allow itself to be opposed by outside forces, outside life movements, can people meet.

It is profoundly true in reality; there are large "families of beings" who work for the same cause, who have gathered in more or less large numbers and who come in groups as it were. It is as though at certain times there were awakenings in the psychic world, as though lots of little sleeping children were being called to wake up: "It is time, quick, quick, go down!" And they hurry down. And sometimes they do not drop at the same place, they are dispersed, yet there is something within which troubles them, pushes them; for one reason or another they are drawn close and that brings them together. But it is something deep in the being, something that is not at all on the surface; otherwise, even if people met they would not perhaps become aware of the bond. People meet and recognise each other only to the extent they become conscious of their psychic being, obey their psychic being, are guided by it; otherwise there is all that comes in to oppose it, all that veils, all that stupefies, all those obstacles to prevent you from finding yourself in your depths and being able to collaborate truly in the work. You are tossed about by the forces of Nature.

There is only one solution, to find your psychic being and

## 18 March 1953

once it is found to cling to it desperately, to let it guide you step by step whatever be the obstacle. That is the only solution.

All this I did not write but I explained it to that lady. She had put to me the question: "How did I happen to come here?" I told her that it was certainly not for reasons of the external consciousness, it was something in her inner being that had pushed her. Only the awakening was not strong enough to overcome all the rest and she returned to the ordinary life for very ordinary reasons of living.

Outwardly, it was a funny thing that had made her come here. She was a young woman like others, she had been betrothed but not married; the man had broken off. She was very unhappy, had wept much and that had spoiled her pretty face, dug wrinkles there. And when the heavy grief had gone, she was no longer so pretty. So she was extremely vexed; she consulted people whose profession it is to make you look pretty. They advised her paraffin injections in the face: "After that, you don't have wrinkles any longer!" She was injected with grease; and instead of the desired effect, she had greasy lumps here and there. She was in despair, for she was uglier than ever. Then she met a charlatan who told her that in England there was no means of restoring her pretty face: "Go to India, there are great Yogis there who will do it for you!" That is why she had come here. The very first thing she told me was: "You see how my face is ruined, can you restore my pretty looks?" I said no! Then she started putting me questions on Yoga and she was moved. That day she told me: "I came to India to get rid of my wrinkles; now what you tell me interests me. But then why did I come? This is not the true motive that made me come here." I explained to her that there was something other than her external being and that it was her psychic being which had led her here. External motives are simply pretexts used by the psychic to realise itself.

But she was quite a wonderful person! In the beginning she had taken an attitude of benevolence and goodwill towards everything and everybody, even the worst scamp; she saw only the good side. Then as she stayed on, her consciousness developed; after a time, she began to see people as they were. So, one day she told me: "Formerly, when I was unconscious, I thought that everybody was good, people seemed to be so nice! Why did you make me conscious?" I answered her: "Do not stop on the way. Go a little further."

Once one has begun Yoga, it is better to go to the end.

# 25 March 1953

> *You have said: "You must be vigilant and see that you do not use the Divine as a cloak for the satisfaction of your desires."*
>
> Questions and Answers 1929 (14 April)

Many people accept certain theories, some of which are very convenient, and they say, "Everything is the result of the divine Will"; others say, "The Divine is everywhere and in everything and does everything"; yet others say, "My will is one with the divine Will, it is He who inspires me." Indeed, there are many theories and they say that. Naturally, their ego is as alive. They do all that they want to do, saying, "It is the Divine who is doing it in me." Whatever is supplied by their brain is the "divine Will". It is not a personal inspiration: "Everything is the result of the divine Will." "It is not I who am acting, it is the Divine who is acting through me." They do all that they wish to do. There are many people like that. Therefore I said, "Do not use the Divine as a pretty cloak to hide your desires."

> *"The question is to be sincere. If you are not sincere, do not begin Yoga."*
>
> Ibid.

Sincerity is perhaps the most difficult of all things and perhaps it is also the most effective.

If you have perfect sincerity, you are sure of victory. It is infinitely difficult. Sincerity consists in making all the elements of the being, all the movements (whether outer or inner), all the parts of the being, all of them, have one single will to belong to the Divine, to live only for the Divine, to will only what the Divine wills, to express only the divine Will, to have no other source of energy than that of the Divine.

And you find that there is not a day, not an hour, not a minute when you do not need to intensify, rectify your sincerity — a total refusal to deceive the Divine. The first thing is not to deceive oneself. One knows one cannot deceive the Divine; even the cleverest of the Asuras cannot deceive the Divine. But even when one has understood that, one sees that quite often in one's life, in the course of the day, one tries to deceive oneself without even knowing it, spontaneously and almost automatically. One always gives favourable explanations for all that one does, for one's words, for one's acts. That is what happens first. I am not speaking of obvious things like quarrelling and saying, "It is the other one's fault", I am speaking of the very tiny things of daily life.

I know a child who knocked against a door and he gave a good kick to the door! It is the same thing. It is always the other one who is in the wrong, who has committed the mistake. Even when you have passed the stage of the child, when you have a little reason, you still give the stupidest of all excuses: "If he had not done that, I wouldn't have done this." But it should be just the other way round!

This is what I call being sincere. When you are with someone, if you are sincere, instantaneously your way of reacting should be to do the right thing, even when you are with someone who does not do it. Take the most common example of someone who gets angry: instead of saying things that hurt, you say nothing, you keep calm and quiet, you do not catch the contagion of the anger. You have only to look at yourself to see if this is easy. It is quite an elementary thing, a very small beginning to know whether you are sincere. And I am not speaking of those who catch every contagion, even that of coarse joking nor of those who commit the same stupidity as the others.

I tell you: if you look at yourself with sharp eyes, you will catch in yourself insincerities by the hundred, even though you are trying to be sincere in your general attitude. You will see how difficult it is.

## 25 March 1953

I tell you: If you are sincere in all the elements of your being, to the very cells of your body and if your whole being integrally wants the Divine, you are sure of victory but for nothing less than that. That is what I call being sincere.

I am not speaking of glaring things like obeying your impulses, your caprices and then saying: "I do not belong to myself any more, I belong to the Divine; it is the Divine who is doing everything in me, who is acting in me", that indeed is crude enough. I am speaking of more refined people, a little more noble, who put on a pretty cloak to cover their desires.

How many things in the course of the day, how many thoughts, sensations, gestures are turned exclusively towards the Divine in an aspiration? How many? I believe if you have a single one in the whole day, you may mark that in red letters.

When I say, "If you are sincere, you are sure of victory", I mean true sincerity: to be constantly the true flame that burns like an offering. That intense joy of existing only by the Divine and for the Divine and feeling that without Him nothing exists, that life has no longer any meaning, nothing has any purpose, nothing has any value, nothing has any interest, unless it is this call, this aspiration, this opening to the supreme Truth, to all that we call the Divine (because you must use some word or other), the only reason for the existence of the universe. Remove that and everything disappears.

# 1 April 1953

> *"Ambition has been the undoing of many Yogis. That canker can hide long. Many people start on the Path without any sense of it. But when they get powers, their ambition rises up, all the more violently because it had not been thrown out in the beginning."*
> 
> Questions and Answers 1929 (14 April)

*What do you call a "canker"?*

It is an image, as of a fine mango, very beautiful to look at, and when one opens it, there is a worm inside. That is because the fly laid an egg before the fruit was formed; outside there is no trace. Everything seems candid, disinterested. But within, right at the bottom, there is a great ambition, the desire to have an exceptional position, to be respected by everybody... that is, the ego. This is the canker, it remains very quiet, but it is there. When the power comes, instead of realising that one is nothing, does not deserve anything and that all that one has to do is to remain as passive as possible, one deceives oneself, feels the need of others taking note of it also. It is this I call the canker. It eats up all that is inside and leaves the appearance intact.

*You say that it is necessary to establish "homogeneity in our being"?*

*Ibid.*

Don't you know what a homogeneous thing is, made up of all similar parts? That means the whole being must be under the same influence, same consciousness, same tendency, same will. We are formed of all kinds of different pieces. They become active one after another. According to the part that is active, one

*1 April 1953*

is quite another person, becomes almost another personality. For instance, one had an aspiration at first, felt that everything existed only for the Divine, then something happens, somebody comes along, one has to do something, and everything disappears. One tries to recall the experience, not even the memory of the experience remains. One is completely under another influence, one wonders how this could have happened. There are examples of double, triple, quadruple personalities, altogether unconscious of themselves.... But it is not about this I am speaking; I am speaking about something which has happened to all of you: you have had an experience, and for some time you have felt, understood that this experience was the only thing that was important, that had an absolute value — half an hour later you try to recall it, it is like a smoke that vanishes. The experience has disappeared. And yet half an hour ago it was there and so powerful.... It is because one is made of all kinds of different things. The body is like a bag with pebbles and pearls all mixed up, and it is only the bag which keeps all that together. This is not a homogeneous, uniform consciousness but a heterogeneous one.

You can be a different person at different moments in your life. I know people who took decisions, had a strong will, knew what they wanted and prepared to do it. Then there was a little reversal in the being; another part came up and spoilt all the work in ten minutes. What had been accomplished in two months was all undone. When the first part comes back it is in dismay, it says: "What!... " Then the whole work has to be started again, slowly. Hence it is evident that it is very important to become aware of the psychic being; one must have a kind of signpost or a mirror in which all things are reflected and show themselves as they truly are. And then, according to what they are, one puts them in one place or another; one begins to explain, to organise. That takes time. The same part comes back three or four times and every part that comes up says: "Put me in the first place; what the others do is not important, not at all important, it is I who will decide, for I am the most important." I am sure that if you look at yourself, you will see that there's not one among you who has not had the experience. You want to become conscious, to have goodwill, you have understood, your aspiration is shining — all is brilliant, illuminated; but all of a sudden something happens, a useless conversation, some unfortunate reading, and that upsets everything. Then one thinks that it was an illusion one lived in, that all things were seen from a certain angle.

This is life. One stumbles and falls at the first occasion. One tells oneself: "Oh! One can't always be so serious", and when the other part returns, once again, one repents bitterly: "I was a fool, I have wasted my time, now I must begin again.... " At times there is one part that's ill-humoured, in revolt, full of worries, and another which is progressive, full of surrender. All that, one after the other.

There is but one remedy: that signpost must always be there, a mirror well placed in one's feelings, impulses, all one's sensations. One sees them in this mirror. There are some which are not very beautiful or pleasant to look at; there are others which are beautiful, pleasant, and must be kept. This one does a hundred times a day if necessary. And it is very interesting. One draws a kind of big circle around the psychic mirror and arranges all the elements around it. If there is something that is not all right, it casts a sort of grey shadow upon the mirror: this element must be shifted, organised. It must be spoken to, made to understand, one must come out of that darkness. If you do that, you never get bored. When people are not kind, when one has a cold in the head, when one doesn't know one's lessons, and so on, one begins to look into this mirror. It is very interesting, one sees the canker. "I thought I was sincere!" — not at all.

Not a thing happens in life which is not interesting. This mirror is very, very well made. Do that for two years, three, four years, at times one must do it for twenty years. Then at the end of a few years, look back, turn your gaze upon what you were

# 1 April 1953

three years ago: "How I have changed!... Was I like that?... " It is very entertaining. "I could speak like that? I could talk like that, think like that?... But I was indeed stupid! How I have changed!" Isn't it very interesting, isn't it?

11

# 8 April 1953

*"One of the commonest forms of ambition is the idea of service to humanity. All attachment to such service or work is a sign of personal ambition."*
Questions and Answers 1929 (14 April)

*Why do you say that this is ambition?*

Why do you want to serve humanity, what is your idea? It is ambition, it is in order to become a great man among men. It is difficult to understand?... I can see that!

*The Divine is everywhere. So if one serves humanity, one serves the Divine, isn't that so?*

That's marvellous! The clearest thing in this business is to say: "The Divine is in me. If I serve myself, I am also serving the Divine!" (*Laughter*) In fact, the Divine is everywhere. The Divine will do His own work very well without you.

I see quite well that you do not understand. But truly, if you do understand that the Divine is there, in all things, with what are you meddling in serving humanity? To serve humanity you must know better than the Divine what must be done for it. Do you know better than the Divine how to serve it?

The Divine is everywhere. Yes. Things don't seem to be divine.... As for me, I see only one solution: if you want to help humanity, there is only one thing to do, it is to take yourself as completely as possible and offer yourself to the Divine. That is the solution. Because in this way, at least the material reality which you represent will be able to grow a little more like the Divine.

We are told that the Divine is in all things. Why don't things change? Because the Divine does not get a response, everything

**8 April 1953**

does not respond to the Divine. One must search the depths of the consciousness to see this. What do you want to do to serve humanity? Give food to the poor? — You can feed millions of them. That will not be a solution, this problem will remain the same. Give new and better living conditions to men? — The Divine is in them, how is it that things don't change? The Divine must know better than you the condition of humanity. What are you? You represent only a little bit of consciousness and a little bit of matter, it is that you call "myself". If you want to help humanity, the world or the universe, the only thing to do is to give that little bit entirely to the Divine. Why is the world not divine?... It is evident that the world is not in order. So the only solution to the problem is to give what belongs to you. Give it totally, entirely to the Divine; not only for yourself but for humanity, for the universe. There is no better solution. How do you want to help humanity? You don't even know what it needs. Perhaps you know still less what power you are serving. How can you change anything without indeed having changed yourself?

In any case, you are not powerful enough to do it. How do you expect to help another if you do not have a higher consciousness than he? It is such a childish idea! It is children who say: "I am opening a boarding-house, I am going to build a crèche, give soup to the poor, preach this knowledge, spread this religion...." It is only because you consider yourself better than others, think you know better than they what they should be or do. That's what it is, serving humanity. You want to continue all that? It has not changed things much. It is not to help humanity that one opens a hospital or a school.

*All the same it has helped, hasn't it? If all the schools were abolished...*

I don't think that humanity is happier than it was before nor that there has been a great improvement. All this mostly gives you the feeling "I am something." That's what I call ambition.

If these very people who are ready to give money for schools were told that there was a divine Work to be done, that the Divine has decided to do it in this particular way, even if they are convinced that it is indeed the Divine's Work, they refuse to give anything, for this is not a recognised form of beneficence — one doesn't have the satisfaction of having done something good! This is what I call ambition. I had instances of people who could give lakhs of rupees to open a hospital, for that gives them the satisfaction of doing something great, noble, generous. They glorify themselves, that's what I call ambition.

I knew a humorist who used to say: "It won't be so soon that the kingdom of God will come, for those poor philanthropists — what would remain for them? If humanity suffered no longer, the philanthropists would be without work." It is difficult to come out of that. However, it is a fact that never will the world come out of the state in which it is unless it gives itself up to the Divine. All the virtues — you may glorify them — increase your self-satisfaction, that is, your ego; they do not help you truly to become aware of the Divine. It is the generous and wise people of this world who are the most difficult to convert. They are very satisfied with their life. A poor fellow who has done all sorts of stupid things all his life feels immediately sorry and says: "I am nothing, can do nothing. Make of me what You want." Such a one is more right and much closer to the Divine than one who is wise and full of his wisdom and vanity. He sees himself as he is.

The generous and wise man who has done much for humanity is too self-satisfied to have the least idea of changing. It is usually these people who say: "If indeed I had created the world, I wouldn't have made it like this, I would have created it much better than that", and they try to set right what the Divine has done badly! According to their picture, all this is stupid and useless.... It is not with that attitude that you can belong to the Divine. There will always be between you and Him the conscious ego of one's own intellectual superiority which judges

## 8 April 1953

the Divine and is sure of never being mistaken. For they are convinced that if they had made the world, they would not have committed all the stupidities that God has perpetrated. And all this comes from pride, vanity, self-conceit; and there is exactly the seed of that in people who want to serve humanity.

What are they going to give to humanity? Nothing at all! Even if they gave every drop of their blood, all the ideas in their head, all the money in their pocket, that could not change one individual, who is but a second of time in eternity. They believe they can serve eternity? There are even beings higher than man who have come, have brought the light, given their life, and that has not changed things much. So how can a little man, a microscopic being, truly help? It is pride. The argument given is: "If everyone did his best, all would go well." I don't think so and, even, it is impossible. In a certain way, each thing in the universe does its best. But that best doesn't come to anything at all. Unless everything changes, nothing will change. It is this best that must change. In the place of ignorance must be born knowledge and power and consciousness, otherwise we shall always turn in a circle around the same stupidity.

You may open millions of hospitals, that will not prevent people getting ill. On the contrary, they will have every facility and encouragement to fall ill. We are steeped in ideas of this kind. This puts your conscience at rest: "I have come to the world, I must help others." One tells oneself: "How disinterested I am! I am going to help humanity." All this is nothing but egoism.

In fact, the first human being that concerns you is yourself. You want to diminish suffering, but unless you can change the capacity of suffering into a certitude of being happy, the world will not change. It will always be the same, we turn in a circle — one civilisation follows another, one catastrophe another; but the thing does not change, for there is something missing, something not there, that is the consciousness. That's all.

At least, that's my opinion. I am giving it to you for what it is worth. If you want to build hospitals, schools, you may do so; if that makes you happy, so much the better for you. It has not much importance. When I saw the film *Monsieur Vincent*, I was very interested. He found out that when he fed ten poor men, a thousand came along. That was what Colbert told him: "It seems you create them, your poor ones, by feeding them!" And it is not altogether false. However! If it is your destiny to found schools and give instruction, to care for the sick, to open hospitals, it is good, do it. But you must not take that very seriously. It is something grandiose you are doing for your own pleasure. Say: "I am doing it because it gives me pleasure." But do not speak of yoga. It is not yoga you are doing. You believe you are doing something great, that's all, and it is for your personal satisfaction.

*It is said that the Rishi Vishvamitra also created a new world.*

What did he do? Tell me. He was not happy with this world and created another, did he? Where is this world?

Naturally, the first idea is to be greater than the one who has created the world. For one thinks that it is badly done. It is possible, you may say it is done badly. If you believe that you can do better than the Divine, I am not saying that you will be wrong. I am saying that you cannot say that you are not ambitious. I do not say they were wrong; I say they are ambitious. It is nothing else but that. The proof is that these are people who do good, these are the generous, good, disinterested ones who are the most difficult to convert; their ego is formidable. Their idea of justice, generosity, etc. is so big that there is no place for anything else, for the Divine.

Before being capable of doing good, one must go deep within oneself and make a very important discovery. It is that one does not exist. There is *one* thing which exists, that is the Divine, and so long as you have not made that discovery, you cannot advance on the path. But it is so hard a carapace!... If you have the philosophic mind, you will ask yourself: "What do I call 'myself'? Is it my body? — it changes all the time, it is never the same thing. Is it my feelings? — they change so often. Is it my thoughts? — they are built and destroyed continuously. That is not myself. Where is the self? What is it that gives me this sense of continuity?" If you continue sincerely, you go back a few years. The problem becomes more and more perplexing. You continue to observe, you tell yourself: "It is my memory." But even if one loses one's memory, one would be oneself. If one sincerely continues this profound search, there comes a moment when everything disappears and one single thing exists, that is the Divine, the divine Presence. Everything disappears, dissolves, everything melts away like butter in the sunlight.... When one has made this discovery, one becomes aware that one was nothing but a bundle of habits. It is always that which does not know the Divine and is not conscious of the Divine which speaks. In everyone there are these hundreds and hundreds of "selves" who speak and in hundreds of completely different ways — "selves" unconscious, changing, fluid. The self which speaks today is not the same as yesterday's; and if you look further, the self has disappeared. There is only one who remains. That is the Divine. It is the only one that may be seen always the same. And unless you have gone so far...

*If everything comes from Him, why are there so many errors?*

You must not believe that everything that happens to you in life comes to you naturally from the Divine, that is, that it is the Truth-Consciousness which is directing your life. For if everything came from Him, it would be impossible for you to make a mistake.

How does it happen that there's error everywhere? Why do things go in opposition to the Divine and to what they ought to be?... Because there are numerous elements which cross each other and intervene. Wills cross each other, the strongest gets the best of it. It is this complexity of norms that has created a determinism. The divine Will is completely veiled by this host of things. So I have said here (*Mother takes her book*): "You must accept all things — and only those things — that come from the Divine. Because things can come from concealed desires. The desires work in the subconscious and attract things to you of which possibly you may not recognise the origin, but which do not come from the Divine but from disguised desires."

If you have a strong desire for something you cannot get, you project your desire outside yourself. It goes off like a tiny personality separated from you and roams about in the world. It will take a little round, more or less large, and return to you, perhaps when you have forgotten it. People who have a kind of passion, who want something, — that goes out from them like a little being, like a little flame into the surroundings. This little being has its destiny. It roams about in the world, tossed around by other things perhaps. You have forgotten it, but it will never forget that it must bring about that particular result.... For days you tell yourself: "How much I would like to go to that place, to Japan, for instance, and see so many things", and your desire goes out from you; but because desires are very fugitive things, you have forgotten completely this desire you had thrown out with such a force. There are many reasons for your thinking about something else. And after ten years or more, or less, it comes back to you like a dish served up piping hot. Yes, like a piping-hot dish, well arranged. You say: "This does not interest me any longer." It does not interest you ten or twenty years *later*. It was a small formation and it has gone and done its work as it could.... It is impossible to have desires without their being realised, even if it be quite a tiny desire. The formation has done what it could; it took a lot of trouble, it has worked hard, and after years it returns. It is like a servant you have sent out and who has done his best. When he returns you tell him: "What have you done?" — "Why? But, sir, it was because you wanted it!"

*8 April 1953*

You cannot put forth a strong thought without its going out from you like a little balloon, as it were. We have certain stories which are not unbelievable, like the one about that miser who thought of nothing but his money; he had hidden his hoard somewhere and always used to go to see it. After his death he continued to come as a ghost (that is to say, his vital being), to watch over his money. Nobody could go near the place without meeting with a catastrophe. It is like that, if you have worked to bring out something, it is always realised. It may be realised even after your death! Yes, for when your body ceases to exist, none of the vibrations stops existing. They are realised somewhere. That was what the Buddha said: the vibrations continue to exist, to be perpetuated. They are contagious. They continue in others, pass into others, and everyone adds a little to them.

*Can one help the world with a vibration of goodwill?*

With good wishes one can change many things, only it must be an extremely pure and unmixed goodwill. It is quite obvious that a thought, a perfectly pure and true prayer, if it is sent forth into the world, does its work. But where is this perfectly pure and true thought when it passes into the human brain? There are degradations. If through an effort of inner consciousness and knowledge, you can truly overcome in yourself a desire, that is to say, dissolve and abolish it, and if through inner goodwill, through consciousness, light, knowledge, you are able to dissolve the desire, you will be, first of all in yourself personally, a hundred times happier than if you had satisfied this desire, and then it will have a marvellous effect. It will have a repercussion in the world of which you have no idea. It will spread forth. For the vibrations you have created will continue to spread. These things grow larger like the snowball. The victory you win in your character, however small it be, is one which can be gained in the whole world. And it is this I meant just now: all things which are done outwardly without changing the inner nature —

hospitals, schools, etc. — are done through vanity, for the feeling of being great, whilst these small unnoticed things overcome in oneself gain an infinitely greater victory, though the effects are hidden. Every movement in you which is false and opposed to the truth is a negation of the divine life. Your small efforts have considerable results which you don't even have the satisfaction of knowing, but which are true and have precisely an impersonal and general effect.

If you really want to do something good, the best thing you can do is to win your small victories in all sincerity, one after another, and thus you will do for the world the maximum you are able to.

*Will our victory act for the whole world?*

It will not change the whole world. For your victory is too small for the whole world. Millions of such victories are needed. It is a very small victory if compared with the whole. But it gets mingled with other things.... It could be said that it is like bringing into the world the *capacity* of doing a thing. But for this to act effectively, at times centuries are necessary; it is a question of proportion. You can try it out (and it is much more difficult) even with those around you. You must be absolutely sincere, not do it with the idea of getting a result, but because you want to gain a victory. If you gain it, it will necessarily have an effect on those around you. But if a bargaining element is mixed up in it, if you do this thing because you want to get that other: "I want to overcome my defects, but that person must also overcome his", then that doesn't work. It is a merchant's attitude: "I give this, but I shall take that." That spoils everything. There is neither sincerity nor purity. It is bargaining.

Nothing must be mixed with your sincerity, your aspiration, your motive. You do things for love of the Divine, for truth, for perfection, without any other motive, any other idea. And that brings results.

# 15 April 1953

*You have written: "Do not try to pull at the forces of the Divine."*
Questions and Answers 1929 (14 April)

*Can one pull the divine forces by violence?*

Yes, if you call very strongly, if you aspire very strongly, you may pull down a large number of forces into you, but you will not be able to digest them, assimilate them. It is the same thing as with food; when you swallow all that you have at hand in one gulp, that causes indigestion, it chokes you. You cannot bear it. So if you want to go fast, if you hurry, you send a kind of call and pull towards you too great a number of forces, forces which otherwise would have come less quickly.

Just a little hidden ambition is enough to... There are people who do not do Yoga for the sake of Yoga but to obtain a result, to have powers, to know one thing or another.

*But then that means they are not sincere? How is it then that the Divine responds?*

You think that the Divine has a small human judgment! You must not project human ideas upon the Divine.

If you are not sincere, what happens is that your own consciousness is veiled. Take, for example, a man who tells lies; his consciousness gets veiled and after a while, he can no longer distinguish falsehood from truth. He sees images and calls them truth. One who is wicked loses his aspiration, loses his capacity of realisation, loses all possibility of understanding, feeling and realising. That is the punishment.

One puts veils, obstacles between oneself and the Divine.

That is how one punishes oneself. The Divine does not withdraw; one makes oneself incapable of receiving him. The Divine does not distribute in this way rewards and punishments, it is not at all like that.

When one is insincere, when one has bad will, when one is a traitor, one punishes oneself instantaneously. Insincere people lose even the little bit of consciousness that would make them know that they are wicked; they become as though unconscious. They end up by not knowing anything at all any longer.

*What is it that you call "the basis of equanimity in the external being"?*

*Ibid.*

It is good health, a solid body, well poised; when one does not have the nerves of a little girl that are shaken by the least thing; when one sleeps well, eats well…. When one is quite calm, well balanced, very quiet, one has a solid basis and can receive a large number of forces.

If anyone among you has received spiritual forces, forces of the Divine, Ananda, for example, he knows from experience that unless he is in good health he cannot contain them, keep them. He begins to weep and cry, gets restless to expend what he has received. He must laugh and talk and gesticulate, otherwise he cannot keep them, he feels stifled. And so by laughing, weeping, moving about he throws out what he has received.

To be well balanced, to be able to absorb what one receives, one must be very quiet, very calm. One must have a solid basis, good health. One must have a very solid basis. That is very important.

*What is the difference between outer equality and the equality of the soul?*

The equality of the soul is a psychological thing. It is the power

**15 April 1953**

to bear all happenings, good or bad, without being sad, discouraged, desperate, upset. Whatever happens, you remain serene, peaceful.

The other is the equality in the body. It is not psychological, it is something material; to have a physical poise, to receive forces without being troubled.

The two are equally necessary if one wants to progress on the path. And other things still. For example, a mental poise; such that all possible ideas, even the most contradictory, may come from all sides without one's being troubled. One can see them and put each in its place. That is mental poise.

## 22 April 1953

The following brief passage about sleep and dreams, is part of a longer, incompletely recorded talk.

*When one sleeps, how can one distinguish the nature of the visions?*

They do not leave the same impression at all.

In order to know things well, one must educate oneself, develop the conscious being. But there are all kinds of different things, there are mental and vital projections exactly as in the cinema; then there are visions you may have if you are exteriorised in the mental and vital regions; the great difference is that these dreams are imposed upon you, you are taken in ... [1] Then there are countless dreams without any connection which have no interest. For your brain is like a recording instrument: something comes and strikes hundreds of cells, each thing must strike a small note. Things will strike the brain convolutions — a remembrance, an impression, all kinds of tiny memories — it depends on your condition. But you have the control, ideas follow each other in accordance with a certain logic; there is also a mechanism which puts memories into movement through contagion, and the movement through contagion is made according to logic (what you call logic). But when you sleep, that faculty usually goes to sleep, so all those little cells are left to themselves and the connections — like the connections of electric wires — don't work any longer, things come the wrong way round or in any direction at all. You must not look for a meaning. It was a contagion: because this one was vibrating, that other also vibrated, one vibration gives rise to another. Your logic works no longer. And you have fantastic dreams, absurd dreams.

[1] Here a whole passage is missing.

## 22 April 1953

It is very difficult to put one's mind into repose. The majority of men get up very tired, more tired than when they went to sleep. One must learn how to quieten one's mind, make it completely blank, and then when one wakes up, one feels refreshed. One must relax the whole mind in the pure white silence, then one has the least number of dreams.

# 29 April 1953

*Sweet Mother, you have said that one can exercise one's conscious will and change the course of one's dreams.*

Ah, yes, I have already told you that once. If you are in the middle of a dream and something happens which you don't like (for instance, somebody shouts that he wants to kill you), you say: "That won't do at all, I don't want my dream to be like that", and you can change the action or the ending. You can organise your dream as you want. One can arrange one's dreams. But for this you must be conscious that you are dreaming, you must know you are dreaming.

*But these dreams are not of much importance, are they?*

Yes, they are, and one must be conscious of what can happen. Suppose that you have gone for a stroll in the vital world; there you meet beings who attack you (that's what happens usually), if you know that it is a dream, you can very easily gather your vital forces and conquer. That's a true fact; you can with a certain attitude, a certain word, a certain way of being do things you would not do if you were just dreaming.

*If in the dream someone kills you it doesn't matter, for it is just a dream!*

I beg your pardon! Usually, the next day you are ill, or may be a little later. That's a warning. I know someone whose eye was thus hurt in a dream, and who really lost his eye a few days later. As for me, once I happened to dream getting blows on my face. Well, when I woke up the next morning, I had a red mark in the same place, on the forehead and the cheek.... Inevitably,

## 29 April 1953

a wound received in the vital being is translated in the physical body.

*But how does it happen? There must be some intermediary?*

It was in the vital that I was beaten. It is from within that this comes. Nothing, nobody touched anything from outside. If you receive a blow in the vital, the body suffers the consequence. More than half of our illnesses are the result of blows of this kind, and this happens much more often than one believes. Only, men are not conscious of their vital, and as they are not conscious they don't know that fifty per cent of their illnesses are the result of what happens in the vital: shocks, accidents, fighting, ill-will.... Externally this is translated by an illness. If one knows how it reacts on the physical, one goes to its source and can cure oneself in a few hours.

*How is it that the symbolism of dreams varies according to traditions, races, religions?*

Because the form given to the dream is mental. If you have learnt that such and such a form represents such and such a mythological person, you see that form and say: "It is that." In your mind there is an association between certain ideas and certain forms, and this is continued in the dream. When you translate your dream you give it an explanation corresponding to what you have learnt, what you have been taught, and it is with the mental image you have in your head that you know. Moreover, I have explained this to you a little later in the vision of Joan of Arc (*Mother takes her book and reads*):

*"The beings who were always appearing and speaking to Jeanne d'Arc would, if seen by an Indian, have quite a different appearance; for when one sees, one projects the*

> *forms of one's mind.... You have the vision of one in India whom you call the Divine Mother; the Catholics say it is the Virgin Mary, and the Japanese call it Kwannon, the Goddess of Mercy; and others would give other names. It is the same force, the same power, but the images made of it are different in different faiths."*
>
> Questions and Answers 1929 (21 April)

And then? You are not very talkative today! Is that all?

*You say that "each person has his own world of dream-imagery peculiar to himself."*

> Ibid.

Each individual has his own way of expressing, thinking, speaking, feeling, understanding. It is the combination of all these ways of being that makes the individual. That is why everyone can understand only according to his own nature. As long as you are shut up in your own nature, you can know only what is in your consciousness. All depends upon the height of the nature of your consciousness. Your world is limited to what you have in your consciousness. If you have a very small consciousness, you will understand only a few things. When your consciousness is very vast, universal, only then will you understand the world. If the consciousness is limited to your little ego, all the rest will escape you.... There are people whose brain and consciousness are smaller than a walnut. You know that a walnut resembles the brain; well these people look at things and don't understand them. They can understand nothing else except what is in direct contact with their senses. For them only what they taste, what they see, hear, touch has a reality, and all the rest simply does not exist, and they accuse us of speaking fancifully! "What I cannot touch does not exist", they say. But the only answer to give them is: "It does not exist *for you*, but there's no reason why it shouldn't exist for others." You must not insist with these

## 29 April 1953

people, and you must not forget that the smaller they are the greater is the audacity in their assertions.

One's cocksureness is in proportion to one's unconsciousness; the more unconscious one is, the more is one sure of oneself. The most foolish are always the most vain. Your stupidity is in proportion to your vanity. The more one knows... In fact, there is a time when one is quite convinced that one knows nothing at all. There's not a moment in the world which does not bring something new, for the world is perpetually growing. If one is conscious of that, one has always something new to learn. But one can become conscious of it only gradually. One's conviction that one knows is in direct proportion to one's ignorance and stupidity.

*Mother, have the scientists, then, a very small consciousness?*

Why? All scientists are not like that. If you meet a true scientist who has worked hard, he will tell you: "We know nothing. What we know today is nothing beside what we shall know tomorrow. This year's discoveries will be left behind next year." A real scientist knows very well that there are many more things he doesn't know than those he knows. And this is true of all branches of human activity. I have never met a scientist worthy of the name who was proud. I have never met a man of some worth who has told me: "I know everything." Those I have seen have always confessed: "In short, I know nothing." After having spoken of all that he has done, all that he has achieved, he tells you very quietly: "After all, I know nothing."

*There are people who say at times that they know nothing, just to appear modest, but they don't believe what they say!*

There are insincere and hypocritical people everywhere in the

29

world. So much the worse for them. These shut the door completely to all progress. That is all.

*For us who attend classes, is it dangerous then to study?*

No, quite the contrary! For if you begin to study well, your consciousness awakens, and you can become more aware of what you still lack. This reminds me of the lady who, having gradually become conscious, told me: "Before I heard you, I had trust in men, everybody was very kind, I was happy. Now that I have begun to see clearly and become conscious, I have lost all my serenity! It is awful to become conscious!"

What is to be done? — Become still more conscious. It is very bad to learn just a little. One must learn more until one comes to the point where one sees that one knows nothing.... I spoke to you about the novice who wants to pass on to others what he has learnt — until the day he sees he has not much to pass on. Usually all religious teaching is based on that. A very little knowledge, with precise formulas which are well written (often quite well written) and crystallise in the brain, and assert: "That is indeed the truth." You have only to study what is there in the book. How easy it is! In every religion there is a book — whether it be the Catechism, the Hindu texts, the Koran, in short, all the sacred books — you learn it by heart. You are told that this-is-the-truth, and you are sure it is the truth and remain comfortable. It is very convenient, you don't need to try to understand. Those who don't know the same thing as you, are in the falsehood, and you even pray for those who are outside the "Truth"! This is a common fact in all religions. But in all religions there are people who know better and don't believe in these things. I had met one of these particularly, one belonging to the Catholic faith. He was a big man. I spoke to him about what I knew and asked him: "Why do you use this method? Why do you perpetuate ignorance?" He answered: "It is a policy of peace of mind. If we didn't do that, people wouldn't listen to

## 29 April 1953

us. This, indeed, is the secret of religions." He told me: "There are in our religion, as in the ancient initiations, people who know. There are schools where the old tradition is taught. But we are forbidden to speak about it. All these religious images are symbols representing something other than what is taught. But that is not taught outside."

The reason for this is very generous and kind (according to them): "People who have a tiny brain — and there are plenty — if we tell them something that's too high, too great, it troubles them, disturbs them, and they become unhappy. They will never be able to understand. Why worry them uselessly? They don't have the capacity to find the truth. Whilst, if you tell them: 'If you have faith in this, you will go to heaven', they are quite happy." There, you see. It is very convenient. That is why it is perpetuated, otherwise there would be no religions.

I am not telling you this to encourage one particular religion rather than another. But this is a procedure that *seems* generous.... Otherwise there would be no religions; there would be masters and disciples, people who have a higher teaching and an exceptional experience. That would be a very good thing. But as soon as the master is gone, what happens is that the knowledge he gave is changed into a religion. Rigid dogmas are established, religious rules come into being and one cannot but bow down before the Tables of the Law. Yet at the beginning it was not like that. You are told: "This is true, this is false, the Master has said...." Some time later the master becomes a god, and you are told: "God has said this."

Note that I am telling you this because I know that here you are all liberated from religions. If I had before me someone having a religion he believed in, I would tell him: "It is very good, keep your religion, continue." Happily for all of you, you don't have one. And I hope you will never have one, for it means a door shut upon all progress.

# 6 May 1953

*"People often meet in these planes, before they meet upon earth. They may join there, speak to each other and have all the relations you can have upon earth. Some know of these relationships, some do not know. Some, as are indeed most, are unconscious of the inner being and the inner intercourse, and yet it happens that when they meet the new face in the outer world, they find it very familiar, quite well known."*

*Questions and Answers 1929 (21 April)*

That depends very much upon the level of consciousness in one's inner being. For most people, all that is a mixture in the mental, vital and physical planes; they are not at all conscious of what is happening. Some are conscious and usually they have a similar feeling when they are told: "Why, it was like that that I knew you, yes, I know you already intimately, and I have a feeling, but the impression is very vague." Very few people are developed enough to say: "Well, I saw you under such and such circumstances." Yet this has happened.

And then there are those who have learnt a little, who are more or less occultists or believe in rebirth in a childish way, believe that it is a tiny person who has put on a physical robe, that is, a body, and when this garment falls off, it goes away and puts on another and then another... like a doll whose dress is changed. For them it is like that: one changes one's body, as one changes one's clothes. Some people have even written books very seriously telling you about all their lives since they were monkeys! That indeed is absolute childishness. For in nine hundred and ninety-nine cases out of a thousand, it is just the tiny psychic formation at the centre of the being that continues after death; all the rest is dissolved, goes to pieces, scattered here and there, the

6 May 1953

individuality exists no longer. Now, how often in the physical life does the psychic being take part consciously in what the physical being does?... I am not speaking of people who do yoga and are a little disciplined; I am speaking of average people who have a psychic capacity in the sense that their psychic is already sufficiently developed to be able to intervene in life and guide it — some pass years and years without the psychic intervening. And they come and tell you in which country they were born and what their father and mother were like and the house they lived in, the roof of the church and the forest that was by the side and all the most casual events of their life! It is absolutely idiotic, for it is all rubbed off, these things don't exist any longer; whilst the memory that one may still have is that of the particular moment in life when there is a special circumstance, "vital" moments, so to say, in which the psychic suddenly takes part, through an inner call or an absolute necessity — all of a sudden the psychic intervenes — and that then is engraved in the psychic memory. When you have the psychic memory you remember a set of circumstances at one *moment* of life, particularly of the inner emotion, of the consciousness that acted at that moment. And then that passes into the consciousness along with some associations, with all that was around you, perhaps a word spoken, a phrase heard; but what was most important was the state of the soul in which you were: for that indeed remains very clearly engraved. These are the landmarks of the psychic life, things that have left a deep impression and taken part in its formation. Hence when you find your psychic being in you again constantly, continuously, clearly, it is things like these that you remember. There may be quite a few, but they are flashes in one's life, and one cannot say: "I was such and such a person, I did such and such a thing, I was called by this name and I was doing this or that." Or otherwise it would mean that at that moment (a rare one) there was a combination of circumstances good enough for one to be able to fix the date or the place, the country and the age. That can happen.

Naturally the psychic takes a greater and greater part, and the larger does the set of memories grow. And then one can retrace one's life, but not in all its details. One can say that at certain moments, "it was like this," or "I was that." Certain moments, yes, very important moments of a life.... What's necessary is a being wholly identified with the psychic, one that has organised its whole existence around it, unified its whole being — all the tiniest parts, all the elements, all the movements of the being around the psychic centre — that has made of itself a single being, solely turned to the Divine; then, if the body falls off, that remains. It is only a completely formed conscious being that can remember exactly in another life all that has happened before. It can even pass consciously from one life to another without losing anything of its consciousness. How many people upon earth have reached that state?... Not many, I believe. And usually they are not in the least inclined to narrate their adventures.

*There are people who tell the life of others.*

Yes, I know. I know many things, I have heard all that one can hear. They tell stories after stories.... They look at you and say: "You were so-and-so in that life, you did such and such a thing." Well I guarantee, it is not true. For I know how one can find out where one has seen a person and what he was and how it is — it is not just a little story that you can write in a book. When you look within a person, when you have the perception, precisely of the psychic world, which enables you to recognise the psychic there where it was, then all of a sudden you can see a scene, an image, a form, a word; there is a sort of association due to which even in the present being of this person there still remain certain sympathies and attractions which come from previous lives. But, as I was saying, these are "moments" of life. And so one sees, one can see these various moments, but one cannot narrate a whole life.

I believe Sri Aurobindo has written something very amus-

**6 May 1953**

ing about this, the number of Caesars one knew, the number of all the great beings, the Napoleons and all the important personages, the Shakespeares, all the people whose names have survived in history! How many are there! There are hundreds of them! And you hear their stories: "I was this, I was that, I did this", or in séances the so-called spirits come and speak to you. A large number of people indulge in this playing with "spirits", practising automatic writing and particularly in communicating with spirits. Now, there are garrulous spirits. They come to many places at the same time, especially people like Napoleon (I do not know why they have a partiality for Napoleon), everywhere Napoleon arrives and tells you extraordinary stories of his life and usually very contradictory stories and perhaps all at the same time! These are really very active people. Well, it is extremely comic — and it is impossible.

The truth is that these are small vital entities, a class of beings formed by the decomposition of desires that have persisted after a man's death and retained their form; of imaginations that have remained coagulated and try to manifest and reappear. Sometimes they are small beings of the vital world, not very well- disposed; as soon as they see people playing at such things — automatic writing, spirit-communication — they come and play. And as they are in a domain from where it is easy to read human thought, they tell you very well what you have in your head. They respond to what you expect. You wish to have a particular answer: they give you the answer even before you have put the question! They can give you precise details, they can tell you that such and such a thing happened to you, that such and such a member of your family... They know quite well. They do excellent thought-reading and tell you things altogether convincingly. "I did not say that I was married and had three sons and four daughters, how did he know all that?" — Because it was in your head.

Psychic memories have a very special character and a wonderful intensity. But that cannot be narrated in this way.... They are unforgettable moments of life when the consciousness is intense, luminous, strong, active, powerful, and sometimes turning-points in life that have changed the direction of one's life. But one will never be able to say what dress one was wearing or the gentleman with whom one spoke and the neighbours and the kind of field where one was.

*Why do we forget our dreams?*

Because you do not dream always at the same place. It is not always the same part of your being that dreams and it is not at the same place that you dream. If you were in conscious, direct, continuous communication with all the parts of your being, you would remember all your dreams. But very few parts of the being are in communication.

For example, you have a dream in the subtle physical, that is to say, quite close to the physical. Generally, these dreams occur in the early hours of the morning, that is between four and five o'clock, at the end of the sleep. If you do not make a sudden movement when you wake up, if you remain very quiet, very still and a little attentive — quietly attentive — and concentrated, you will remember them, for the communication between the subtle physical and the physical is established — very rarely is there no communication.

Now, dreams are mostly forgotten because you have a dream while in a certain state and then pass into another. For instance, when you sleep, your body is asleep, your vital is asleep, but your mind is still active. So your mind begins to have dreams, that is, its activity is more or less coordinated, the imagination is very active and you see all kinds of things, take part in extraordinary happenings.... After some time, all that calms down and the mind also begins to doze. The vital that was resting wakes up; it comes out of the body, walks about, goes here and there, does all kinds of things, reacts, sometimes fights, and finally eats. It does all kinds of things. The vital is very adventurous. It watches.

**6 May 1953**

When it is heroic it rushes to save people who are in prison or to destroy enemies or it makes wonderful discoveries. But this pushes back the whole mental dream very far behind. It is rubbed off, forgotten: naturally you cannot remember it because the vital dream takes its place. But if you wake up suddenly at that moment, you remember it. There are people who have made the experiment, who have got up at certain fixed hours of the night and when they wake up suddenly, they do remember. You must not move brusquely, but awake in the natural course, then you remember.

After a time, the vital having taken a good stroll, needs to rest also, and so it goes into repose and quietness, quite tired at the end of all kinds of adventures. Then something else wakes up. Let us suppose that it is the subtle physical that goes for a walk. It starts moving and begins wandering, seeing the rooms and... why, this thing that was there, but it has come here and that other thing which was in that room is now in this one, and so on. If you wake up without stirring, you remember. But this has pushed away far to the back of the consciousness all the stories of the vital. They are forgotten and so you cannot recollect your dreams. But if at the time of waking up you are not in a hurry, you are not obliged to leave your bed, on the contrary you can remain there as long as you wish, you need not even open your eyes; you keep your head exactly where it was and you make yourself like a tranquil mirror within and concentrate there. You catch just a tiny end of the tail of your dream. You catch it and start pulling gently, without stirring in the least. You begin pulling quite gently, and then first one part comes, a little later another. You go backward; the last comes up first. Everything goes backward, slowly, and suddenly the whole dream reappears: "Ah, there! it was like that." Above all, do not jump up, do not stir; you repeat the dream to yourself several times — once, twice — until it becomes clear in all its details. Once that dream is settled, you continue not to stir, you try to go further in, and suddenly you catch the tail of something else. It is more distant, more vague, but you can still seize it. And here also you hang on, get hold of it and pull, and you see that everything changes and you enter another world; all of a sudden you have an extraordinary adventure — it is another dream. You follow the same process. You repeat the dream to yourself once, twice, until you are sure of it. You remain very quiet all the time. Then you begin to penetrate still more deeply into yourself, as though you were going in very far, very far; and again suddenly you see a vague form, you have a feeling, a sensation... like a current of air, a slight breeze, a little breath; and you say, "Well, well...." " It takes a form, it becomes clear — and the third category comes. You must have a lot of time, a lot of patience, you must be very quiet in your mind and body, very quiet, and you can tell the story of your whole night from the end right up to the beginning.

Even without doing this exercise which is very long and difficult, in order to recollect a dream, whether it be the last one or the one in the middle that has made a violent impression on your being, you must do what I have said when you wake up: take particular care not even to move your head on the pillow, remain absolutely still and let the dream return.

Some people do not have a passage between one state and another, there is a little gap and so they leap from one to the other; there is no highway passing through all the states of being with no break of the consciousness. A small dark hole, and you do not remember. It is like a precipice across which one has to extend the consciousness. To build a bridge takes a very long time; it takes much longer than building a physical bridge.... Very few people want to and know how to do it. They may have had magnificent activities, they do not remember them or sometimes only the last, the nearest, the most physical activity, with an uncoordinated movement — dreams having no sense.

But there are as many different kinds of nights and sleep as there are different days and activities. There are not many days that are alike, each day is different. The days are not the same,

6 May 1953

the nights are not the same. You and your friends are doing apparently the same thing, but for each one it is very different. And each one must have his own procedure.

*Why are two dreams never alike?*

Because all things are different. No two minutes are alike in the universe and it will be so till the end of the universe, no two minutes will ever be alike. And men obstinately want to make rules! One must do this and not that.... Well! we must let people please themselves.

You could have put to me a very interesting question: "Why am I fourteen years old today?" Intelligent people will say: "It is because it is the fourteenth year since you were born." That is the answer of someone who believes himself to be very intelligent. But there is another reason. I shall tell this to you alone.... I have drowned you all sufficiently well! Now you must begin to learn swimming!

*If one finds the truth in things, does it mean that one has found the Divine?*

Surely! In everything, whatever it is that is the only way. There is not a thing that does not carry in itself an eternal truth, otherwise it could not exist. The universe could not exist for even a thousandth part of a second if it did not contain a truth in itself.

*If one were in contact with the Divine, what would be its effect?*

For each one a different effect. Because we are in the presence of a fact: there is a universe, at least there is an earth, of that we are almost sure, you cannot dispute that, granted?... Have you ever asked yourself why there is an earth? No! Probably it was quite wise. Once I spoke to you of that occultist whom I knew.

He was a wise man in his own way. People used to come and ask him:

First of all, why is there a universe? Answer: What is that to you?

Secondly, then why is it as it is? Reply: It is as it is. What does it matter to you?

Thirdly, I do not find it satisfactory.

That's very good. We begin to touch the practical. To those who do not find it satisfactory, I would say: There is only one thing to do, start working for its change, find a way for it to be otherwise and to be good. Things are as they are. Why are they so?... Perhaps one might know — it is not certain. In any case they are so. The most remarkable thing is that if you are sincere you will find out why they are so and how they are so: the cause, the origin and the process. For it is one single thing. There is what we call the Truth, the basis of everything; because if this were not there, there would be nothing. Once you have found the Truth, you find the origin, you find the means of changing the cause — how it is so, why it is so and the means of changing it. If you are in contact with the Divine, you have the key to everything. You know the how, the why and the process to change.

There is something to do: to work, it is so interesting. You represent a small agglomerated mass of substance that makes up yourself. Enter within and find the key. You have only to go down inside there. You cannot say: "That is beyond me, it is too big for me." Go within your little person and you will find the key which opens all the doors.

# 13 May 1953

*"There are some who, when they are sitting in meditation, get into a state which they think very fine and delightful."*

Questions and Answers 1929 (21 April)

*What is this state?*

Whatever it may be, they think their state is delightful and remarkable. They have a very high opinion of themselves. They believe they are remarkable people because they are able to sit quietly without moving; and if they don't think of anything, that is remarkable. But usually it is a kind of kaleidoscope that is going on in their head, they do not even notice it. Still, those who can remain for a moment without moving, without speaking and thinking, have certainly a very high opinion of themselves. Only, as I have said, if they are pulled out of it, if someone comes and knocks at the door and they are told, "There is somebody waiting for you", or "Madam, your child is crying", they immediately get furious and say: "There, my meditation is spoilt! Completely spoilt." I am telling you things I have seen with my own eyes. People who were very serious in their meditation, and could not be interrupted in their meditation without their getting violently angry.... Naturally this is not a sign of great spiritual progress. They stormed against everybody because they had been pulled out of their beatific meditation.

Among people who meditate there are some who know how to meditate, who concentrate not on an idea, but in silence, in an inner contemplation in which they say they reach even a union with the Divine; and that is perfectly all right. There are others, just a few, who can follow an idea closely and try to find exactly what it means; that too is all right. Most of the time people try to concentrate and enter into a kind of half sleepy and, in any case, very tamasic state. They become some kind of inert thing; the mind is inert, the feeling is inert, the body is immobile. They can remain like that for hours, for there is nothing more durable than inertia! All this that I am telling you now — these are experiences of people I have met. And these people, when they come out of their meditation, sincerely believe they have done something very great. But they have simply gone down into inertia and unconsciousness. People who know how to meditate are very few in number. Besides, admitting that through much discipline and years of effort you have in your meditation succeeded in coming into conscious relation with the divine Presence, evidently this is a result, and this result should necessarily have an effect upon your character and your life. But this effect is very different according to individuals. There are cases in which the person is split into two in so radical a way that while in meditation such people can enter into contact with the Divine and obtain this supreme felicity of identification, but when they come out of this and lead their normal life, begin to live and act, they can be the most ordinary men with the most ordinary and sometimes even the most vulgar reactions. Indeed, I know people who become altogether ordinary men, and then they do, for example, all the things one should not do, like passing their time in gossiping about others, thinking of themselves only, having all selfish reactions and wanting to organise their life for their petty personal well-being; they do not think of others at all and never do anything for anybody, have no large idea. And yet, in their meditation, they have had this contact. And that is why people who have discovered how very difficult it is to change this petty outer nature that one takes up along with the body, how difficult it is to transcend oneself, to transform one's movements, say: "It is not possible, it is no use trying; in coming to the world, you have taken a body of dust, you have only to let it fall off and prepare to go away, leaving the world as it is; and the only thing to do is to run away as

## 13 May 1953

quickly as one can; and if everybody runs away, there will no longer be a world and therefore no more misery." That's logical. If they are told: "But perhaps what you propose to do is very selfish, to go away and leave others floundering?" — "Well, they have only to do what I do. If everybody did what I am doing, they would get out of it, there would be no longer any world, no longer any misery." As though it depended upon the will of individuals who have not even taken any part in the making of the world! How can they hope to stop it? At least if it was they who had made it, they could know how it was made and could try to undo it (although it is not always easy to undo what one has done), but it is not they who have made it, they do not even know how it has been made and they have the presumption to want to undo it, because they imagine that they themselves can run away from it.... I do not think it is possible. One cannot run away, even if one tries. That however is another subject. In any case, for me, my experience (which is sufficiently long, for it is now almost fifty-three years since I have been dealing with people, with their yoga, their inner efforts; I have seen much here and there, a little everywhere in the world); well, I do not believe that it is by meditation that you can transform yourself. I am absolutely convinced of the contrary.

If while doing what you have to do — whatever it may be, whatever work it is — if you do it and while doing it are careful not to forget the Divine, to offer to Him what you do and try so to give yourself to Him that He may change all your reactions — instead of their being selfish, petty, stupid and ignorant, making them luminous, generous — then in that way you will make progress. Not only will you have made some progress but you will have helped in the general progress. I have never seen people who have left everything in order to go and sit down in a more or less empty contemplation (for it is more or less empty); I have never seen such people making any progress, or in any case their progress is very trifling. I have seen persons who had no pretensions of doing yoga, who were simply filled with enthusiasm by the idea of terrestrial transformation and of the descent of the Divine into the world and who did their little bit of work with that enthusiasm in the heart, giving themselves wholly, without reserve, without any selfish idea of a personal salvation; these I have seen making magnificent progress, truly magnificent. And sometimes they are wonderful. I have seen sannyasis, I have seen people who live in monasteries, I have seen people who professed to be yogis, well, I would not exchange one of the others for a dozen such people (I mean, from the standpoint of terrestrial transformation and world progress, that is to say, from the standpoint of what we want to do, to try that this world may no longer be what it is and may become truly the instrument of the divine Will, with the divine Consciousness). It is not by running away from the world that you will change it. It is by working there, modestly, humbly but with a fire in the heart, something that burns like an offering. *Voilà.*

*So meditation is of no use?*

No, and to the extent it is necessary, it will come spontaneously. All of a sudden, you will be seized by something that makes you still, makes you concentrate in the vision of an idea or of a psychological state. That captures you. You must not resist. Then you make the needed progress. At such a moment you see, you understand something; and then the next minute you start your work again with that something gained in you, but without any pretension. What I most fear are those who believe themselves very exceptional because they sit down and meditate. Of all things this is the most dangerous, because they become so vain and so full of self-satisfaction that they close up in this way all avenues of progress.... There is one thing that has always been said, but always misunderstood, it is the necessity of humility. It is taken in the wrong way, wrongly understood and wrongly used. Be humble, if you can be so in the right way; above all, do not be so in the wrong way, for that leads you nowhere.

**13 May 1953**

But there is one thing: if you can pull out from yourself this weed called vanity, then indeed you will have done something. But if you knew how difficult it is! You cannot do a thing well, cannot have a fine idea, cannot have a right movement, cannot make a little progress without getting puffed up inside (even without being aware of it), with a self-satisfaction full of vanity. And you are obliged then to hammer it hard to break it. And still broken bits remain and these begin to germinate. One must work the whole of one's life and never forget to work in order to uproot this weed that springs up again and again and again so insidiously that you believe it is gone and you feel very modest and say: "It is not I who have done it, I feel it is the Divine, I am nothing if He is not there", and then the next minute, you are so satisfied with yourself simply for having thought that!

*What is the right and the wrong way of being humble?*

It is very simple, when people are told "be humble", they think immediately of "being humble before other men" and that humility is wrong. True humility is humility before the Divine, that is, a precise, exact, *living* sense that one is nothing, one can do nothing, understand nothing without the Divine, that even if one is exceptionally intelligent and capable, this is nothing in comparison with the divine Consciousness, and this sense one must always keep, because then one always has the true attitude of receptivity — a humble receptivity that does not put personal pretensions in opposition to the Divine.

> *You have said: "If you surrender you have to give up effort, but that does not mean that you have to abandon also all willed action."*
> 
> *Questions and Answers 1929 (21 April)*
> 
> *But if one wants to do something, it means personal*

45

*effort, doesn't it? What then is the will?*

There is a difference between the will and this feeling of tension, effort, of counting only on oneself, having recourse to oneself alone which personal effort means; this kind of tension, of something very acute and at times very painful; you count only on yourself and you have the feeling that if you do not make an effort every minute, all will be lost. That is personal effort.

But the will is something altogether different. It is the capacity to concentrate on everything one does, do it as best one can and not stop doing it unless one receives a very precise intimation that it is finished. It is difficult to explain it to you. But suppose, for example, through a concurrence of circumstances, a work comes into your hands. Take an artist who has in one way or another got an inspiration and resolved to paint a picture. He knows very well that if he has no inspiration and is not sustained by forces other than his own, he will do nothing much. It will look more like a daub than a painting. He knows this. But it has been settled, the painting is to be done; there may be many reasons for that, but the painting has to be done. Then if he had the passive attitude, well, he would place his palette, his colours, his brushes, his canvas and then sit down in front of it and say to the Divine: "Now you are going to paint." But the Divine does not do things this way. The painter himself must take up everything and arrange everything, concentrate on his subject, find the forms, the colours that will express it and put his whole will for a more and more perfect execution. His will must be there all the time. But he has to keep the sense that he must be open to the inspiration, he will not forget that in spite of all his knowledge of the technique, in spite of the care he takes to arrange, organise and prepare his colours, his forms, his design, in spite of all that, if he has no inspiration, it will be one picture among a million others and it will not be very interesting. He does not forget. He attempts, he tries to see, to feel what he wants his painting to express and in what way it should be expressed.

### 13 May 1953

He has his colours, he has his brushes, he has his model, he has made his sketch which he will enlarge and make into a picture, he calls his inspiration. There are even some who manage to have a clear, precise vision of what is to be done. But then, day after day, hour after hour, they have this will to work, to study, to do with care all that must be done until they reproduce as perfectly as they can the first inspiration.... That person has worked for the Divine, in communion with Him, but not in a passive way, not with a passive surrender; it is with an active surrender, a dynamic will. The result generally is something very good. Well, the example of the painter is interesting, because a painter who is truly an artist is able to see what he is going to do, he is able to connect himself to the divine Power that is beyond all expression and inspires all expression. For the poet, the writer, it is the same thing and for all people who do something, it is the same.

If you tried that for your lessons, don't you think it would succeed?

*Two days later the Mother took up the subject again in the "Friday Class".*

If you said to yourself, my children, "We want to be as perfect instruments as possible to express the divine Will in the world", then for this instrument to be perfect, it must be cultivated, educated, trained. It must not be left like a shapeless piece of stone. When you want to build with a stone you chisel it; when you want to make a formless block into a beautiful diamond, you chisel it. Well, it is the same thing. When with your brain and body you want to make a beautiful instrument for the Divine, you must cultivate it, sharpen it, refine it, complete what is missing, perfect what is there.

For example, you go to your class. If you are not in a very good mood, you say, "Oh, how tedious it is going to be!" Supposing it is a professor who does not know how to entertain you (one can be a very good professor without knowing how to amuse you, for it is not always easy... there are days when one does not like to be amusing), one would like to be somewhere else rather than at the school. Still, you go to your class, in that way, you go because you have to go, for if you go about according to your whims, you will never have control over yourself, it will be your whims that will control you, it won't be you who will control yourself. You go to your class. But then, on your way there, instead of saying, "Oh, how bored I am going to be, oh, dear! it is not going to be at all interesting", etc., if you say, "There is not a minute in life, there is not a circumstance in one's existence that cannot bring an opportunity for progress; what then is the progress that I am going to make today?... I offer all my little person to the Divine. I want it to be a good instrument for Him to express Himself, that I may be ready one day for the transformation. What am I going to do today? I am going to that class, it is a subject that does not enthuse me; but if I do not know how to take interest in this work, it is perhaps because there is something lacking in me, because somewhere in my brain some cells are missing. But then, if that is so, I am going to try to find out; I am going to listen properly, concentrate properly and above all drive away from my mind this kind of frivolity, this outward levity which makes me feel bored when there's something I do not grasp. Why do I get bored?... Because I do not progress." When one does not progress, one gets bored — old and young, everybody — because we are here upon earth to progress. If we do not progress every minute, well, it is indeed boring, monotonous; it is not always pleasant, it is far from being fine. "So I am going to find out today what progress I can make in this class; there is something I do not know and which I can learn."

If you want to learn, you can learn at every moment. As for me I have learnt even by listening to little children's chatter. Every moment something may happen; someone may say a word to you, even an idiot may say a word that opens you to something enabling you to make some progress. And then,

**13 May 1953**

if you knew, how life becomes interesting! You can no longer get bored, that is gone, everything is interesting, everything is wonderful — because every minute you can learn, at each step make progress. For example, when you are in the street, instead of being simply there and not knowing what you are doing, if you look around, if you observe... I remember having been thus obliged to be in the street on a shopping errand or going to see someone or to purchase something, that's not important; indeed, it is not always pleasant to be in the street, but if you begin to observe and to see how this person walks, how that one moves, how this light plays upon that object, how this little bit of a tree there suddenly makes the landscape pretty, how hundreds of things shine... then every minute you can learn something. Not only can you learn, but I remember to have once had — I was just walking in the street — to have had a kind of illumination, because there was a woman walking in front of me and truly she knew how to walk. How lovely it was! Her movement was magnificent! I saw that and suddenly I saw the whole origin of Greek culture, how all these forms descend towards the world to express Beauty — simply because here was a woman who knew how to walk! You understand, this is how all things become interesting. And so, instead of going to the class and doing stupid things there (I hope none of you does that, I am sure all who come here to my class will never go and do stupid things at school, that it is exceptions that prove the rule; however, I know that unfortunately too many go there and do all the idiotic things one might invent), so, instead of that, if you could go to the class in order to make progress, every day a new little progress — even if it be the understanding why your professor bores you — it would be wonderful, for all of a sudden he will no longer be boring to you, all of a sudden you will discover that he is very interesting! It is like that. If you look at life in this way, life becomes something wonderful. That is the only way of making it interesting, because life upon earth is made to be a field for progress and if we progress to the maximum we draw the maximum benefit from our life upon earth. And then one feels happy. When one does the best one can, one is happy.

*When one is bored, Mother, does that mean one does not progress?*

At that time, yes, certainly without a doubt; not only does one not progress, but one misses an opportunity for progressing. There was a concurrence of circumstances which seemed to you dull, boring, stupid and you were in their midst; well, if you get bored, it means that you yourself are as boring as the circumstances! And that is a clear proof that you are simply not in a state of progress. There is nothing more contrary to the very reason of existence than this passing wave of boredom. If you make a little effort within yourself at that time, if you tell yourself: "Wait a bit, what is it that I should learn? What does all that bring to me so that I may learn something? What progress should I make in overcoming myself? What is the weakness that I must overcome? What is the inertia that I must conquer?" If you say that to yourself, you will see the next minute you are no longer bored. You will immediately get interested and you will make progress! This is a commonplace of consciousness.

And then, you know, most people when they get bored, instead of trying to rise a step higher, descend a step lower, they become still worse than what they were, and they do all the stupid things that others do, go in for all the vulgarities, all the meannesses, everything, in order to amuse themselves. They get intoxicated, take poison, ruin their health, ruin their brain, they utter crudities. They do all that because they are bored. Well, if instead of going down, one had risen up, one would have profited by the circumstances. Instead of profiting, one falls a little lower yet than where one was. When people get a big blow in their life, some misfortune (what men call "misfortune", there are people who do have misfortunes), the first thing they

**13 May 1953**

try to do is to forget it — as though one did not forget quickly enough! And to forget, they do anything whatsoever. When there is something painful, they want to distract themselves — what they call distraction, that is, doing stupid things, that is to say, going down in their consciousness, going down a little instead of rising up.... Has something extremely painful happened to you, something very grievous? Do not become stupefied, do not seek forgetfulness, do not go down into the inconscience; you must go to the end and find the light that is behind, the truth, the force and the joy; and for that you must be strong and refuse to slide down. But that we shall see a little later, my children, when you will be a little older.

## 20 May 1953

*You have said: "And as for those who have the will of running away, even they, when they go over to the other side, may find that the flight was not of much use after all."*

*Questions and Answers 1929 (28 April)*

*What do you call "the other side"?*

We speak of the other side of the veil, the other side of existence.

It is being no longer in the physical: being in the vital, for example, or in the conscious part of the vital. One becomes conscious of two sides and so knows what is happening. There are people who go out of their body methodically to have the experience of the separation between the two. But as for that, one must know how to do it, and one must not do it all alone. Someone should be there to look after and watch the body.

*Are not offering and surrender to the Divine the same thing?*

They are two aspects of the same thing, but not altogether the same. One is more active than the other. They do not belong to quite the same plane of existence.

For example, you have decided to offer your life to the Divine, you take that decision. But all of a sudden, something altogether unpleasant, unexpected happens to you and your first movement is to react and protest. Yet you have made the offering, you have said once for all: "My life belongs to the Divine", and then suddenly an extremely unpleasant incident happens (that can happen) and there is something in you that reacts, that does not want it. But here, if you want to be truly logical with

**20 May 1953**

your offering, you must bring forward this unpleasant incident, make an offering of it to the Divine, telling him very sincerely: "Let Your will be done; if You have decided it that way, it will be that way." And this must be a willing and spontaneous adhesion. So it is very difficult.

Even for the smallest thing, something that is not in keeping with what you expected, what you have worked for, instead of an opposite reaction coming in — spontaneously, irresistibly, you draw back: "No, not that" — if you have made a complete surrender, a total surrender, well, it does not happen like that: you are as quiet, as peaceful, as calm in one case as in the other. And perhaps you had the notion that it would be better if it happened in a certain way, but if it happens differently, you find that this also is all right. You might have, for example, worked very hard to do a certain thing, so that something might happen, you might have given much time, much of your energy, much of your will, and all that not for your own sake, but, say, for the divine work (that is the offering); now suppose that after having taken all this trouble, done all this work, made all these efforts, it all goes just the other way round, it does not succeed. If you are truly surrendered, you say: "It is good, it is all good, it is all right; I did what I could, as well as I could, now it is not my decision, it is the decision of the Divine, I accept entirely what He decides." On the other hand, if you do not have this deep and spontaneous surrender, you tell yourself: "How is it? I took so much trouble to do a thing which is not for a selfish purpose, which is for the Divine Work, and this is the result, it is not successful!" Ninety-nine times out of a hundred, it is like that.

True surrender is a very difficult thing.

*For self-surrender, should one continue to do what one ought to do?*

Continue to do what one *ought* to, what is clearly shown as the thing that ought to be done, what is to be done — whether one succeeds or does not succeed, whether the result is what one thinks or expects or isn't — that has no importance; one continues.

*But when one tries, if one makes a mistake unconsciously, how can one know?*

If you are quite sincere, you know. Not to know one's fault is always the sign of an insincerity somewhere. And generally, it is hidden in the vital. When the vital consents to collaborate (which is already a big step), when it decides that it too is going to work, to devote all its effort and all its energy to accomplish the work, even then there is underneath, well hidden somewhere, a sort of — how shall we call it? — an expectation that things will turn out well and the result will be favourable. And that veils the complete sincerity. For this expectation is an egoistic, personal thing, and this veils the full sincerity. Then you do not know.

But if one is altogether, absolutely sincere, as soon as what one is doing is not exactly what should be done, one feels it very clearly — not violently but very clearly, very precisely: "No, not this." And then if one has no attachment, immediately it stops, instantaneously it stops.

Only one has attachment, even for a disinterested work. That's what you must understand. You have given your life for a cause that is not egoistic, but the ego is there all the same. And you have a way of doing the thing which is special, personal to you; and you have within you a hope (not to speak of a desire) that the result will be like this, that you will get this and it will be done. Even a work that is not done for yourself but which you have undertaken, you expect that it will succeed, that you will have success — not personally — for the thing you have undertaken, the work that you are doing. Well, that brings in just a little bit of something like that, down below, quite hidden, quite a tiny thing which is a little... not very straight, a little bent, twisted. And then you do not know. But if that were not there, as soon as you failed to do exactly what should be done, you would know. You would know it absolutely precisely. It is as delicate a movement as the thousandth part of a millimetre would be. Yes, it is there, and that is sufficient, you know: "I was mistaken." But you must have that absolute sincerity which precisely does not want at any cost to blunder, which will do anything, give up everything, everything, rather than live in any kind of illusion. But it is very difficult; it takes time and much labour. When you are doing a thing, always those two, the mind and the vital are there, trying to draw some benefit or other out of what you are doing: the benefit of personal satisfaction, the benefit of happiness, the benefit of a good opinion that you have of yourself. It is difficult not to deceive oneself.

*What is the exact way of feeling that we belong to the Divine and that the Divine is acting in us?*

You must not feel with your head (because you may think so, but that's something vague); you must feel with your sense-feeling. Naturally one begins by wanting it with the mind, because that is the first thing that understands. And then one has an aspiration here (*pointing to the heart*), with a flame which pushes you to realise it. But if you want it to be truly *the* thing, well, you must feel it.

You are doing something, suppose, for example, you are doing exercises, weight-lifting. Now suddenly without your knowing how it happened, suddenly you have the feeling that there is a force infinitely greater than you, greater, more powerful, a force that does the lifting for you. Your body becomes something almost non-existent and there is this Something that lifts. And then you will see; when that happens to you, you will no longer ask how it should be done, you will know. That does happen.

It depends upon people, depends upon what dominates in

their being. Those who think have suddenly the feeling that it is no longer they who think, that there is something which knows much better, sees much more clearly, which is infinitely more luminous, more conscious in them, which organises the thoughts and words; and then they write. But if the experience is complete, it is even no longer they who write, it is that same Thing that takes hold of their hand and makes it write. Well, one knows at that moment that the little physical person is just a tiny insignificant tool trying to remain as quiet as possible in order not to disturb the experience.

Yes, at no cost must the experience be disturbed. If suddenly you say: "Oh, look, how strange it is!"...

*How can we reach that state?*

Aspire for it, want it. Try to be less and less selfish, but not in the sense of becoming nice to other people or forgetting yourself, not that: have less and less the feeling that you are a person, a separate entity, something existing in itself, isolated from the rest.

And then, above all, above all, it is that inner flame, that aspiration, that need for the light. It is a kind of — how to put it? — luminous enthusiasm that seizes you. It is an irresistible need to melt away, to give oneself, to exist only in the Divine.

At that moment you have the experience of your aspiration.

But that moment should be absolutely sincere and as integral as possible; and all this must occur not only in the head, not only here, but must take place everywhere, in all the cells of the body. The consciousness integrally must have this irresistible need.... The thing lasts for some time, then diminishes, gets extinguished. You cannot keep these things for very long. But then it so happens that a moment later or the next day or some time later, suddenly you have the opposite experience. Instead of feeling this ascent, and all that, this is no longer there and you have the feeling of the Descent, the Answer. And nothing but the

## 20 May 1953

Answer exists. Nothing but the divine thought, the divine will, the divine energy, the divine action exists any longer. And you too, you are no longer there.

That is to say, it is the answer to our aspiration. It may happen immediately afterwards — that is very rare but may happen. If you have both simultaneously, then the state is perfect; usually they alternate; they alternate more and more closely until the moment there is a total fusion. Then there is no more distinction. I heard a Sufi mystic, who was besides a great musician, an Indian, saying that for the Sufis there was a state higher than that of adoration and surrender to the Divine, than that of devotion, that this was not the last stage; the last stage of the progress is when there is no longer any distinction; you have no longer this kind of adoration or surrender or consecration; it is a very simple state in which one makes no distinction between the Divine and oneself. They know this. It is even written in their books. It is a commonly known condition in which everything becomes quite simple. There is no longer any difference. There is no longer that kind of ecstatic surrender to "Something" which is beyond you in every way, which you do not understand, which is merely the result of your aspiration, your devotion. There is no difference any longer. When the union is perfect, there is no longer any difference.

*Is this the end of self-progress?*

There is never any end to progress — never any end, you can never put a fullstop there.

*Can that happen before the transformation of the body?*

Before the transformation of the body?... This is a phenomenon of consciousness. For instance, the physical consciousness may have this experience even for years before the cells change. There is a great difference between the physical consciousness (the body consciousness) and the material body. This takes a long time, because it is a thing that has never been done. That state, as I have already told you, is a commonly known state which has been realised by some people, the most advanced, the highest among the mystics; but the transformation of the body has never been done by anyone.

And it takes a terribly long time. Sri Aurobindo said — one day I asked him: "How long will it take to transform the body?" He did not hesitate, he said: "Oh! something like three hundred years."

*Three hundred years from when?*

Three hundred years from the time one has the consciousness I was just speaking about. (*Laughter*)

No, the conclusion, what you must succeed in doing, is to be able to prolong life at will: not to leave the body until one wants to.

So, if one has resolved to transform the body, well, one must wait with all the necessary patience — three hundred years, five hundred years, a thousand years, it does not matter — the time needed for the change. As for me, I see that three hundred years is a minimum. To tell you the truth, with the experience I have of things, I think it is truly a minimum.

Just imagine. You have never thought about what it means, have you? How is your body built? In a purely animal way, with all the organs and all the functions. You are absolutely dependent: if your heart stops for even the thousandth part of a second, you are gone and that's the end. The whole thing works and works automatically without your conscious will (happily for you, for if you had to supervise the functioning, it would have gone the wrong way long ago). All that is there. Everything is necessary, because it was organised in that manner. You cannot do without an organ, at least totally; there must be something in you representing it.

## 20 May 1953

Transformation implies that all this purely material arrangement is replaced by an arrangement of concentrations of force having certain types of different vibrations substituting each organ by a centre of conscious energy moved by a conscious will and directed by a movement coming from above, from higher regions. No stomach, no heart any longer, no circulation, no lungs, no... All this disappears. But it is replaced by a whole set of vibrations representing what those organs are symbolically. For the organs are only the material symbols of centres of energy; they are not the essential reality; they simply give it a form or a support in certain given circumstances. The transformed body will then function through its *real* centres of energy and not any longer through their symbolic representatives such as were developed in the animal body. Therefore, first of all you must know what your heart represents in the cosmic energy and what the circulation represents and what the stomach and the brain represent. To begin with, you must first be conscious of all that. And then, you must have at your disposal the original vibrations of that which is symbolised by these organs. And you must slowly gather together all these energies in your body and change each organ into a centre of conscious energy which will replace the symbolic movement by the real one.... You believe it will take only three hundred years to do that? I believe it will take much more time to have a form with qualities which will not be exactly those we know, but will be much superior; a form that one naturally dreams to see plastic: as the expression of your face changes with your feelings, so the body will change (not the form but within the same form) in accordance with what you want to express with your body. It can become very concentrated, very developed, very luminous, very sane, with a perfect plasticity, with a perfect elasticity and a lightness as one wills... Have you never dreamt of giving a kick to the ground and then soaring into the air, flying away? You move about. You push a little with your shoulder, you go this way; you push again, you go that way; and you go wherever you like, quite easily; and finally when you have finished you come back, enter your body. Well, you must be able to do that with your body, and also certain things related to respiration — but there will no longer be lungs; there's a true movement behind a symbolic movement which gives you this capacity of lightness; you do not belong any longer to the system of gravitation, you escape it.[1] And so for each organ.

There is no end to imagination: to be luminous whenever one wants it, to be transparent whenever one wants it. Naturally there is no longer any need of any bones also in the system; it is not a skeleton with skin and viscera, it is another thing. It is concentrated energy obeying the will. This does not mean that there will no longer be any definite and recognisable forms; the form will be built by qualities rather than by solid particles. It will be, if one may say so, a practical or pragmatic form; it will be supple, mobile, light at will, in contrast to the fixity of the gross material form.

So, to change this into what I have just described, I believe three hundred years are truly very little. It seems many more than that are needed. Perhaps with a very, very, very concentrated work...

*Three hundred years with the same body?*

Well, there is change, it is no longer the same body.

But, you see, when our little humanity says three hundred years with the same body, you say: "Why! when I am fifty it

---

[1] According to Sri Aurobindo, this true movement behind respiration is the same as the one governing electrical and magnetic fields; it is what the ancient yogis used to call Vayu, the Life-Energy. The breathing exercises (*prāṇāyāma*) are simply one system (among others) for acquiring mastery over Vayu which eventually enables you to be free from gravitation and gives certain powers known to the ancients: the power to be extremely light or extremely heavy, very big or very tiny (*garimā, laghimā, mahimā, aṇimā*). As an appendix to this talk we publish an extract from a conversation of Sri Aurobindo with a French scientist-disciple, dealing with some of these "true movements" behind the external movements of Matter.

**20 May 1953**

already begins to decompose, so at three hundred it will be a horrible thing!" But it is not like that. If it is three hundred years with a body that goes on perfecting itself from year to year, perhaps when the three hundredth year is reached one will say: "Oh! I still need three or four hundred more to be what I want to be." If each year that passes represents a progress, a transformation, one would like to have more and more years in order to be able to transform oneself more and more. When something is not exactly as you want it to be — take, for example, simply one of the things I have just described, say, plasticity or lightness or elasticity or luminosity, and none of them is exactly as you want it, then you will still need at least two hundred years more so that it may be accomplished, but you never think: "How is it? It is still going to last two hundred years more!" On the contrary, you say: "Two hundred years more are *absolutely* necessary so that it may be truly done." And then, when all is done, when all is perfect, then there is no longer any question of years, for you are immortal.

But there are many objections that may be raised. It may be said that it would be impossible for the body to change unless something changes in the surroundings also. What would be your relation with other objects if you have changed so much? With other beings also? It seems necessary that a whole set of things changes, at least in relative proportions, so that one can exist, continue to exist. This then brings much complication, for it is no longer one individual consciousness that has to do the work, it becomes a collective consciousness. And so it is much more difficult still.

(*Silence*)

*If we are not conscious of all that the Divine is doing for us, do we not progress?*

You progress, but you are not conscious of your progress; and so it is not a willed progress. That is, it is a progress that the Divine brings about in you without your collaboration. That takes much more time. It does occur, but it takes much more time. When you are conscious and collaborate and indeed do consciously what you should do, it is done much more quickly.

There are many people who are not even conscious, the immense majority of people are not even conscious of the action of the divine Force in them. If you speak to them about it, they look at you in round-eyed wonder, they think you are half mad, they don't know what you are talking about. That is the vast majority of human beings. And yet the Consciousness is at work, working all the time. It moulds them from within whether they want it or not. But then, when they become conscious of this, there are people who are shocked by it, who are so stupid as to revolt and say: "Ah! no, I want it to be *myself*!" Myself, that is, an imbecile who knows nothing. And then, that stage too passes. At last there comes a moment when one collaborates and says: "Oh! What joy!" And you give yourself, you want to be as passive and receptive as possible so as not to stand in the way of this divine Will, this divine Consciousness that is acting. You become more and more attentive, and exactly to the extent you become more attentive and more sincere, you feel in what direction, in what movement this divine Consciousness is working, and you give yourself to it wholly. The thing ripens more quickly. And in this way you are truly able to do in a few minutes the work that would otherwise take years. And that is the goal of yoga: one can do the work in a few hours, in a concentrated, shortened time; one can do in another way what Nature is doing — Nature will do it, Nature will succeed in transforming all this, but when one sees the time she has taken to do what she has done till now, if one wants to do all that in another way.... Evidently, for the divine Consciousness time means very little, but for the consciousness here, it is very long. There is a point of view from which you say: "Bah! That will be done, it is sure to come about, so it is all right, one has

**20 May 1953**

only to let things go on." But then it is not the external human consciousness, it does not take part, for this tiny consciousness which has been formed by the body (this body that's at present made in this way), well, it will have gone away long before the thing is done. Because after all the progress of Nature is not accomplished from one century to another. If we look back, we do not see that there has been really much progress in comparison with what man was some three thousand years ago — just a little, something; something that happens particularly in the head which understands a little better; and then a kind of control over what Nature does, an understanding of her processes; one begins to understand her tricks. Then as one begins to learn her tricks, one begins to intervene. But as one does not have the true knowledge, when one intervenes one may very easily make a lot of blunders.... Indeed, I do not know what will happen when men will know all the secrets of the formation of matter, for example. They have already invented a very fine way of destroying themselves. We shall see what is going to happen. But this is just a very small step; it happens particularly here (*pointing to the head*), with very relative material results.

*How should one practise this consciousness?*

You must establish this will to be conscious constantly and then change the mental will into an aspiration. You must have this movement. And then never to forget. You must look, look at yourself, and look at your life with the sincerity not to make a mistake, never to deceive yourself. Oh! how difficult it is!

Did you ever have spontaneously — spontaneously without effort — the perception that you had made a mistake? I am not speaking of an external reaction that gives you a knock, wakes you up suddenly and you say: "Ah! damn it, what have I done?" I am not speaking of that. When you do a thing, feel a thing, when you say a thing — take simply the petty quarrels like those I hear about at least a dozen of them a day (at least), idiotic, (I wonder how, having one's reason, one can quarrel about such things), well, at the time you utter those words that should not be uttered, that are simply silly, do you see that you are truly stupid — not to say anything worse — spontaneously?... You always give an excuse. You have always the feeling that the other person is wrong, and that you are right and that, indeed, he must be told that he is wrong, yes? Otherwise he would never know it! Isn't that so? I am putting the thing rather glaringly, as though under a small microscope, so that it may look a little bigger. But it is like that. And so long as it is like that, you are a million miles away from the true consciousness. When you are unable immediately, instantaneously to step back, put yourself in the place of the other person, understand why he has this feeling, have a glimpse of your own weakness, compare the two and come to the conclusion: "Well, it is that, that's the true thing", it means that you are still very far behind. When you are able to do it spontaneously, instantaneously, when it does not take time, when it is a natural movement, then you may feel satisfied that you have made a little progress.... How many times do you have the experience during the day? Even if you do not come to an open quarrel, how many times is the reaction there in the head, there, something that leaps up in the head, instead of this wisdom of equanimity which, at the very moment things are happening and it is observing them, understands how they are happening and why all this occurs — and that impersonally enough to be able to smile always and never have a violent reaction, never.

And even if you perceive the Truth, which is far beyond and far above, and the Truth that is not realised and you want to realise, if you have its clear vision and can see constantly the difference between what is true and what should be and what is false and deformed and must give place to the other, see it so clearly, there is no reaction any longer, and even things that seem to you most stupid, most idiotic, most obscure, most ignorant, most vulgar, most crude can make you smile, for you are able to see the whole length of the way you have to cover so that That which is up there may come down here. And if you had had violent reactions, long ago there would have been no world any more. Because, in truth, if the world could exist only on condition of its being true, then long ago it would have ceased to exist! For it has never been true even to this very day.

But if you remain in that consciousness and look from there, then you begin to understand something of the truth. And this consciousness has to be so total, that even if things come directly against you, even the physical movement of someone coming to beat you (you must not allow him to kill you, no; you have perhaps to do what is necessary not to get killed), but if you are yourself in this perfect consciousness and have no personal reaction, well, I give you the guarantee the other cannot kill you. He will not be able to, even if he tries. He will not be able to beat you, even if he tries. Only, you must not have a single violent or wrong vibration, you understand? Even if there is just a little false vibration, that opens the door and the thing enters and all goes wrong. You must be fully conscious, have the full knowledge, the perfect mastery over everything, the clear vision of the Truth — and perfect peace.

You must make an effort all the time.
*Voilà.*

## APPENDIX

*(Extract from a talk of Sri Aurobindo with a French scientist disciple)*

8 May 1926

In the West the highest minds are turned not towards spiritual truth but towards material science. The scope of science is very narrow, it touches only the most exterior part of the physical plane.

And even there, what does science know really? It studies the functioning of the laws, builds theories ever renewed and each time held up as the last word of truth! We had recently the atomic theory, now comes the electronic.

There are, for instance, two statements of modern science that would stir up deeper ranges for an occultist:

1. Atoms are whirling systems like the solar system.
2. The atoms of all the elements are made out of the same constituents. Different arrangement is the only cause of different properties.

If these statements were considered under their true aspect, they could lead science to new discoveries of which there is no idea at present and in comparison with which the present knowledge is poor.

According to the experience of ancient Yogis, sensible matter was made out of five elements, Bhutani: Prithivi, Apas, Agni (Tejas), Vayu, Akasha.

Agni is threefold:

1. Ordinary fire, Jada Agni,
2. Electric fire, Vaidyuta Agni,
3. Solar fire, Saura Agni.

Science has only entered upon the first and the second of these fires. The fact that the atom is like the solar system could

20 May 1953

lead it to the knowledge of the third.[2]

Beyond Agni is Vayu of which science knows nothing. It is the support of all contact and exchange, the cause of gravitation and of the fields (magnetic and electric). By it, the action of Agni, the formal element, the builder of forms, is made possible.

And beyond Vayu is the ether: Akasha.

But these five constitute only the grossest part of the physical plane. Immediately behind is the physical-vital, the element of life buried in matter. J. C. Bose is contacting this element in his experiments. Beyond is the mind in matter. This mind has a far different form than the human mind, still it is a manifestation of the same principle of organisation. And deep below there are two more hidden layers....

That is the occult knowledge concerning the physical plane only. Science is far behind this knowledge.

The Hindu Yogis who had realised these truths did not elaborate them and turn them into scientific knowledge. Other fields of action and knowledge having been open before them, they neglected what for them was the most exterior aspect of the manifestation.

There is a difference between the scientific mind and the cast of mind of an occultist. There is little doubt that one who could unite these two groups of faculties would lead science towards great progress.

---

[2] [It is remarkable to observe that since then (1926) we have indeed discovered a third "fire", that which accompanies nuclear reactions — and that this fire is in fact that of the sun, the enormous radiation of which is liberated in course of the fusion of hydrogen nuclei into helium (Bethe cycle). The first fire is that of chemical reactions wherein molecules get destroyed and reconstituted without the constituent atoms being changed. The second fire comes from the modifications of the peripheral levels of the electrons in the atom, modifications which are at the origin of all electro-magnetic phenomena.]

## 27 May 1953

*"There is a state of consciousness in union with the Divine in which you can enjoy all you read, as you can all you observe, even the most indifferent books or the most uninteresting things. You can hear poor music, even music from which one would like to run away, and yet you can, not for its outward self but because of what is behind, enjoy it. You do not lose the distinction between good music and bad music, but you pass through either into that which it expresses. For there is nothing in the world which has not its ultimate truth and support in the Divine."*

Questions and Answers 1929 (28 April)

*What is there "behind" the external form of music?*

Music is a means of expressing certain thoughts, feelings, emotions, aspirations. There is even a region where all these movements exist and from there, as they are brought down, they take a musical form. One who is a very good composer, with some inspiration, will produce very beautiful music, for he is a good musician. A bad musician may also have a very high inspiration; he may receive something which is good, but as he possesses no musical capacity, what he produces is terribly commonplace, ordinary, uninteresting. But if you go beyond, if you reach just the place where there is this origin of music — of the idea and emotion and inspiration — if you reach there, you can taste these things without being in the least troubled by the forms; the commonplace musical form can be linked up again with that, because that was the inspiration of the writer of the music. Naturally, there are cases where there is no inspiration, where the origin is merely a kind of mechanical music. It is not

*27 May 1953*

always interesting in every case. But what I mean is that there is an inner condition in which the external form is not the most important thing; it is the origin of the music, the inspiration from beyond, which is important; it is not purely the sounds, it is what the sounds express.

*So the expression cannot be better than the inspiration?*

There are musical pieces which have no inspiration, they are like mechanical works. There are musicians who possess a great virtuosity, that is, who have thoroughly mastered the technique and who, for example, can execute without making a mistake the fastest and most difficult things. They can play music but it expresses nothing: it is like a machine. It means nothing, except that they have great skill. For what is most important is the inspiration, in everything that one does; in all human creations the most important thing is inspiration. Naturally, the execution must be on the same level as the inspiration; to be able to express truly well the highest things one must have a very good technique. I do not say that technique is not necessary; it is even indispensable, but it is not the only indispensable thing, it is less important than inspiration.

The essential quality of music depends upon where the music comes from, upon its origin.

*What does "its origin" mean?*

Its starting point. Just as the spring is the source of the river.

*Are there many sources for everything?*

All physical life has the vital and mental life as its origin. The mental and the vital reality have themselves another origin, and so on. Nothing can be manifested physically upon earth that has not a higher truth at its origin, otherwise the world would not exist. If it were a flat thing having its origin in itself, it would very soon cease to exist. It is because there is a force which pushes, an energy which pushes towards manifestation, that life continues to exist. Otherwise it would exhaust itself very soon.

> *If everything that is manifested in the physical world has its origin in the higher Truth, what is it that makes it ugly when it expresses itself? Why are there ugly things at all?*

Because there are forces that intervene between the origin and the manifestation.

If I ask you, "Do you know the truth of your being?" What will you say?... Do you know it? Well, the same holds for everything. And yet you are already a sufficiently evolved thinking being who has passed through all kinds of refinements. You are no longer quite like, let us say, a lizard that runs on the wall; and yet you would not be able to say what the truth of your being is. That is just the secret of all deformations in the world. It is because there is all the inconscience created by the fact of separation from the Origin. It is due to this inconscience that the Origin, though always there, is not able to manifest itself. It is there, that is why the world exists. But in its expression it is deformed because it manifests itself through the inconscience, ignorance and obscurity.

It is something I shall try to explain in the next number of the *Bulletin*.[1] But still, very briefly summed up, it is this:

In creating the universe as it was, the Will was an individual projection — individual, you understand, a scattering: instead of being a unity containing all, it was a unity made of innumerable small unities which are individualisations, that is, things that feel themselves separated. And the very fact of being separated from all others is what gives you the feeling that you are an

---

[1] See *The Four Austerities* (the *tapasyā* of love).

individual. Otherwise you would have the feeling that you were a fluid mass. For example, instead of being conscious of your external form and of everything in your being which makes of you a separate individuality, if you were conscious of the vital forces which move everywhere or of the inconscient that is at the base of all, you would have the feeling of a mass moving with all kinds of contradictory movements but which could not be separated from each other; you would not have the feeling of being an individual at all: you would have the feeling of something like a vibration in the midst of a whole. Well, the original Will was to form individual beings capable of becoming conscious once again of their divine origin. Because of the process of individualisation one must feel separate if one is to be an individual. The moment you are separated, you are cut off from the original consciousness, at least apparently, and you fall into the inconscient. For the only thing which is the Life of life is the Origin, if you cut yourself off from that, consciousness naturally is changed into unconsciousness. And then it is due to this very unconsciousness that you are no longer aware of the truth of your being.... It is a process. You cannot argue whether it is inevitable or evitable; the fact is it is like that. This process of formation and creation is the reason why purity no longer manifests in its essence and in its purity but through the deformation of unconsciousness and ignorance.... If you had answered immediately: "Yes, of course, I know the truth of my being!" it would have finished there, there wouldn't have been any problem.

That is why there is all this ugliness, there is death; that is why there is illness; that is why there is wickedness; that is why there is suffering. There is no remedy, there is only one way for all these things. All this is there in different domains and with different vibrations, but the cause of all is the same. It is inconscience produced because of the necessity of individual formation. Once again I do not say that it was indispensable. That is another problem which perhaps later on we shall be ready to solve; but for the moment we are obliged to state that that's how it is.

And so, the remedy? Since such is the cause, the only way of putting everything right is to become conscious once again. And this is very simple, very simple.

Suppose that there are in the universe two opposing and contradictory forces, as some religions have preached: there was good and evil, and there always will be good and evil, there will be a conflict, a battle, a struggle. The one that is stronger, whether it be the good or the evil, will win; if there is more of the good, the good will win and if there is more of the evil, the evil will win; but the two will always exist. If it were like that, it would be hopeless; one wouldn't have to say then that it is either difficult or easy, it would be impossible. One would not be able to get out of it. But actually that is not so.

Actually there is but one Origin and this origin is the perfection of Truth, for that is the only thing which truly exists; and by exteriorising, projecting, scattering itself, it brings forth what we see, and a crowd of tiny heads, very gentle, very brilliant, in search of something they have not yet seized but which they can seize, because what they are in search of is within them. That is a certainty. It may take more or less time, but it is sure to come. The remedy is at the very core of the evil. *Voilà*.

It has been called by various names, each one has presented it in his own way. According to the angle of seeing, one's experience differs. All those who have found the Divine within themselves have found Him in a certain way, following a certain experience and from a certain angle, and this angle was self-evident to them. But then, if they are not well on their guard, they begin to say: "To find the Divine, one must do this and do that. And it is like that and it is that path one should follow", because for them that was the path of success. When one goes a little further, has a little more experience, one becomes aware that it is not necessarily like that, it can be done through millions of ways.... There is only one thing that is certain, it is that what is

### 27 May 1953

found is always the same. And that's remarkable, that whatever the path followed, whatever the form given to it, the result is always the same. Their experience and everyone's is the same. When they have touched the Thing, it is for all the same thing. And this is just the proof that they have touched That, because it is the same thing for all. If it is not the same thing, it means that they have not yet touched That. When they have touched That, it is the same thing. And to That, you may give all the names you like, it makes no difference.

Words are words. After all, they mean nothing, unless there is something behind. Have you never noticed that when you speak to certain people, you may express yourself quite clearly and yet they understand nothing; and to others you say just two words and they understand immediately? You have not had this experience? No? I have had it often. Therefore, it does not depend upon the external form, the words one speaks, but on the force of the thought one puts into them; and the greater, stronger, more precise and clear the thought-force, the more the chance of what you say being understood by people who are able to receive that force. But if one speaks without thinking, usually it is impossible to understand what he says. It makes a kind of noise, that is all. For example, when you have the habit of speaking with someone, exchanging ideas with him, when between the two of you there is a certain mental adjustment, that is, when you have taken the precaution of saying, "When I use this word, I mean this", and the other person has said, "When I use that word, I mean that", and so on; when you are used to an interchange, when you have established a kind of contact between brain and brain — even if it be only that — you understand each other quite easily. But with people who come altogether from elsewhere, with whom you have never spoken, you need a little time to adjust and adapt yourself to understand what they mean by the words they use.... What is it that makes you understand? It is just the kind of mental sense that is behind the words. When the thought is strongly thought out, there is a powerful vibration and it is that which is sensed; the word is only an intermediary means. You can develop this sense to the point of having a direct mental contact with a minimum of words or even without any words at all; but then you must have a very great force of thought-concentration. And for everything one does, it is like that. When there is a developed consciousness behind, when one has the power to concentrate it, one can do anything at all — this consciousness will act.[2] Certainly it is not the bodily mechanism that makes you act; the mechanism is simply an instrument, nothing more. The day you catch that (it is invisible, but you can catch it), and when you catch it and put it into your movement, this movement becomes conscious and you do well whatever you do. The day you do not catch it, it slips from you like water through your fingers; and then you are clumsy, you do not understand, you do not know what to do. Hence, it is not the physical mechanism that counts, it is what is behind.

*From what plane does music generally come?*

There are different levels. There is a whole category of music that comes from the higher vital, which is very catching, somewhat (not to put it exactly) vulgar, it is something that twists your nerves. This music is not necessarily unpleasant, but generally it seizes you there in the nervous centres. So there is one type of music which has a vital origin. There is music which has a psychic origin — it is altogether different. And then there is music which has a spiritual origin: it is very bright and it carries you away, captures you entirely. But if you want to execute this music correctly you must be able to make it come through the vital passage. Your music coming from above may become

---

[2] At the time of the first publication of this talk, in 1968, Mother added the following commentary: "What is important is to keep the consciousness of the Presence, that is, the Presence must be concrete, and then all that one does and all that one says — whatever one may do and whatever one may say — it is this Presence that expresses itself."

externally quite flat if you do not possess that intensity of vital vibration which gives it its splendour and strength. I knew people who had truly a very high inspiration and it became quite flat, because the vital did not stir. I must admit that by their spiritual practices they had put to sleep their vital completely — it was literally asleep, it did not act at all — and the music came straight into the physical, and if one were connected with the origin of that music, one could see that it was something wonderful, but externally it had no force, it was a little melody, very poor, very thin; there was none of the strength of harmony. When you can bring the vital into play, then all the strength of vibration is there. If you draw into it this higher origin, it becomes the music of a genius.

For music it is very special; it is difficult, it needs an intermediary. And it is like that for all other things, for literature also, for poetry, for painting, for everything one does. The true value of one's creation depends on the origin of one's inspiration, on the level, the height where one finds it. But the value of the execution depends on the vital strength which expresses it. To complete the genius both must be there. This is very rare. Generally it is the one or the other, more often the vital. And then there are those other kinds of music we have — the music of the *café-concert*, of the cinema — it has an extraordinary skill, and at the same time an exceptional platitude, an extraordinary vulgarity. But as it has an extraordinary skill, it seizes you in the solar plexus and it is this music that you remember; it grasps you at once and holds you and it is very difficult to free yourself from it, for it is well-made music, music very well made. It is made vitally with vital vibrations, but what is behind is frightful.

But imagine this same vital power of expression, with the inspiration coming from far above — the highest inspiration possible, when all the heavens open before us — then that becomes wonderful. There are certain passages of César Franck, certain passages of Beethoven, certain passages of Bach, there are pieces by others also which have this inspiration and power. But it is only a moment, it comes as a moment, it does not last. You cannot take the entire work of an artist as being on that level. Inspiration comes like a flash; sometimes it lasts sufficiently long, when the work is sustained; and when that is there, the *same effect* is produced, that is, if you are attentive and concentrated, suddenly that lifts you up, lifts up all your energies, it is as though someone opened out your head and you were flung into the air to tremendous heights and magnificent lights. It produces in a few seconds results that are obtained with so much difficulty through so many years of yoga. Only, in general, one may fall down afterwards, because the consciousness is not there as the basis; one has the experience and afterwards does not even know what has happened. But if you are prepared, if you have indeed prepared your consciousness by yoga and then the thing happens, it is almost definitive.

*What is the cause of the great difference between European and Indian music? Is it the origin or the expression?*

It is both but in an inverse sense.

This very high inspiration comes only rarely in European music; rare also is a psychic origin, very rare. Either it comes from high above or it is vital. The expression is almost always, except in a few rare cases, a vital expression — interesting, powerful. Most often, the origin is purely vital. Sometimes it comes from the very heights, then it is wonderful. Sometimes it is psychic, particularly in what has been religious music, but this is not very frequent.

Indian music, when there are good musicians, has almost always a psychic origin; for example, the *rāgas* have a psychic origin, they come from the psychic. The inspiration does not often come from above. But Indian music is very rarely embodied in a strong vital. It has rather an inner and intimate origin. I have heard a great deal of Indian music, a great deal; I have rarely heard Indian music having vital strength, very rarely; perhaps

**27 May 1953**

not more than four or five times. But very often I have heard Indian music having a psychic origin, it translates itself almost directly into the physical. And truly one must then concentrate, and as it is — how to put it? — very tenuous, very subtle, as there are none of those intense vital vibrations, one can easily glide within it and climb back to the psychic origin of the music. It has that effect upon you, it is a kind of ecstatic trance, as from an intoxication. It makes you enter a little into trance. Then if you listen well and let yourself go, you move on and glide, glide into a psychic consciousness. But if you remain only in the external consciousness, the music is so tenuous that there is no response from the vital, it leaves you altogether flat. Sometimes, there was a vital force, then it became quite good.... I myself like this music very much, this kind of theme developing into a play. The theme is essentially very musical: and then it is developed with variations, innumerable variations, and it is always the same theme which is developed in one way or another. In Europe there were musicians who were truly musicians and they too had the thing: Bach had it, he used to do the same sort of thing, Mozart had it, his music was purely musical, he had no intention of expressing any other thing, it was music for music's sake. But this manner of taking a certain number of notes in a certain relation (they are like almost infinite variations), personally I find it wonderful to put you in repose, and you enter deep within yourself. And then, if you are ready, it gives you the psychic consciousness: something that makes you withdraw from the external consciousness, which makes you enter elsewhere, enter within.

*In what form does music come to the great composers? That is, is it only the melody that comes or is it what we hear?*

But that depends upon the musician. This is just what I was saying. For example, here in India, the science of harmony does not exist much, so the thing is translated by melody. As soon as the vital intervenes, there comes a kind of harmonic complexity in the music. That gives it a richness, a plenitude which it did not have.

*But is it the melody that comes?*

No, it is the music, and music is not necessarily melody. It is a relation of sounds which is not necessarily melodic. Melody is a part of this relation of sounds.

> *"When the resolution has been taken, when you have decided that the whole of your life shall be given to the Divine, you have still at every moment to remember it and carry it out in all the details of your existence. You must feel at every step that you belong to the Divine; you must have the constant experience that, in whatever you think or do, it is always the Divine Consciousness that is acting through you."*
> Questions and Answers 1929 (28 April)

*When one is conscious does one perceive the Divine in His form in everything?*

Oh! that is, you expect to see a divine form in everything!... I do not know, that may happen. But I have the feeling that a great deal of imagination enters into it, for it is not like that. You change consciousness, you change the state of consciousness and change the states of perception.

If I understand well what you mean, you expect to see a form, like the form of Krishna for example, or the form of Christ, of Buddha, in every person? That seems to me childishness. But still I do not say that it cannot happen; I think it should happen. But there is in it much human consciousness added to the perception, for that would no longer be exactly

## 27 May 1953

what I have just told you: for those who have the consciousness of the Divine, when they are in contact with the Divine, whoever they may be, whatever age, whatever country they may belong to, the experience is the same. Whereas if it were as you say, then Indians would see one of their divinities, Europeans one of theirs, the Japanese one of their own, and so on. Then it would no longer be a pure perception, there would already be an addition of their own mental formation. It is no longer the Thing in its essence and purity, which is beyond all form.

But one may have a perception, and a very concrete perception of the Divine Presence, yes. One may have a very personal contact with the Divine, yes. But not in this way. And it is inexpressible, except for those who have had the experience. If you do not have an experience, I could speak to you for hours about it, you would understand nothing; it escapes all explanation. It is only when one has the experience that one can understand. And what do you expect? When you speak or write about things, there is necessarily a mental addition, otherwise you would not be able to speak, you would not be able to write. Well, it is this mental addition that has made people try to give an explanation of their experience, and then they have said or written things like this: "I see images of God." These are ways of speaking. It is possible that the thing you are speaking about may happen: to be suddenly in a particular state and see a Divine Presence and this Presence taking a form that's familiar to you — one is accustomed to associate certain forms with the Divine, due to one's education, tradition, and that takes an external form. But it is not the supreme essence of the experience, it is the form, and this gives a sort of limitation to the experience, it must take away from it its universality and a great deal of its power.

*"Obviously, what has happened had to happen; it would not have happened, if it had not been intended. Even the mistakes that we have committed and the adversities*

*that fell upon us had to be, because there was some necessity in them, some utility for our lives. But in truth these things cannot be explained mentally and should not be. For all that happened was necessary, not for any mental reason, but to lead us to something beyond what the mind imagines. But is there any need to explain after all? The whole universe explains everything at every moment and a particular thing happens because the whole universe is what it is."*

Ibid.

*How does the universe explain at every moment the universe?*

That is not what I have said. If you want an explanation of something, it is the universe that explains this something. And each thing is explained by everything; and you can explain nothing except by the whole universe and the entire universe is explained by everything.... Just see: if you read all the explanations given in all the sciences, all the branches of human knowledge, always one thing is explained by another, and if you want to explain this other you explain it by yet another and if you want to explain this other one too, you explain it by yet another. So you continue in this way and go round the universe in order to explain one thing. Only, usually people get tired after a time, they accept the last explanation and stick to it. Otherwise, if they continued to find an explanation, they would have to make the full round of all things and would come back always to the same point. Things are so because they are so, because they had to be so, otherwise they would not be. Things are so, because they are as they are. There's no doubt about it. And that indeed is supreme wisdom.

*Is there not a physical law that is able to explain everything in the universe?*

27 May 1953

Find it out, I shall be very glad.

*Can it be found by science?*

Yes, if it moves in a very definite direction, if it progresses sufficiently, if it does not stop on the way, scientists will find the same thing the mystics have found, and all religious people, everybody, because there is only one thing to find, there are no two. There is only one. So one can go a long way, one can turn round and round and round, and if one turns and turns long enough without stopping, one will be obliged to come to the same spot. Once there, one feels as though there is nothing at all to find. As I have just told you, there is nothing to find. It is That, the Power.[3] It is That, that is all. It is so. Still another question?

*Can the Divine withdraw from us?*

That is an impossibility. Because if the Divine withdrew from a thing, immediately it would collapse, for it would not exist. To put it more clearly: The Divine is the only existence.[4]

---

[3] Later on, a disciple asked Mother what she meant by, "It is That, the Power." Mother answered, "Yes, they will find the same thing the mystics have found and — religious people have found, as everybody has found — it is That, the Power. What one finds is the Power. And to That, essentially, you can give neither a name nor a definition.... That is now the big quarrel about Auroville: in the 'Charter' I put the 'Divine Consciousness' (to live in Auroville one must be a 'willing servitor of the Divine Consciousness', so they say: it makes you think of God. I said (*laughing*), as for me, it does not make me think of God! So some translate it as 'the highest consciousness', others put other things. I agreed with the Russians to put 'Perfect Consciousness', but that is an approximation.... And it is That — which you can neither name nor define — which is the supreme Power. It is Power that one finds. And the supreme Power is only an aspect: the aspect concerning the creation."

Vide "Notes on the Way" (13 and 16 March 1968), *Bulletin of Sri Aurobindo International Centre of Education*, April 1968.

[4] At the time of the publication of this talk, Mother added: "Now I would have answered: it is as if you asked whether the Divine would withdraw from Himself! (*Mother laughs.*) Well, that is the trouble: when you say 'Divine', they understand 'God'.... There is *only* That, That alone exists. That, what is it? That alone exists."

Vide "Notes on the Way" (13 March 1968), *Bulletin*, April 1968.

If the Divine withdrew, it would mean that He would withdraw from the universe; there would no longer be any universe (this is an image to make you understand the thing, I speak of an impossibility). Human beings may withdraw from the Divine and they do it very often. But the Divine withdrawing from human beings, that's an impossibility.

*By following the way of music or art or any other thing, why can't one arrive at the divine realisation and the transformation?*

Who has told you that? Do you know all that is happening in you? Don't you think that there are many people who have realised the Divine, who have never said anything about it, known nothing about it?[5] There are people who have spoken about it — philosophers, whose very profession necessarily is to express what happened to them. But there are people who have had experiences but never said anything. And I know there are artists who purely by their art attained the divine realisation.

As for transformation, I would be glad if you could show me an instance; I would be glad to see it. *One* example. Whatever the way one follows, whether it be the religious way, the philosophical way, the yogic ways, the mystic way, no one has realised transformation.

*Since art does not arrive at transformation, it is not of much value!*

But who has ever reached there till now, will you tell me? Neither philosophy, nor religion, nor yoga. If you put the value in realisation and in the transformation of the world, for example one

---

[5] A disciple asked the Mother how one could realise the Divine and know nothing about it? The Mother answered: "It is once more the same thing. One might add: 'and know nothing about it mentally.' They did not say: 'I have realised the Divine', because that did not correspond to any mental conception."

**27 May 1953**

single individual transformation, admitting that it is possible, and I do not believe it, then nothing has any value, because nothing has ever reached there till today. Don't you understand?

*Yes, I understand that.*

Then why do you suddenly say that art has no value? Nothing has any value, because nothing has led to that? But everything helps. The whole universe is helping the transformation.

*But it may happen that the artist after having reached a certain height where he is master of his art, has to stop his work to proceed towards the transformation of his life.*

Why? For the transformation of his life? Who has told you that? If you were doing manual work, there are any number of artisans who have had a wonderful conversion. There is the example of a shoe-maker who became one of the greatest Yogis of the world. It does not depend on what one does, happily! You have to sit in meditation, like that, with an orange robe on, under a tree, to be able to realise the Divine?
So I do not understand anything of what you say.

*There may come a time when one must change one's activity?*

But by any path whatever, if you follow it sincerely enough and fairly constantly you arrive, by any path whatsoever — I tell you, you may make shoes and find the Divine. There are illuminating examples that are uncontestable. It matters little what one does. There are numerous examples of people who were doing gardening, or cultivating, and who found the Divine even while they were working physically; they had no need to stop their work to do this. You do not understand? You believe one must have what? — a philosophical knowledge?

*No, it is not that, but I do not know how to express myself....*

No, I understand very well what you mean to say, but, excuse me, it is something foolish.

# 3 June 1953

*"Freedom and fatality, liberty and determinism are truths that obtain on different levels of consciousness."*
Questions and Answers 1929 (28 April)

*What are these different levels of consciousness?*

But I have explained it later on. All that follows is the explanation.

I have already spoken to you of the different planes of consciousness. Well, on the material plane, purely material (when separated from the vital plane), it is an absolute mechanism where consequently all things are linked together; and as I was saying the other day, if you want to find the cause of one thing or what is the result of a thing, you will find another and yet another and you will make an entire tour round the universe. And it is like that, everything is absolutely mechanised. Only, in this purely material plane, there can intervene the vital plane, and it already does intervene in the vegetable kingdom. The vital plane has an altogether different determinism, its own particular determinism. But when you introduce the vital determinism into the determinism of the physical, that produces a kind of combination that changes everything. And above the vital plane there is the mental plane. The mental plane also has its own determinism where all things are linked together rigorously.

But that is the movement which could be called "horizontal". If you take a vertical movement, the mind descending into the vital and the vital descending into the physical, you have there three determinisms that intervene and naturally produce something altogether different. And where the mind has intervened the determinism will necessarily be different from the one where it does not intervene; that is, in the higher animal life there is already a mental determinism which intervenes that is altogether different from the determinism of the vegetable plane.

Above these planes there are others — above each plane there are others, following one another right up to the highest plane. The highest plane is the plane of absolute freedom. If in your consciousness you are capable of passing through all these planes, so to say in a vertical line, and reaching the highest plane and, by means of this connection, of bringing down this plane of perfect freedom into the material determinisms, you change everything. And all the intermediaries change everything. Then because of the very changes from level to level, it gives altogether the appearance of complete freedom; for the intervention or descent of one plane into another has unforeseen consequences for the other plane, the lower plane. The higher plane can foresee, but the lower ones cannot. So, as these consequences are unforeseen, that gives altogether the impression of the unexpected and of freedom. And it is only if you remain consciously and constantly on the highest level, that is, in the supreme Consciousness, that there you can see that, at the same time, all is absolutely determined but also, because of the complexity of the interlinking of these determinisms, all is absolutely free. It is the Plane where there are no more contradictions, where all things *are* and are in harmony without contradicting one another.

*In the lower planes can't one say what will happen at a particular moment?*

That depends. On certain planes there are consciousnesses that form, that make formations and try to send them down to earth and manifest them. These are planes where the great forces are at play, forces struggling with each other to organise things in one way or another. On these planes all the possibilities are there, all the possibilities that present themselves but have not yet come to a decision as to which will come down.... Suppose a plane full of the imaginations of people who want certain things

# 3 June 1953

to be realised upon earth — they invent a novel, narrate stories, produce all kinds of phenomena; it amuses them very much. It is a plane of form-makers and they are there imagining all kinds of circumstances and events; they play with the forces; they are like the authors of a drama and they prepare everything there and see what is going to happen. All these formations are facing each other; and it is those which are the strongest, the most successful or the most persistent or those that have the advantage of a favourable set of circumstances which dominate. They meet and out of the conflict yet another thing results: you lose one thing and take up another, you make a new combination; and then all of a sudden, you find, pluff! it is coming down. Now, if it comes down with a sufficient force, it sets moving the earth atmosphere and things combine; as for instance, when with your fist you thump the saw-dust, you know surely what happens, don't you? You lift your hand, give a formidable blow: all the dust gets organised around your fist. Well, it is like that. These formations come down into matter with that force, and everything organises itself automatically, mechanically as around the striking fist. And there's your wished object about to be realised, sometimes with small deformations because of the resistance, but it will be realised finally, even as the person narrating the story up above wanted it more or less to be realised. If then you are for some reason or other in the secret of the person who has constructed the story and if you follow the way in which he creates his path to reach down to the earth and if you see how a blow with the fist acts on earthly matter, then you are able to tell what is going to happen, because you have seen it in the world above, and as it takes some time to make the whole journey, you see in advance. And the higher you rise, the more you foresee in advance what is going to happen. And if you pass far beyond, go still farther, then everything is possible.

    It is an unfolding that follows a highway which is for you unknowable; for all will be unfolded in the universe, but in what order and in what way? There are decisions that are taken up there which escape our ordinary consciousness, and so it is very difficult to foresee. But there also, if you enter consciously and if you can be present up there... How shall I explain that to you? All is there, absolute, static, eternal: but all that will be unrolled in the material world, naturally more or less one thing after another; for in the static existence all can be there, but in the becoming all becomes in time, that is, one thing after another. Well, what path will the unrolling follow? Up there is the domain of absolute freedom.... Who tells you that a sufficiently sincere aspiration, a sufficiently intense prayer is not capable of changing the path of the unrolling?

This means that all is possible.

Now, one must have a sufficient aspiration and a prayer that's sufficiently intense. But that has been given to human nature. It is one of the marvellous gifts of grace given to human nature; only, one does not know how to make use of it.

This comes to saying that in spite of the most absolute determinisms in the horizontal line, if one knows how to cross all these horizontal lines and reach the highest Point of consciousness, one is able to make things change, things apparently absolutely determined. So you may call it by any name you like, but it is a kind of combination of an absolute determinism with an absolute freedom. You may pull yourself out of it in any way you like, but it is like that.

I forgot to say in that book (perhaps I did not forget but just felt that it was useless to say it) that all these theories are only theories, that is, mental conceptions which are merely more or less imaged representations of the reality; but it is not the reality at all. When you say "determinism" and when you say "freedom", you say only words and all that is only a very incomplete, very approximate and very weak description of what is in reality within you, around you and everywhere; and to be able to begin to understand what the universe is, you must come out of your mental formulas, otherwise you will never understand anything.

To tell the truth, if you live only a moment, just a tiny

*3 June 1953*

moment, of this absolutely sincere aspiration or this sufficiently intense prayer, you will know more things than by meditating for hours.

> *"The Supreme Consciousness ... gives to the individual in the active life of the world his sense of freedom and independence and initiative. These things in him are Her pragmatic tools or devices and it is through this machinery that the movements and issues planned and foreseen elsewhere are realised here."*
>
> Questions and Answers 1929 (28 April)

These "things in him", that is in the individual, are: the sense of freedom, independence and initiative. You know what independence is? It is precisely the freedom of choice. Independence means the freedom of choice and initiative means the fact of choosing. First of all, one feels that one is free; and then one feels that no one can prevent him from choosing; and finally one uses his freedom to choose and one decides. These are the three stages. So these three stages: the feeling that you are free, the idea that you are going to use your freedom for choosing and then the choice — these three things I call the pragmatic tools and devices.

I am sorry, my children, all this is said in a form a little too philosophical which I do not now approve of very much. I was obliged to speak a language which now appears to me a little too complicated. But what is to be done, it was like that. I was saying that these three things, the feeling of freedom, the will to choose and the choice made are the devices that Nature uses in us to make us act, otherwise we would not move.

If we did not have this illusion that we are free, this second illusion that we can use our freedom for choosing and the third illusion of choosing, well, we would not move. So Nature gives us these three illusions and makes us move, for she requires us to move.

She, with a capital S, I said it was the Supreme Consciousness, but in fact it is Nature and it is the trick of Nature; for the Supreme Consciousness has no tricks, it is Nature that has tricks. The Supreme Consciousness quite simply enters into all things with all her consciousness, because it is *the* consciousness: and with that She tries to make all this inconscience move towards consciousness, simply, without any tricks. She has no need of tricks, She is everywhere. She is at work everywhere and She puts consciousness into the inconscience. When you light a lamp in a dark room, as soon as you turn on the electricity, the room is no longer dark. As soon as you put consciousness in, there is no longer any unconsciousness. So that is what She does. Wherever She sees unconsciousness, She tries to enter. Sometimes the doors are locked, then it takes a little more time, but sometimes the doors open, then She rushes in immediately, the unconsciousness disappears and consciousness comes — without needing any tricks or any intermediaries. She becomes conscious. But material Nature, physical Nature is not like that, she is full of tricks; she makes you move all the time, she pulls the puppet strings; for her you are so many little dolls: she pulls the strings and makes them move. She puts all kinds of illusions in your head so that you may do the things she wants, without even your wanting it. She does not require that you should want it: she pulls the thread and you do it.

That is why we quarrel at times, but that's something we do not say.

*You have said here that we are "tied to the chain of Karma", but then sometimes when the Divine Grace acts, that contradicts...*

Completely, the Divine Grace completely contradicts Karma; you know, It makes it melt away like butter that's put in the sun.

That is what I was saying just now. What you have just told me is another way of speaking. I was putting myself in your

3 June 1953

place and asking: There you are, if you have an aspiration that's sincere enough or a prayer that's intense enough, you can bring down in you Something that will change everything, everything — truly it changes everything. An example may be given that is extremely limited, very small, but which makes you understand things very well: a stone falls quite mechanically; say, a tile falls; if it gets loose, it will fall, won't it? But if there comes, for example, a vital or mental determinism from someone who passes by and does not want it to fall and puts his hand out, it will fall on his hand, but it will not fall on the ground. So he has changed the destiny of this stone or tile. It is another determinism that has come in, and instead of the stone falling on the head of someone, it falls upon the hand and it will not kill anybody. This is an intervention from another plane, from a conscious will that enters into the more or less unconscious mechanism.

*So the consequences of Karma are not rigorous?*

No, not at all. In all religions there are people who have said that, who have given such absolute rules, but I believe it was in order to substitute themselves for Nature and pull the strings. There is always this kind of instinct that wants to take the place of Nature and pull the strings of people. So they are told: "There is an absolute consequence of all that you do...." It is a concept necessary at a given moment of evolution to prevent people from being in a completely unconscious egoism, in a total unconsciousness of the consequences of what they do. There is no lack of people who are still like that, I believe it is the majority; they follow their impulses and do not even ask themselves whether what they have done is going to have any consequences for them and for others. So it is good that someone tells you straight, with a severe look: "Take care, that has consequences which will last for a very long time!" And then there are others who come and tell you: "You will pay for it in another life." That, however, is one of those fantastic stories.... But it does not matter: this also can be for the good of people. There are other religions which tell you: "Oh! If you commit that sin, you will go to hell for eternity." You can imagine!... So people have such a fright that it stops them a little, it gives them just a moment for reflection before obeying an impulse — and not always; sometimes the reflection comes afterwards, a little late.

It is not absolute. These are still mental constructions, more or less sincere, which cut things into small bits like that, quite neatly cut, and tell you: "Do this or do that. If it is not this, it will be that." Oh! what a nuisance is this kind of life. And so people go mad, they are frightened! "Is it like that or rather this?" And they want it to be neither this nor that, what should they do? — They have only to climb to a higher storey. They must be given the key to open the door. There is a door to the staircase, a key is needed. The key, as I told you just now, is the sufficiently sincere aspiration or the sufficiently intense prayer. I said "or", but I do not think it is "or". There are people who like one better and others, the other. But in both there is a magical power, you must know how to make use of it.

There is something very beautiful in both, I shall speak to you about it one day, I shall tell you what there is in aspiration and what in prayer and why both of them are beautiful.... Some dislike prayer; if they entered deep into their heart, they would find it was pride — worse than that, vanity. And then there are those who have no aspiration, they try and they cannot aspire; it is because they do not have the flame of the will, it is because they do not have the flame of humility.

Both are needed. There must be a very great humility and a very great will to change one's Karma.

*Voilà, au revoir*, my children.

# 10 June 1953

> *"Attacks from adverse forces are inevitable: you have to take them as tests on your way and go courageously through the ordeal. The struggle may be hard, but when you come out of it, you have gained something, you have advanced a step. There is even a necessity for the existence of the hostile forces. They make your determination stronger, your aspiration clearer.*
>
> *"It is true, however, that they exist because you gave them reason to exist. So long as there is something in you which answers to them, their intervention is perfectly legitimate. If nothing in you responded, if they had no hold upon any part of your nature, they would retire and leave you."*
>
> Questions and Answers 1929 (5 May)

*Sometimes when an adverse force attacks us and we come out successful, why are we attacked once again by the same force?*

Because something was left inside. We have said that the force can attack only when there is something which responds in the nature — however slight it may be. There is a kind of affinity, something corresponding, there is a disorder or an imperfection which attracts the adverse force by responding to it. So, if the attack comes, you must keep perfectly quiet and send it back, but it does not necessarily follow that you have got rid of that small part in you which allows the attack to come.

You have something in you which attracts this force; take, for example (it is one of the most frequent things), the force of depression, that kind of attack of a wave of depression that falls upon you: you lose confidence, you lose hope, you have the feeling you will never be able to do anything, you are cast down. It means there is in your vital being something which is naturally egoistic, surely a little vain, which needs encouragement to remain in a good state. So it is like a little signal for those forces which intimates to them: "You can come, the door is open." But there is another part in the being that was watching when these forces arrived; instead of allowing them to enter, the part which sees clearly, which knows, which has power, which resists, says: "No, I do not want that, it is not true, I do not want it", and sends them back. But you have not necessarily been cured of the little thing within you which permitted them to come. You must go very deep within, work within you persistently to be able to efface all possibility of calling. And so long as you have not completely effaced it, the attack will recur almost unexpectedly. You push it back — it is like a ball you throw against the wall, back it returns; you push it back once again and again it returns — until the moment there is no longer anything to attract it. Then it does not return again.

Therefore, the most important thing to do when you are attacked by an adverse force, is to say to yourself: "Yes, the force comes from outside and the attack is there, but there must certainly be a correspondence in my nature, otherwise it could not have attacked me. Well, I am going to look and find within me what allows this force to come and I am going to send it back or transform it or put the light of consciousness upon it so that it may be converted, or drive it away so that it remains no longer within me...." There is a way, isn't there? When the force comes, the adverse force, when it attacks, the part which corresponds rushes out to meet it, it goes forward. A kind of meeting takes place. If at that time, instead of being altogether overwhelmed or taken by surprise and off your guard, you observe very closely what it was within you that vibrated (it makes the sound tat, tat, tat: another thing has entered), then you can catch it. At that moment, you catch it and say to it: "Get out with your friends, I don't want you any longer!" You send away the two together,

### 10 June 1953

the part that attracted and the thing it attracted; they are sent away and you are absolutely clear.

For that, you must be very vigilant and have a little courage, in the sense that at times you have to grip it hard and then pull it out — it hurts a little — and then you throw it out along with the forces you send away. After that, it is finished. And so long as this is not done, it comes back and back again; and then if one is not in oneself sufficiently courageous or vigilant or persevering, the fourth or fifth time one falls flat and says: "That's too much, I have had enough!" So the force installs itself, contented, satisfied with its work; and then you can see it laughing, it enjoys itself immensely, it has succeeded in its deal. Now to send it back again means a very considerable work. But if you follow the other method, if you look closely this way: "Well, I am going to catch the thing that has allowed it to come", you see somewhere within you something rising, wriggling, coming up in response to the evil force which is approaching. That is the moment to seize it and throw it out with all the rest.

*But when we throw it out, it does not die. Then it can go elsewhere once more, for it remains in the world.*

Exactly. It remains in the world and it will surely go elsewhere — until it meets someone who has sufficient spiritual and occult power to dissolve it, and that is very difficult.... One must be very strong, possess a very great knowledge and power to dissolve a movement that has (this can be said at least) its reason for existence in the world — I do not say it is legitimate, but still it has its reason for existence. There are things which can be dissolved; but if somewhere in the world it exists in someone, he can reconstitute it. It is the same thing when people are attacked by small beings of the vital world, hostile beings who attack them, install themselves in their atmosphere, trying to possess them, that is, enter into them and use their body and all the rest. These beings — it is very difficult for the individual to get rid of them: that needs a very, very hard yoga. But one who has the knowledge and the power and who sees them can very well get them out of the atmosphere and destroy them. But if one who is attacked keeps within himself this little affinity which allowed the thing to enter, then he will recall it. I have had several examples of the kind, several.

I had the example of a person who was three-fourths possessed and at the moment manifested a kind of power, a force that was not very good, but all the same it gave the impression of a force, a power, a capacity. Only he recognised that it was bad and was for evil, and prayed to be relieved of it. The opportunity comes: the being shows itself separately from the person it possesses, it can be seized, pulled out and dissolved. Then the one who had been possessed suddenly feels that he is becoming as commonplace as anybody else. That feeling of power he had is now lost and he feels he is becoming quite ordinary and says: "I have no special faculties, I have no special value, I have no special capacity, I am quite an ordinary person and less than ordinary, of a sickening commonness!" Now what does he do? He prays to have his possession back again. And so a few days later, I find him as possessed as ever.

Well, here it is truly not worth the trouble. One has only to leave them to their fate. This has happened many a time. In such people, you know, it is a kind of vanity which generally opens the door to those forces; they wished to be big, powerful, to play an important role, to be somebody; that attracts the force and so they become like that, possessed. The thing is taken away from them: all their remarkable capacity disappears at the same time and their self-satisfied vanity as well. They have the feeling they have become something quite ordinary and a tiny little thing within them says: "Oh! it was better before...." For one that is destroyed, there are always ten ready to come in. That's how it is, it is a strange task!

You know the story of Durga, don't you? Durga who every year has to destroy her asura; and always she is compelled to

## 10 June 1953

begin again. It goes on in this way till the end of the reign allotted to the titans. When they will be banished from this world, it will not be thus any longer. But till then, that is as long as they are useful (as I have said in this book) for intensifying the aspiration, clarifying the consciousness, for putting to the test the sincerity of people, they will be there. The day the test will not be needed, the day the sincerity will be pure and self-existent they will disappear. Then that day, Durga will no longer need to begin her battle over again every year.

*Would it not be better to change them?*

Ah! my child, certainly it would be better, much better. But then...

It is a domain of which I have a thorough experience. After forty years of sustained effort I have found out that it is absolutely impossible to change anyone unless in truth he wants it sincerely. If he does not set himself to the task with an absolute sincerity, well — I have tried for forty years, one can try it for a hundred and forty years, it will be the same thing — he won't stir. It is the very character of these beings to be perfectly satisfied with themselves, and they do not desire, they have not the least intention to change! Even now, among the beings who are concerned with the earth, the asuric beings, the greatest of the asuras who is still busy with the earth at present, who is the asura of falsehood and calls himself the "Lord of the Nations" — he has taken a beautiful name, he is Lord of the Nations — it is he, wherever there is something going wrong, you may be sure it is he or a representative of his who is there. It is also perfectly sure that very soon his hour will come and all will be over for him, that he will have to disappear. And he absolutely refuses to change. He has no intention to do it, for immediately he will lose all his power. It is impossible. And he knows that he will disappear. But he proclaims categorically that before disappearing he will destroy all he can.... At heart, he would not consent to disappear unless everything disappeared at the same time as he. Unfortunately for him, this is not possible. But he will do all that lies in his power to destroy, demolish, ruin, corrupt as many things as he can. That is certain. Afterwards it is the downfall. He accepts the downfall on this condition. It has never crossed his mind that he might be converted. It would no longer be he, don't you see, he would no longer be himself.

There is a great difference between a human being and these beings of the vital plane. I have told you this many times, I am going to repeat it:

In a human being, there is the divine Presence and the psychic being — at the beginning embryonic, but in the end a being wholly formed, conscious, independent, individualised. That does not exist in the vital world. It is a special grace given to human beings dwelling in matter and upon earth. And because of this, there is no human being who cannot be converted, if he wants it; that is, there is a possibility of his wanting it and the moment he wants it, he can do it. He is sure to succeed the moment he wants it, whereas those beings of the vital do not have a psychic being in them, they do not have the direct divine Presence (naturally, at the Origin, they descended directly from the Divine, but that was at the Origin, that is very far away). They are not in direct contact with the Divine within them, they have no psychic being. And if they were converted, there would remain nothing of them! For they are made up entirely of the opposite movement: they are entirely made up of personal self-assertion, despotic authority, separation from the Origin, and, of a great disdain for all that is pure, beautiful and noble. They do not have within them this psychic element which in man, even in the most debased, makes him respect what is beautiful and pure; even the basest man, in spite of himself, against his own will, respects what is pure, noble and beautiful. But those beings do not have that. They are wholly on the other side, totally on the other side. It disgusts them in every way. It is for them something which should not be touched, because it destroys; it is

## 10 June 1953

the thing that makes them disappear. Goodwill, sincerity, purity and beauty are things which make them disappear. So they hate these things.

Now I do not know on what grounds one could convert them. What would be the point of support? I do not find it. Even in the greatest. That is, some of these beings will not disappear until hatred disappears from the earth.... One might put it the other way round. One might say that hatred will disappear from the earth when those beings disappear; but, for the reason I have just given, the power to make light spring forth in the place of darkness, beauty in the place of ugliness, goodness instead of evil, that power man possesses, the Asura does not. Therefore it is man who will do that work, it is he who will change, it is he who will transform his earth and it is he who will compel the Asura to flee into other worlds or to dissolve. After that, all will be quiet. There you are.

Any questions?

*You have said here, in reference to the mind: "Any part of the being that keeps to its proper place and plays its appointed role is helpful; but directly it steps beyond its sphere, it becomes twisted and perverted and therefore false. A power has the right movement when it is set into activity for the Divine purpose; it has the wrong movement when it is set into activity for its own satisfaction."*

*Questions and Answers 1929 (5 May)*

*When a part of the being steps beyond its sphere, why does it get deformed and perverted?*

I use the word "sphere" in the sense of the place and the role one has to play. Each part of the being has its place in the whole and a definite role to play. If instead of playing that role, it wishes to play another, naturally it loses the qualities necessary for it to play its true role, and it cannot take up any others because they are foreign to it. So necessarily it gets deformed and perverted. For example, we say here that the true role of the mind is a formative role in relation to action. An idea enters the mind, the mind seizes it and gives it a form to realise it, changes it into a motive of action and sends it out towards the material field. The mind organises the idea so that it may be realised in action. This is its true role, and so long as it does that and does it with care, it fulfils its role, it abides in its place and is quite useful. But if the mind imagines that it knows, that it has no need of receiving knowledge and ideas from another part of the being — a higher part — if it imagines that it knows and, by the association of inner movements, believes it has found some knowledge, which can never be but a reflection of something else, and if it wants to impose this knowledge upon the physical life, then it leaves its role and becomes a tyrant — this happens quite often to it, it is then completely perverted and instead of helping the sadhana, it brings it down. You can easily make this observation. Naturally, one must be able to follow the true working, the activities within oneself.

It is the same thing with the vital. The vital is meant to put in the drive, the realising force, the enthusiasm, the energy necessary for the idea formed by the mind to be transmitted to the body and realised in action. Well, so long as the vital limits itself to this activity, that is, sets all its energy, enthusiasm, strength to work in order to collaborate with the idea, it is very good. But if instead of that, all of a sudden, it is seized by a desire — and this happens to it quite often — and it uses all its qualities to realise, not the higher idea which wanted to manifest, but its own desire, then it steps beyond its zone of action, it gets perverted, it deforms everything and succeeds in creating catastrophes.

*Sometimes we do not notice that the adverse forces are attacking us; why don't we?*

**10 June 1953**

You do not notice it! That happens when you are not alert, when you are not attentive, when you are busy with altogether external things, the tiny little things of daily practical life. Then the forces can attack you, enter into you, install themselves without even your noticing it. Most often, they do not attack you directly thus, because if they attack you directly, there is a chance of your feeling it (you may feel uneasy suddenly, that may awaken your attention). They go down into the inconscient and then come up, like that, quietly from below. So you do not know at all what is happening to you. When you are aware of it, it is already there, thoroughly installed, quite comfortably.

*Sometimes one cannot distinguish adverse forces from other forces.*

That happens when one is quite unconscious.

There are only two cases when this is possible: you are either very unconscious of the movements of your being — you have not studied, you have not observed, you do not know what is happening within you — or you are absolutely insincere, that is, you play the ostrich in order not to see the reality of things: you hide your head, you hide your observation, your knowledge and you say, "It is not there." But indeed the latter I hope is not in question here. Hence it is simply because one has not the habit of observing oneself that one is so unconscious of what is happening within.

Have you ever practised distinguishing what comes from your mind, what comes from your vital, what comes from your physical?... For it is mixed up; it is mixed up in the outward appearance. If you do not take care to distinguish, it makes a kind of soup, all that together. So it is indistinct and difficult to discover. But if you observe yourself, after some time you see certain things, you feel them to be there, like that, as though they were in your skin; for some other things you feel you would have to go within yourself to find out from where they come;

for other things, you have to go still further inside, or otherwise you have to rise up a little: it comes from unconsciousness. And there are others; then you must go very deep, very deep to find out from where they come. This is just a beginning.

Simply observe. You are in a certain condition, a certain undefinable condition. Then look: "What! how is it I am like that?" You try to see first if you have fever or some other illness; but it is all right, everything is all right, there's neither headache nor fever, the stomach is not protesting, the heart is functioning as it should, indeed, all's well, you are normal. "Why then am I feeling so uneasy?"... So you go a little further within. It depends on cases. Sometimes you find out immediately: yes, there was a little incident which wasn't pleasant, someone said a word that was not happy or one had failed in his task or perhaps did not know one's lesson very well, the teacher had made a remark. At the time, one did not pay attention properly, but later on, it begins to work, leaves a painful impression. That is the second stage. Afterwards, if nothing happened: "All's well, everything is normal, everything usual, I have nothing to note down, nothing has happened: why then do I feel like that?" Now it begins to be interesting, because one must enter much more deeply within oneself. And then it can be all sorts of things: it may be precisely the expression of an attack that is preparing; it may be a little inner anxiety seeking the progress that has to be made; it may be a premonition that there is somewhere in contact with oneself something not altogether harmonious which one has to change: something one must see, discover, change, on which light is to be put, something that is still there, deep down, and which should no longer be there. Then if you look at yourself very carefully, you find out: "There! I am still like that; in that little corner, there is still something of that kind, not clear: a little selfishness, a little ill-will, something refusing to change." So you see it, you take it by the tip of its nose or by the ear and hold it up in full light: "So, you were hiding! you are hiding? But I don't want you any longer." And then it has to go away.

**10 June 1953**

This is a great progress.

*If this sort of thing happens in the class, if one feels uneasy...*

That happens to you in the class? It means you do not listen to your teacher, otherwise it would not happen. If you were very attentive in your class and paid attention to your lesson, that could not happen to you. When you came out of it, then you would feel that, but not in the class. This means that you were dreaming or living within you or following your imagination, but you were not listening to your lessons.... But it is this that's wonderful, my children: when you are learning something, when you are studying, when you are concentrated on your lesson, these things never happen to you. They may happen before, they may happen afterwards; but they won't happen at that time. For if you are quite concentrated, all your energies are concentrated on your study and there is nothing unpleasant there. You understand what you learn and you are interested in what you learn.

*Sometimes, one tries to concentrate but one can't.*

If truly you can't, then you have only to spend your time in seeking within yourself for the reason why it is so! Then if the teacher asks you a question, you have to tell him: "I am sorry, I was not listening."

You don't like to learn?

Yes

Then how can this happen?

*But in some classes, I do not understand.*

Then in some classes, you do not like to learn! You can say

103

generally, "Yes, yes, I like to learn!" but if one really likes to learn, there isn't a class in which one could not learn. Surely, whatever the class, there is always something one does not know, one can always learn. You are not a living encyclopaedia! Even if you go over the same book again (this happens, I believe, in some classes), and you may say: "Oh! I have already gone through this book, this is boring", but that's simply because you do not want to learn: because certainly if you repeat the same book, it means that you have not learnt it properly the first time and you must take particular care to learn what you have not learnt. Even a book of grammar! I do not say that books of grammar are very exciting, but even a grammar-book becomes interesting if you set out to learn it — even the most abstract rules of grammar. You cannot imagine how amusing it is when you truly want to learn, when you want to understand why it is so; instead of just committing to memory, learning by heart, if you want to understand: what are these words put there? For what idea, what real knowledge are they put there? What do they represent?... Any rule whatsoever is simply a human mental formula of something that exists in itself. Take any rule at all, it shows simply that a few heads have made an effort to formulate in the way most clear to them, most condensed, something which exists in itself. So if one goes behind the words and begins searching for this something — the thing existing in itself, which is there, behind the words — how interesting it becomes! It is throbbing, thrilling! It is like passing through a jungle to discover a new country, like going on an exploration to the North Pole! So, if you do that with the laws of grammar, I assure you nothing in the world can bore you afterwards.

Understand instead of learning.

I admit this asks for a very great concentration. It demands a concentration capable of penetrating, digging a hole into the mental shell and passing through to the other side. And afterwards, it becomes worth the trouble.... You have been pushed against something cold, rigid, hard, unelastic. Then you concen-

**10 June 1953**

trate, concentrate, concentrate sufficiently until... suddenly you are on the other side, and then you emerge into the light and you understand: "Ah! that's wonderful! Now I understand." A very tiny thing gives you a great joy.

You see it is possible not to get bored at school.

*At school one has to finish a course in a year. One must hasten a little at times. Before one has been able to understand a question well, one has to go to the next chapter.*

There, my child, I fully agree with you, it is not quite right. But we shall try to change all that; because after all I don't see why one has to finish a book in a year. It is quite arbitrary. One should not leave a chapter until it has been fully grasped; only then take up the next one and so on. And if a chapter is finished, it is finished: and if it is not finished it is not finished.

The truth is that the teacher, instead of basing his course on a text-book, should take the trouble of preparing the course himself. He must know enough and take sufficient pains to prepare his course from day to day, and in this way he will close a subject only when — I do not say when everyone has understood, for that is impossible — but at least when those whom he considers the interesting elements of his class have understood. Then the next subject is taken up. And if that continues, if a particular type of subject extends over two years instead of one or for a year and a half instead of two, it matters little; because it is his own production, his own course written by him and he writes according to the need of his class. That is my conception of teaching. Now, it has indeed its difficulties. But that is the true way of working, because by taking a book and following it, particularly a book which may very well be not at all suited to the students.... I do not say that a particular course could suit all, it is impossible to satisfy everybody. But there are those who want to make an effort; it is these that you must consider. Those who are lazy, somnolent or indolent — well, you must leave them to their laziness or somnolence or indolence. If they want to sleep all their lives, let them sleep until something shakes them up sufficiently and awakens them! But what is interesting in a class is the section that wishes to learn, those who really want to learn and it is for them that the class should be taken. Don't you see, the present method of education is a kind of levelling; everyone must be at the same stage. So those who have their heads higher up have them cut off, and those who are too small are pushed up from below. But that doesn't do any good. One must be concerned only with those who come up, the others will take what they can. And indeed I do not see any necessity for everybody knowing the same thing — for that is not normal. But those who want to know and who can know, those who must work, these should be given all possible means for working, must be pushed up as much as possible, must always be given new food. They are the hungry ones, they must be fed.... Ah! If I had the time I would take a class. That would interest me much, to show how it must be done. Only one cannot be everywhere at the same time!

There you are, my children, now it is very late. Good night.

# 17 June 1953

> *"There is a true movement of the intellect and there is a wrong movement: one helps, the other hinders."*
> Questions and Answers 1929 (5 May)

*What is the true movement of the intellect?*

What exactly do you understand by intellect? Is it a function of the mind or is it a part of the human being? How do you understand it?

*A function of the mind.*

A function of the mind? Then it is that part of the mind which deals with ideas; is that what you mean?

*Not ideas, Mother.*

Not ideas? What else, then?

*Ideas, but...*

There is a part of the mind which receives ideas, ideas that are formed in a higher mind. Still, I don't know, it is a question of definition and one must know what exactly you mean to say.

It is intellect that puts ideas in the form of thoughts, gathering and organising the thoughts at the same time. There are great ideas which lie beyond the ordinary human mentality, which can put on all possible forms. These great ideas tend to descend, they want to manifest themselves in precise forms. These precise forms are the thoughts; and generally it is this, I believe, that is meant by intellect: it is this that gives thought-form to the ideas.

And then, there is also the organisation of the thoughts among themselves. All that has to be put in a certain order, otherwise one becomes incoherent. And after that, there is the putting of these thoughts to use for action; that is still another movement.

To be able to say what the true movement is, one must know first of all which movement is being spoken about. You have a body, well, you don't expect your body to walk on its head or its hands nor to crawl flat on its belly nor indeed that the head should be down and the legs up in the air. You give to each limb a particular occupation which is its own. This appears to you quite natural because that is the habit; otherwise, the very little ones do not know what to do, neither with their legs nor with their hands nor with their heads; it is only little by little that they learn that. Well, it is the same thing with the mind's functions. You must know which part of the mind you are speaking about, what its own function is, and then only can you say what its true movement is and what is not its true movement. For example, for the part which has to receive the master ideas and change them into thought, its true movement is to be open to the master ideas, receive them and change them into as exact, as precise, as expressive a thought as possible. For the part of the mind which has the charge of organising all these thoughts among themselves so that they might form a coherent and classified whole, not a chaos, the true movement is just to make the classification according to a higher logic and in a thoroughly clear, precise and expressive order which may be serviceable each time a thought is referred to, so that one may know where to look for it and not put quite contradictory things together. There are people whose mind does not work like that; all the ideas that come into it, without their being even aware of what the idea is, are translated into confused thoughts which remain in a kind of inner chaos. I have known people who, from the philosophical point of view — although there is nothing philosophical in it — could put side by side the most contradictory things, like ideas

## 17 June 1953

of hierarchic order and at the same time ideas of the absolute independence of the individual and of anarchism, and both were accepted with equal sympathy, knocked against each other in the head in the midst of a wild disorder, and these people were not even aware of it!... You know the saying: "A question well put is three-fourths solved." So now, put your question. What do you want to speak about? I am stretching out a helping hand, you have only to catch it. What is it you are speaking about, what is it that you call intellect? Do you know the difference between an idea and a thought?

*Not quite.*

Ah! That is the first hurdle. Can anybody here tell me? (*To a child*) You, do you know the difference between an idea and a thought?

*A thought is something vague, more vague than an idea.*

No, it is not a question of a vague thought in a vague mind or a clear thought when the mind is clear. It is not like that.

*You said just now that ideas came from above and were translated into thoughts.*

Yes, but how do they come from above?

*From the higher parts of the mind.*

Yes, but could you give me an idea and the thoughts in which it can be expressed? That is what I am asking. Can anyone give me an example? (*Looking at a disciple*) He is longing to speak. Tell us something, we shall see.

> *The manifestation of the Divine upon earth is an idea and the transformation is a thought.*

Ah, you are a monist? If I am not mistaken, this is the principle of monism.

It is a thought of God that has made the universe, but now instead of a thought, we say an idea.

Has anyone something interesting to say?

> (A teacher) *In logic, it is said: "Mortality" is an idea, and "man is mortal", is a thought.*

Now, have you understood the difference between idea and thought? It is clear. The idea is translated into all kinds of thoughts. They may be the most contradictory thoughts and the whole thing is to organise them in a coherent way. I think I have told you many times that contradictory thoughts may be found in union if one rises high enough, climbs towards the idea.... One could perhaps play at this little game, it would be very interesting. We have a thesis, we are going to find an antithesis, and then we shall find the synthesis.

Who will propose the thesis?... Ah! I am going to propose this immediately: "Man is mortal." The antithesis is: "Man is immortal." Now find the place where the two agree: the synthesis.

> *It is ignorance that prevents man from uniting with immortality.*

It is a rather vague way of putting the thing. One could say it more intellectually. One could say: in his reality, man is immortal; and because of ignorance or of unconsciousness, he has become mortal. That's better? And then one can go a little further: Why is he immortal? Why is he mortal? And how being mortal can he become immortal?

17 June 1953

Whatever the part of the being, whether it be the intellect or any other part, whether it is in the mind or the vital or anywhere else, the true movement is a double movement: first, it must not intercept the divine Truth in its manifestation, and secondly, it must help in its manifestation. A negative side, consisting in not being a screen, not intercepting anything, not blocking the passage of the divine force seeking to express itself; on the other side, to be sufficiently clear and pure to be able to help this manifestation.

One can apply this everywhere, it is very convenient. *Voilà.* Now, any other question?

*If men did not die, with age their body would become useless?*

Ah! No. You are looking from the wrong side. They could escape dying only if their body did not decay. It is just because their body decays that they die. It is because their body becomes useless that they die. If they are not to die, their body should not become useless. This is just the contrary. It is precisely because the body decays, declines and ends in a complete degradation that death becomes necessary. But if the body followed the progressive movement of the inner being, if it had the same sense of progress and perfection as the psychic being, there would be no necessity for it to die. One year added to another need not bring a deterioration. It is only a habit of Nature. It is only a habit of what is happening at *this* moment. And that is exactly the cause of death. One can foresee quite well, on the contrary, that the movement for perfection which is at the beginning of life might continue under another form. I have already told you that one does not foresee an uninterrupted growth, for that would need changing the height of the houses after some time! But this growth in height may be changed into a growth in perfection: the perfection of the form. All the imperfections of the form may be gradually corrected, all the weaknesses replaced by strength, all the incapacities by skill. Why should it not be like this? You do not think in that way because you have the habit of seeing things otherwise. But there is no reason why this should not happen.

Have you ever seen a tree growing, a palm tree? There is one in the Ashram courtyard, in the Samadhi courtyard, quite close to the door by which you come up every day, have you never seen how it grows? This tree, you know, is some forty, forty-five or fifty years old perhaps. You see how small it is. These trees can become even much taller than the building. They can live several hundred years, easily, in their natural state, if there is no accident. Have you never seen what it does? I see it from above. It is quite pretty. It happens once a year. At first, you see a kind of small brown ball. Then this small brown ball begins to grow and becomes slightly lighter in colour, less deep. Little by little, you see that it is made of a mass of somewhat complex small lines, with their tips bent inward, as though turned back upon themselves; and that begins to grow, it comes out, becomes more and more limpid, until it begins to turn green, a little pale yellowish green and it takes the form of the bishop's cross. Then you see it multiplying and separating; it is yet a little brown, a little queer (almost like you), something like a caterpillar. And suddenly, it is as though it sprang out, it leaps forth. It is pale green; it is frail. It has a delightful colour. It lengthens out. This lasts for a day or two; and then on the following day there are leaves. These leaves I have never counted, I do not know how many they are. Every time there is a new range of leaves. They remain very pale; they are exquisite. They are like a little child, with that something tender, pretty and graceful a child has. And you have still the feeling that it is fragile; and indeed, if it receives a blow, it is spoilt for life. It is very frail, but it is delightfully tender. It has its charm and you say: "But why does not Nature remain like that?" The following morning... pluff! they are separated, they are bright green, they look wonderful with all the strength and force of youth, a magnificent brilliant

## 17 June 1953

green. It should stop there — not at all. It continues. Then comes the dust, the deterioration from people who pass by. So it begins to fall, to become yellowish, another kind of yellow, the yellow of dryness until it is completely withered and falls away. It is replaced by the trunk. Every year the trunk increases a little. And it will take several hundred years to reach the end. But every year, it repeats the same thing, passes through all the stages of beauty, charm, attractiveness and you say: "But why does it not stop there?" And the next minute, it is something else. You cannot say it is better, but it is different. And so it passes from one thing to another through all the stages of flowering. Then the accidents begin; with the accidents comes deterioration, and with deterioration there is death.

It is like that. But accidents are not indispensable. And even what looks like death helps in the growth of the tree. One sheds off something, but it's in order to grow again and have something more. One must be able to keep the harmony and the beauty till the end. There is no reason why one should have a body which has no longer any purpose in being, in existing; because it would no longer be good for anything. To be no longer good for anything, that is exactly what makes it disappear. One could have a body that grows from perfection to perfection. There are many things in the body that make you say: "Ah, if it were like that! Ah, I would like it to be thus!" (I am not speaking of your character, for there are so many things that need changing; I am speaking only of your physical appearance). You see some disharmony somewhere and you say: "If this disharmony disappeared, how much better would it be!"... But why don't you think that it could be done? If you look at yourself in quite an objective way — not with that sort of attachment one has for one's little person, but quite objectively, — you look at yourself as you would look at another person and tell yourself: "But this thing is not altogether in harmony with that", and if you look yet more closely, it becomes very interesting: you discover that this disharmony is the expression of a defect in your character. It is because in your character there is something a bit twisted, not quite harmonious, and in your body this is reproduced somewhere. You try to arrange it in your body and you find out that to get back to the source of this physical disharmony, you have to find out the defect in your inner being. And then you begin to work and the result is obtained.

You don't know to what an extent the body is plastic! From another standpoint, I would say it is terribly rigid and that is why the body deteriorates. But that is because we do not know how to make use of it. We do not know, when we are still fresh like little leaves, how to will for a luxuriant, magnificent, faultless flowering. And instead of telling oneself with a somewhat miserable look: "It is a pity my arms are too thin or my legs are too long or my back is not straight or my head is not quite harmonious", if one said: "It must be otherwise, my arms must be proportionate, my body harmonious, every form in me must express a higher beauty", then one will succeed. And you will succeed if you know how to do it with the true will that is persistent, tranquil, that is not impatient, does not care for appearances of defeat, continues its work quietly, very quietly, continues to will that it be so, to look for the inner reason, to discover it, to work with energy. Immediately, as soon as you see a little black worm somewhere, which does not look pretty and makes a small rather unpleasant, disgusting stain, you pick it up, pull it out and throw it away and put a lovely light in its place. And after a time you discover: "Why! that disharmony I had in my face is disappearing; that sign of brutality, unconsciousness which was in my expression, it is going away." And then ten years later you don't recognise yourself any longer.

You are all, here, youthful matter; you must know how to profit by it — and not for petty, selfish and stupid reasons but for the love of beauty, for the need of harmony.

If the body is to last, it must not deteriorate. There must not

*17 June 1953*

be any decay. It must win on one side: it must be a transformation, it must not be a decay. With decay there is no possibility of immortality.

*Where does one go after death?*

Ah, my child, you need a book! It is not one question! Well, it will be for next time. Besides, I believe there is a chapter which speaks about it, if I remember aright. We shall have occasion to speak about it.... I shall tell you one thing immediately: when you are born upon earth, do you know where you are going? And all the people on earth, do they all go to the same place? Tell me that!

Everyone follows his way. Everyone has a different destiny. Why should it be the same for all when they are dead? For each one it is a different thing.

Good night.

## 24 June 1953

*"The beings of the vital world are powerful by their very nature; when to their power they add knowledge, they become doubly dangerous. There is nothing to be done with these creatures; you should avoid having any dealings with them unless you have the power to crush and destroy them. If you are forced into contact with them, beware of the spell they can cast. These vital beings, when they manifest on the physical plane, have always a great hypnotic power; for the centre of their consciousness is in the vital world and not in the material and they are not veiled or dwarfed by the material consciousness as human beings are."*

Questions and Answers 1929 (12 May)

*Mother, you say: "These beings are very powerful"; what kind of power have they?*

The power that the vital has over Matter. And, in fact, you can do nothing without the vital power. If there were no vital power, Matter would be inert and unconscious. The vital power is what men usually call "power" in short.

*Cannot the vital power be replaced by some other higher power?*

No. The vital must be transformed. I have always said that nothing can be done without the vital, but the vital must be converted; that is, instead of being an instrument of those beings, it should become an instrument of the divine will. One can do nothing in the physical world without the vital. It is exactly here that the error of the ascetics lies; as they know it is

24 June 1953

a power full of desires and indeed full of the need of realising itself, they abolish it, so deaden it that it exists no longer. All ascetic methods are invented for abolishing and deadening the vital. For that evidently is the most convenient way of cutting off all connection with material life: one becomes worse than a vegetative kind of being.

What is needed is that the vital, instead of serving its own ends or being an instrument of anti-divine forces, should become an instrument of the Divine and put all its force at the service of the Divine. This is quite possible.

*When we are afraid, is that due to the mischief of these beings?*

Yes, my child. Fear is the prettiest gift these beings have given to the world. It is their first present, and the most powerful. It is through fear that they hold human beings. First of all, they create a movement of fear; the movement of fear weakens you, then hands you over little by little into their power. And it is not even a reasonable fear; it is a kind of fear which seizes you, you don't know why, something that makes you tremble, gives you anxiety. You do not know why, it has no apparent reason. It is their action.

*When one feels frightened, what should one do?*

That depends upon who you are. There are many ways of curing oneself of fear.

If you have some contact with your psychic being, you must call it immediately and in the psychic light put things back in order. This is the most powerful way.

When one does not have this psychic contact, but is still a reasonable being, that is, when one has a free movement of the reasoning mind, one can use it to reason with, to speak to oneself as one would to a child, explaining that this fear is a bad thing

117

in itself and, even if there is a danger, to face the danger with fear is the greatest stupidity. If there is a real danger, it is only with the power of courage that you have a chance of coming out of it; if you have the least fear, you are done for. So with that kind of reasoning, manage to convince the part that fears that it must stop being afraid.

If you have faith and are consecrated to the Divine, there is a very simple way, it is to say: "Let Your will be done. Nothing can frighten me because it is You who are guiding my life. I belong to You and You are guiding my life." That acts immediately. Of all the means this is the most effective: indeed, it is. That is, one must be truly consecrated to the Divine. If one has that, it acts immediately; all fear vanishes immediately like a dream. And the being with the bad influence also disappears like a dream along with the fear. You should see it running away at full speed, prrt! *Voilà*.

Now, there are people having a strong vital power in them and they are fighters who immediately lift up their heads and say: "Ah! an enemy is here, we are going to knock him down." But for that one must have the knowledge and a very great vital power. One must be vitally a giant. That does not happen to everyone.

So there are many different ways. They are all good, if you know how to make use of the one that suits your own nature.

*In gymnastics when I want to take a jump and feel frightened, why does this happen?*

Ah! there, my children, it depends.... You must distinguish two very different things and you must deal with them very differently.

If it is a vital fear, you must reason with yourself and go about it all the same. But if it is a physical instinct (that is possible, it happens very often that there is a kind of physical instinct), in that case you must listen to it, for the instinct of the

## 24 June 1953

body is a very sure thing, if it is not disturbed by thought or vital will. The body left to itself knows very well what it can and what it cannot do. And not only that but even a thing that one can do and does usually, if one day you feel a sort of repulsion, as if you were shrinking back, you must definitely not do it; it is an indication that for some reason or other — a purely material reason of a disorder in the functioning of the body — you are not fit to do the thing at that time. Then you must not do it. In that case, it is not even a fear, it is something that shrinks, that withdraws, there is nothing in the head, it does not correspond to any kind of thought like: "What is going to happen?" When the head starts working and you say: "What is going to happen?", you must sweep it away because it is worth nothing; you must use all the means of reason and good sense you have to drive that away. But if it is a purely physical sensation, as though something were contracting, a kind of physical repugnance, if the body itself is refusing, so to say, you should never force it, never, because it is usually when you force it that there's an accident. That may very well be a kind of premonition that there's going to be an accident, that if you do the thing, you will not go far. And in such a case you must not do it. You must not put into it the least *amour-propre*. You must realise: "Today I am not in a good condition."

But if it is a vital fear, if for example you have a competition or a tournament, and you felt this kind of fear and then: "What is going to happen?", you must sweep it away quickly, it means nothing.

*But sometimes, it is laziness that prevents us from doing a thing.*

Ah! if you are tamasic, that is yet something else. If you have a tamasic nature, you must use another procedure. You must exert your consciousness, your will, your force, gather your energy, shake yourself a little and whip yourself and say: "Hup! hup!

forward, march." If it is laziness that keeps you back from, say, doing the vaulting, you must immediately do something much more tiring and say: "Well, you don't want to do that? All right, you are going to do 1500 metres running!" Or else: "I don't want to do the weight-lifting today, I don't feel like doing it: good, I shall do skipping 4000 times at a stretch."

*The same method should be used for studies also?*

Yes, exactly. If you don't feel like learning your lesson, you take a book ten times more tiring, something dry and compel yourself to read it with attention. There are books of this kind, so dry, of such an arid kind of knowledge... Well, if you don't feel like reading your book of history or geography, which are after all very easy and very entertaining, instead of that take one of those books that are given to you (*Mother looks at a teacher*) — I do not dare to say anything, because your teacher is there! — extremely arid, and compel yourself to study at least half the book. Afterwards, everything else appears charming to you.

*Would it not be better to continue the work even if one feels lazy?*

That depends on the work; there we enter another domain.

If it is a work that you are doing for the collectivity and not for yourself personally, then you must do it, whatever happens. It is an elementary discipline. You have undertaken to do this work or have been given the work and have taken it up, therefore you have accepted it, and in that case you must do it. At all times, unless you are absolutely ill, ill in the last degree and unable to move, you must do it. Even if you are rather ill, you must do it. An unselfish work always cures you of your petty personal maladies. Naturally, if you are really compelled to be in bed without being able to move, with a terrible fever or a very serious illness, then that's quite different. But otherwise, if

## 24 June 1953

you are just a little indisposed: "I am not feeling quite well, I have a little headache or I have indigestion, or I have a bad cold, I am coughing", things like that — then doing your work, not thinking of yourself, thinking of the work, doing it as well as you can, that puts you right immediately.

In reality illness is only a disequilibrium; if then you are able to establish another equilibrium, this disequilibrium disappears. An illness is simply, always, in every case, even when the doctors say that there are microbes — in every case, a disequilibrium in the being: a disequilibrium among the various functions, a disequilibrium among the forces.

This is not to say that there are no microbes: there are, there are many more microbes than are known now. But it is not because of that you are ill, for they are always there. It happens that they are always there and for days they do nothing to you and then all of a sudden, one day, one of them gets hold of you and makes you ill — why? Simply because the resistance was not as it used to be habitually, because there was some disequilibrium in some part, the functioning was not normal. But if, by an inner power, you can re-establish the equilibrium, then that's the end, there is no more difficulty, the disequilibrium disappears.

There is no other way of curing people. It is simply when one sees the disequilibrium and is capable of re-establishing the equilibrium that one is cured. Only there are two very different categories you come across... Some hold on to their disequilibrium — they hold on to it, cling to it, don't want to let it go. Then you may try as hard as you will, even if you re-establish the equilibrium the next minute they get into disequilibrium once again, because they love that. They say: "Oh no! I don't want to be ill", but within them there is something which holds firmly to some disequilibrium, which does not want to let it go. There are other people, on the contrary, who sincerely love equilibrium, and directly you give them the power to get back their equilibrium, the equilibrium is re-established and in a few minutes they are cured. Their knowledge was not sufficient or their power was not sufficient to re-establish order — disequilibrium is a disorder. But if you intervene, if you have the knowledge and re-establish the equilibrium, quite naturally the illness will disappear; and those who allow you to do it get cured. Only those who do not let you do it are not cured and this is visible, they do not allow you to act, they cling to the illness. I tell them: "Ah! you are not cured? Go to the doctor then." And the funniest part of the thing is that most often they believe in the doctors, although the working remains the same! Every doctor who is something of a philosopher will tell you: "It is like that; we doctors give only the occasion, but it is the body that cures itself. When the body wants to be cured, it is cured." Well, there are bodies that do not allow equilibrium to be re-established unless they are made to absorb some medicine or something very definite which gives them the feeling that they are being truly looked after. But if you give them a very precise, very exact treatment that is sometimes very difficult to follow, they begin to be convinced that there is nothing better to do than to regain the equilibrium and they get back the equilibrium!

I knew a doctor who was a neuropath and treated illnesses of the stomach. He used to say that all illnesses of the stomach came from a more or less bad nervous state. He was a doctor for the rich and it was the rich and unoccupied people who went to him. So they used to come and tell him: "I have a pain in the stomach, I cannot digest", and this and that. They had terrible pains, they had headache, they had, well, all the phenomena! He used to listen to them very seriously. I knew a lady who went to him and to whom he said: "Ah! your case is very serious. But on which floor do you live? On the groundfloor? All right. This is what you have to do to cure your illness of the stomach. Take a bunch of fully ripe grapes (do not take your breakfast, for breakfast upsets your stomach), take a bunch of grapes; hold it in your hand, like this, very carefully. Then prepare to go out — not by your door, never go out by your door! You must go

## 24 June 1953

out by the window. Get a stool. And go out by the window. Go out in the street, and there you must walk while eating one grape every two steps — not more, yes, not more! You will have stomach-ache! One single grape every two steps. You must take two steps, then eat one single grape and you should continue till there are no more grapes. Do not turn back, go straight on till there are no more grapes. You must take a big bunch. And when you have finished, you may return quietly. But do not take a conveyance! Come back on foot, otherwise the whole trouble will return. Come back quietly and I give you the guarantee that if you do that every day, at the end of three days you will be cured." And in fact this lady was cured!

> (A child) *Sometimes there is a lot of work. One does not know what to do.*

A lot of work... Truly a lot of work?

> *Many kinds of work. For example, in our studies, we have many subjects to read.*

What do you do the whole day, from morning till evening? How much time do you devote to your toilet, to take your bath, to dress? Approximately, not exactly to a minute.

> *About three quarters of an hour.*

How much time do you take for eating?

> *Fifteen minutes.*

Every time? How many times per day? Four? All right. How much time do you spend in gossiping?... That you don't know!

## Questions and Answers 1953

*I don't gossip.*

You don't gossip! You are a marvel, indeed. I shall put you on a pedestal. You don't gossip?

*Yes, I gossip, but when I have work, I don't gossip.*

Yes. And how many hours per day do you need to work to be able to do your tasks?

*In the morning sometimes I get up at half-past four.*

To do your home-work? You are still half asleep, aren't you, at half-past four? Are you quite awake?... No! Ah! And then, you start working immediately?

*Yes, sometimes.*

Because I am leading exactly towards that... When you work, if you are able to concentrate, you can do absolutely in ten minutes what would otherwise take you one hour. If you want to gain time, learn to concentrate. It is through attention that one can do things quickly and one does them much better. If you have a task that should take you half an hour — I don't say if you have to write for half an hour of course — but if you have to think and your mind is floating about, if you are thinking not only of what you are doing but also of what you have done and of what you will have to do and of your other subjects, all that makes you lose thrice as much time as you need to do your task. When you have too much to do, you must learn how to concentrate exclusively on what you are doing, with an intensity in your attention, and you can do in ten minutes what would otherwise take you one hour.

So I do not know, I cannot decide without full knowledge of the matter, if you have too much work, unless you bring me

*24 June 1953*

all the work you have to do; but I do not believe that you are overburdened with work. I say I do not believe it. Now, I do not assert this because I do not know what all the teachers do. But in any case, if you have much to do, you must learn how to concentrate much, all the more, and when you are doing a thing, to think of that only, and focus all your energy upon what you do. You gain at least half the time. So if you tell me: "I have too much work", I answer: "You do not concentrate enough."

(Another child) *For a mathematical problem, sometimes the solution comes quickly, sometimes it takes too long.*

Yes, it is exactly that: it depends on the degree of concentration. If you observe yourself, you will notice this quite well: when it does not come, it is because of a kind of haziness in the brain, something cloudy, like a fog somewhere, and then you are there as in a dream. You push forward trying to find it, and it is as though you were pushing into cottonwool, you do not see clearly there; and so nothing comes. You may remain in that state for hours.

Concentration consists precisely in removing the cloud. You gather together all the elements of your intelligence and fix them on one point, and then you do not even try actively to find the thing. All that you do is to concentrate in such a way as to see only the problem — but seeing not only its surface, seeing it in its depth, what it conceals. If you are able to gather together all your mental energies, bringing them to a point which is fixed on the enunciation of the problem, and you stay there, fixed, as though you were about to drill a hole in the wall, all of a sudden it will come. And this is the only way. If you try: Is it this, is it that, is it this, is it that?... You will never find anything or else you will need hours. You must get your mental forces to a point with strength enough to pierce through the words and strike upon the thing that is behind. There is a thing to be found; swoop down upon it.

And it is always the days you are a little hazy that it becomes difficult. You are hazy: as though there is something you seem to catch and which escapes you.

Naturally, if it is materially impossible — you do not have to deal with monsters! I believe your teachers are reasonable enough and if you go to them and say, "Well, I could not do it, I had no time, I did what I could, I did not have the time", they won't scold you, I don't think so. But here ninety-nine times out of a hundred, it is a kind of half-inertia of the mind which makes you think that you have too much work. If you observe yourself, you will find out that there is always something which pulls this way, something which pulls that way and then this kind of haziness as though you were living in cottonwool, in the clouds: nothing is clear.

The usefulness of work is nothing else but that: to crystallise this mental power. For, what you learn (unless you put it in practice by some work or deeper studies), half of what you learn, at least, will vanish, disappear with time. But it will leave behind one thing: the capacity of crystallising your thought, making something clear out of it, something precise, exact and organised. And that is the true usefulness of work: to organise your cerebral capacity. If you remain in your hazy movement in that kind of cloudy fluidity, you may labour for years, it will be quite useless to you; you will not come out of it more intelligent than when you entered it. But if you are able, even for half an hour, to concentrate your attention on things that seem to you of very little interest, like a rule of grammar, for example (the rules of grammar are some of the dry things I was speaking about, there are other things much more arid, but indeed the rules of grammar are sufficiently arid), if you take one of them and try to understand it — not learn it by heart and apply mechanically what you have learnt by heart, that will be of no use — but try to understand the thought behind the words: "Why was this rule formulated in this way?" and try to find out your own formula for the thing; that is so interesting. "Why has this gentleman who wrote this rule written it in this way? But I am studying, trying to understand why. Why has he put this word after that and that word after that other, and why has he stated the rule in this way? It is because he thought that it was the most complete and the most clear way of expressing the thing." And so that's the thing you must find. And when you find it, you suddenly exclaim: "That is what it means! It must be seen in this way, then it becomes very clear."

I am going to explain it to you: when you have understood, it forms a little crystal in you, like a little shining point. And when you have put in many, many, many of these, then you will begin to be intelligent. That is the utility of work, not simply to stuff the head with a heap of things that take you nowhere.

*How is it that in people occupied with scientific studies artistic imagination is lacking? Are these two things opposed to each other?*

Not necessarily.

*In general?*

They do not belong to the same domain. It is exactly as though you had what is called "a torchlight", a small beacon-light in your head at the place of observation. Scientists who want to do a certain work turn the beacon in a particular way, they always put it there and the beacon remains thus: they turn it towards matter, towards the details of matter. But people with imagination turn it upward, because up above there is everything, you know, all inspirations of artistic and literary things: this comes from another domain. It comes from a much more subtle domain, much less material. So these turn upward and want to receive the light from above. But it is the same instrument. The others turn it downwards, and it is just a lack of gymnastic skill. It is the same instrument. It is the same power of a luminous ray upon something. But as one has made it a habit of concentrating it in a certain direction, one is no longer supple, one loses the habit of doing things otherwise.

But you can at any time do both the things. When you are doing science, you turn it in one direction and when you do literature and art, you turn it in the other direction; but it is the same instrument: all depends on the orientation. If you have concentration, you can move this power of concentration from one place to another and in every way it will be effective. If you are occupied with science, you use it in a scientific way, and if you want to do art, you use it in an artistic way. But it is the same instrument and it is the same power of concentration. It is simply because people do not know this that they limit themselves. So the hinges get rusty, they do not turn any more. Otherwise, if one keeps the habit of turning them, they continue to turn. Moreover, even from the ordinary point of view, it is not rare to find a scientist having as his hobby some artistic occupation — and the reverse also. It is because they have found that the one was not harmful to the other and that it was the same faculty which could be utilised in both.

Essentially, from the general point of view, particularly from the intellectual viewpoint, the most important thing is the capacity of attention and concentration, it is that which one must work at and develop. From the point of view of action (physical action), it is the will: you must work and build up an unshakable will. From the intellectual point of view, you must work and build up a power of concentration which nothing can shake. And if you have both, concentration and will, you will be a genius and nothing will resist you.

# 1 July 1953

"The human being is at home and safe in the material body; the body is his protection. There are some who are full of contempt for their bodies and think that things will be much better and easier after death without them. But in fact the body is your fortress and your shelter. While you are lodged in it the forces of the hostile world find it difficult to have a direct hold upon you.... Directly you enter any realm of this [vital] world, its beings gather round you to get out of you all you have, to draw what they can and make it a food and a prey. If you have no strong light and force radiating from within you, you move there without your body as if you had no coat to protect you against a chill and bleak atmosphere, no house to shield you, even no skin covering you, your nerves exposed and bare. There are men who say, 'How unhappy I am in this body', and think of death as an escape! But after death you have the same vital surroundings and are in danger from the same forces that are the cause of your misery in this life....

"It is here upon earth, in the body itself, that you must acquire a complete knowledge and learn to use a full and complete power. Only when you have done that will you be free to move about with entire security in all the worlds."

Questions and Answers 1929 (12 May)

(A child) *After death people enter the vital world, but those who do good go to paradise?*

Where is your paradise? Who has taught you that? They have spoken to you of heaven and hell and purgatory?... No? Not of all that? From where did you gather your idea of paradise? From which book?

*I have heard about it.*

But from whom?

*I do not remember now.*

It is generally what religious priests say to the faithful to encourage them to do good. For it is a notorious fact that life is not more easy for the good than for the wicked; usually it is the contrary: the wicked succeed better than the good! So people who are not very spiritual say to themselves: "Why should I take the trouble of being good? It is better to be wicked and have an easy life." It is very difficult to make them understand that there are many kinds of good and that sometimes it is worth the trouble perhaps to make an effort to be good. So to make this intelligible to the least intelligent, they are told: "There, it is very simple. If you are quite obedient, quite nice, quite unselfish, if you always do good deeds, and if you believe in the dogmas we teach, well, when you die, God will send you to Paradise. If you have sometimes good will, sometimes bad, if, sometimes you do good, sometimes you don't and if you think very much of yourself and very little of others, then when you die, you will be sent to Purgatory for another experience. And then if you are thoroughly wicked, if you are always doing harm to others, doing all kinds of bad things and you do not care about the good of anyone and particularly if you do not believe in the dogma that we teach you, then you will go straight to Hell and for eternity."

This is one of the prettiest inventions I have ever heard of: they have invented *eternal hell*. That is to say, once you are in hell, it is for eternity.... You understand what that means, for eternity? You will be tortured and burnt (in the hot countries

## 1 July 1953

you are burnt, in the cold countries you are frozen), and that for eternity. That is it. So I do not know who taught you those pretty things; but they are simply inventions to make people obey, to keep them under control.

There are teachings which are not like that. There are religions which are not like that. But still one can, in a poetic, picturesque, descriptive manner speak of a paradise; because this paradise means a wonderful place where there is utmost joy and happiness and comfort.... And yet that depends upon the religion to which you belong. For there are heavens where you pass your time singing praises to God, you do nothing else — but in the end that must be somewhat wearisome; however, there you pass your time playing music and singing the praises of God. There are other heavens, on the contrary, where you enjoy all possible pleasures, all that you desired to have during your life, you have in heaven. There are heavens where you are constantly in blissful meditation — but for people who are not keen on meditating, that must be rather tiresome. However, that depends, you know: they have invented all kinds of things so that people may really want to be wise and obey the laws given to them.

And man's imagination is so creative, such a form-maker, that there really are in the world places like these heavens. There are places also like these hells and there are places like these purgatories. Man creates out of nothing the things he imagines. If your consciousness is enlightened, then you can be pulled out of these places; otherwise you are shut up, imprisoned there by the very belief you had when alive. You will tell me that it is equal to a life, but it is an altogether illusory and extremely limited existence. It is real only for those who think like that. As soon as you think differently, it does not exist for you any longer; you can come out of it. You can pull a person out of these places, and immediately he perceives that he was imprisoned in his own formation.

Man has an extraordinary power of creation. He has created

a whole set of godheads in his own image, having the same faults as himself, doing on a bigger scale, with greater power whatever he does. These beings have a relative existence, but still it is an independent existence, just like your thought. When you have a thought, a well-made mental formation which goes out of you, it becomes an independent entity and continues on its way and it does that for which it was made. It continues to act independently of you. That is why you must be on your guard. If you have made such a formation and it has gone out, it has gone out to do its work; and after a time you find out that it was perhaps not a very happy thing to have a thought like that, that this formation was not very beneficial; now that it has gone out, it is very difficult for you to get hold of it again. You must have considerable occult knowledge. It has gone out and is moving on its way.... Supposing in a moment of great anger (I do not say that you do so, but still) when you were in quite a rage against someone, you said: "Ah! couldn't some misfortune befall him?" Your formation has gone on its way. It has gone out and you have no longer any control over it; and it goes and organises some misfortune or other: it is going to do its work. And after sometime the misfortune arrives. Happily, you do not usually have sufficient knowledge to tell yourself: "Oh! It is I who am responsible", but that is the truth.

Note that this power of formation has a great advantage, if one knows how to use it. You can make good formations and if you make them properly, they will act in the same way as the others. You can do a lot of good to people just by sitting quietly in your room, perhaps even more good than by undergoing a lot of trouble externally. If you know how to think correctly, with force and intelligence and kindness, if you love someone and wish him well very sincerely, deeply, with all your heart, that does him much good, much more certainly than you think. I have said this often; for example, to those who are here, who learn that someone in their family is very ill and feel that childish impulse of wanting to rush immediately to the spot to attend to

## 1 July 1953

the sick person. I tell you, unless it is an exceptional case and there is nobody to attend on the sick person (and at times even in such a case), if you know how to keep the right attitude and concentrate with affection and good will upon the sick person, if you know how to pray for him and make helpful formations, you will do him much more good than if you go to nurse him, feed him, help him wash himself, indeed all that everybody can do. Anybody can nurse a person. But not everybody can make good formations and send out forces that act for healing.

In any case, to come back to our paradise, it is a childish deformation — ignorant or political — of something which is true in a sense but not quite like that.... I have told you many times and I could not repeat it too often, that one is not built up of one single piece. We have within us many states of being and each state of being has its own life. All this is put together in one single body, so long as you have a body, and acts through that single body; so that gives you the feeling that it is one single person, a single being. But there are many beings and particularly there are concentrations on different levels: just as you have a physical being, you have a vital being, you have a mental being, you have a psychic being, you have many others and all possible intermediaries. But it is a little complicated, you might not understand. Suppose you were living a life of desire, passion and impulse: you live with your vital being dominant in you; but if you live with spiritual effort, with great good will, the desire to do things well and an unselfishness, a will for progress, you live with the psychic being dominant in you. Then, when you are about to leave your body, all these beings start to disperse. Only if you are a very advanced yogi and have been able to unify your being around the divine centre, do these beings remain bound together. If you have not known how to unify yourself, then at the time of death all that is dispersed: each one returns to its domain. For example, with regard to the vital being, all your different desires will be separated and each one run towards its own realisation, quite independently, for the physical being will no longer be there to hold them together. But if you have united your consciousness with the psychic consciousness, when you die you remain conscious of your psychic being and the psychic being returns to the psychic world which is a world of bliss and delight and peace and tranquillity and of a growing knowledge. So, if you like to call that a paradise, it is all right; because in fact, to the extent to which you are identified with your psychic being, you remain conscious of it, you are one with it, and it is immortal and goes to its immortal domain to enjoy a perfectly happy life or rest. If you like to call that paradise, call it paradise. If you are good, if you have become conscious of your psychic and live in it, well, when your body dies, you will go with your psychic being to take rest in the psychic world, in a blissful state.

But if you have lived in your vital with all its impulses, each impulse will try to realise itself here and there... For example, a miser who is concentrated upon his money, when he dies, the part of the vital that was interested in his money will be stuck there and will continue to watch over the money so that nobody may take it. People do not see him, but he is there all the same, and is very unhappy if something happens to his precious money. I knew quite well a lady who had a good amount of money and children; she had five children who were all prodigals each one more than the other. The same amount of care she had taken in amassing the money, they seemed to take in squandering it; they spent it at random. So when the poor old lady died, she came to see me and told me: "Ah, now they are going to squander my money!" And she was extremely unhappy. I consoled her a little, but I had a good deal of difficulty in persuading her not to keep watching over her money so that it might not be wasted.

Now, if you live exclusively in your physical consciousness (it is difficult, for you have, after all, thoughts and feelings, but if you live exclusively in your physical), when the physical being disappears, you disappear at the same time, it is finished.... There is a spirit of the form: your form has a spirit which persists for seven days after your death. The doctors have declared that you are dead, but the spirit of your form lives, and not only does it live but it is conscious in most of the cases. But that lasts for seven or eight days and afterwards it is dissolved. I am not speaking of yogis; I am speaking of ordinary people. Yogis have no laws, it is quite different; for them the world is different. I am speaking to you of ordinary men living an ordinary life; for these it is like that.

So the conclusion is that if you want to preserve your consciousness, it would be better to centralise it on a part of your being that is immortal; otherwise it will vanish like a flame in the air. And it is very fortunate, for if it were otherwise, there would be perhaps gods or types of superior men who would create hells and heavens as they do in their material imagination, where they would imprison you; you would be imprisoned in heaven or in hell according as you pleased or displeased them. It would be a very critical situation and happily it is not like that.

*It is said that there is a god of Death. Is it true?*

Yes, I call it the spirit of Death. I know it very well. And that is an extraordinary organisation. You do not know to what an extent it is organised.

I believe there are many of these spirits of death, I believe there are hundreds. I have met at least two of them. One I met in France and the other in Japan, and they were very different; which leads one to believe that probably in accordance with the mental culture, the education, the country and beliefs there should be different spirits. But there are spirits of all the manifestations of Nature: there are spirits of fire, spirits of air, of water, of rain, of wind; and there are spirits of death.

Each spirit of death, whatever it may be, has a claim to a certain number of deaths per day. Indeed it is a fantastic organisation; it is a kind of alliance between the vital forces and the forces of Nature. For example, if the spirit of death has decided: "That is the number of people to which I am entitled", let us say four or five or six, or one or two persons, it depends on the day; it has decided that certain persons would die, it goes straight and settles down beside the person about to die. But if you happen to be conscious (not the person), if you see the spirit going to a person and you do not want him to die, then you can, if you possess a certain occult power, tell it: "No, I forbid you to take him." It is a thing that has happened, not once but several times, in Japan and here. It was not the same spirit. That is what makes me say that there must be many.

— I don't want him to die.

— But I have a right to one death!

— Go and find someone who is ready to die.

So I have seen several cases: sometimes it is just a neighbour who dies suddenly in place of the other, sometimes it is an acquaintance and sometimes it is an enemy. Naturally, there is a relation, good or bad, of neighbourhood (or anything else) which externally looks like chance. But it is the spirit who has taken *its* dead. The spirit has a claim to one death, it will have one death. You can tell it: "I forbid you to take this one", and have the power of sending it away, and the spirit can do nothing but go away; but it does not give up its due and goes elsewhere. There is another death.

It is the same thing with fire. I saw the spirit of fire, particularly in Japan because fire is an extraordinary thing in that country. When a fire starts, some eighty houses burn: a whole quarter. It is something fantastic. The houses are of wood and they burn like match-boxes; you see a fire kindling and then all of a sudden, puff!... You have never seen a match-box catching fire? a flash! like that, a flash! one, two, three, ten, twenty houses burnt down before my eyes!... So there are spirits of fire. One day, I was in my bed. I was concentrating, looking at people. Suddenly I saw something like a cloud of flames drawing close to the house. I looked and I saw it was a conscious being.

— Eh! what are you here for?

— I have the right to burn the house, start a fire.

**1 July 1953**

— That's possible, I told it, but not here.
And it could not resist.
It is a question of who proves the stronger. I said: "No, here you can't burn, that's all!" Five minutes later I heard cries: "Ah! Ah!" Two or three houses farther away, a house had caught fire. It had gone there as I had forbidden it to come to my house. It had a claim to one house. There we are!

*Sometimes when people are dying, they know that they are about to die. Why don't they tell the spirit to go away?*

Ah! well, that depends upon the people. Two things are necessary. First of all, nothing in your being, no part of your being should want to die. That does not happen often. You have always a defeatist in you somewhere: something that is tired, something that is disgusted, something that has had enough of it, something that is lazy, something that does not want to struggle and says: "Well! Ah! Let it be finished, so much the better." That is sufficient, you are dead.

But it is a fact: if nothing, absolutely nothing in you consents to die, you will not die. For someone to die, there is always a second, perhaps the hundredth part of a second when he gives his consent. If there is not this second of consent, he does not die.

I knew people who should have really died according to all physical and vital laws; and they refused. They said: "No, I will not die", and they lived. There are others who do not need at all to die, but they are of that kind and say: "Ah! Well! Yes, so much the better, it will be finished", and it is finished. Even that much, even nothing more than that: you need not have a persistent wish, you have only to say: "Well, yes, I have had enough!" and it is finished. So it is truly like that. As you say, you may have death standing by your bedside and tell him: "I do not want you, go away", and it will be obliged to go away.

But usually one gives way, for one must struggle, one must be strong, one must be very courageous and enduring, must have a great faith in the necessity of life; like someone, for example, who feels very strongly that he has still something to do and he must absolutely do it. But who is sure he has not within him the least bit of a defeatist, somewhere, who just yields and says: "It is all right"?... It is here, the necessity of unifying oneself.

Whatever the way we follow, the subject we study, we always arrive at the same result. The most important thing for an individual is to unify himself around his divine centre; in that way he becomes a true individual, master of himself and his destiny. Otherwise, he is a plaything of forces that toss him about like a piece of cork on a river. He goes where he does not want to go, he is made to do things he does not want to do, and finally he loses himself in a hole without having any strength to recover. But if you are consciously organised, unified around the divine centre, ruled and directed by it, you are master of your destiny. That is worth the trouble of attempting.... In any case, I find it preferable to be the master rather than the slave. It is a rather unpleasant sensation to feel yourself pulled by the strings and made to do things whether you want to or not — that is quite irrelevant — but to be compelled to act because something pulls you by the strings, something which you do not even see — that is exasperating. However, I do not know, but I found it very exasperating, even when I was quite a child. At five, it began to seem to me quite intolerable and I sought for a way so that it might be otherwise — without people getting a chance to scold me. For I knew nobody who could help me and I did not have the chance that you have, someone who can tell you: "This is what you have to do!" There was nobody to tell me that. I had to find it out all by myself. And I found it. I started at five. And you, you were five long ago.... *Voilà.*

# 8 July 1953

*"The mind is an instrument of action and formation and not an instrument of knowledge; at each moment it is creating forms. Thoughts are forms and have an individual life, independent of their author: sent out from him into the world, they move in it towards the realisation of their own purpose of existence. When you think of anyone, your thought takes a form and goes out to find him; and, if your thinking is associated with some will that is behind it, the thought-form that has gone out from you makes an attempt to realise itself."*
Questions and Answers 1929 (19 May)

*Do prayers and aspirations also take a form like thoughts?*

Yes. At times they take even the form of the person who has the aspiration or makes the prayer — often. That depends. Aspirations sometimes take the form of that to which one aspires, but most often, and specially prayers, clearly take the form of the one who prays.

*What is the difference between prayer and aspiration?*

I have written this somewhere. There are several kinds of prayers.

There is the purely mechanical, material prayer, with words which have been learnt and are mechanically repeated. That does not signify anything much. And that has usually only one single result, that of quietening the person who prays, for if a prayer is repeated several times, the words end up by making you calm.

There is a prayer which is a spontaneous formula for expressing something precise which one wants to ask for: one prays for this thing or that, one prays for one thing or another; one can pray for somebody, for a circumstance, for oneself.

There is a point where aspiration and prayer meet, for there are prayers which are the spontaneous formulation of a lived experience: these spring up all ready from within the being, like something that's the expression of a profound experience, and which offers thanksgiving for that experience or asks its continuation or asks for its explanation also; and that indeed is quite close to aspiration. But aspiration is not necessarily formulated in words; or if it is formulated in words, it is almost a movement of invocation. You aspire for a certain state; for instance, you have found something in yourself that is not in keeping with your ideal, a movement of darkness and ignorance, perhaps even of ill-will, something that's not in harmony with what you want to realise; then that is not going to be formulated in words; that will be like a springing flame and like an offering made of a living experience, asking to grow larger, be magnified and ever more and more clear and precise. All that may be put into words *later*, if one tries to remember and note down one's experience. But aspiration always springs up like a flame that rises high and carries in itself the thing one desires to be or what one desires to do or desires to have. I use the word "desire", but truly it is here that the word "aspire" should be used, for that does not have either the quality or the form of a desire.

It is truly like a great purifying flame of will, and it carries in its core the thing that asks to be realised.

For instance, if you have done something you regret having done, if that has unhappy consequences which disturb things, and several people are implicated, you do not know the reactions of the others, but you yourself wish that what has been done may take a turn for the best, and that if there is a mistake, it may be understood, and that no matter what the mistake, this may be for you an opportunity for a greater progress, a greater

8 July 1953

discipline, a new ascent towards the Divine, a door open on a future that you want to be more clear and true and intense; so all this is gathered here (*pointing to the heart*) like a force, and then it surges up and rises in a great movement of ascent, and at times without the shadow of a formulation, without words, without expression, but like a springing flame.

That indeed is true aspiration. That may happen a hundred, a thousand times daily if one is in that state in which one constantly wants to progress and be more true and more fully in harmony with what the Divine Will wants of us.

Prayer is a much more external thing, generally about a precise fact, and always formulated for it is the formula that makes the prayer. One may have an aspiration and transcribe it as a prayer, but aspiration goes beyond prayer in every way. It is much closer and much more as it were self-forgetful, living only in the thing one wants to be or do, and the offering of all that one wants to do to the Divine. You may pray in order to ask for something, you may also pray to thank the Divine for what He has given you, and that prayer is much greater: it may be called an act of thanksgiving. You may pray in gratitude for the aspect of kindness the Divine has shown to you, for what He has done for you, for what you see in Him, and the praise you want to offer Him. And all this may take the form of a prayer. It is decidedly the highest prayer, for it is not exclusively preoccupied with oneself, it is not an egoistic prayer.

Certainly, one may have an aspiration in all the domains, but the very centre of aspiration is in the psychic being, whilst one may pray in all the domains, and the prayer belongs to the domain in which one prays. One may make purely material, physical prayers, vital prayers, mental prayers, psychic prayers, spiritual prayers, and each one has its special character, its special value.

There is a kind of prayer at once spontaneous and unselfish which is like a great call, usually not for one's own self personally, but like something that may be called an intercession with the Divine. It is extremely powerful. I have had countless instances of things which have been realised almost instantaneously due to prayers of this kind. It implies a great faith, a great ardour, a great sincerity, and a great simplicity of heart also, something that does not calculate, does not plan, does not bargain, does not give with the idea of receiving in exchange. For, the majority of men give with one hand and hold out the other to get something in exchange; the largest number of prayers are of that sort. But there are others of the kind I have described, acts of thanksgiving, a kind of canticle, and these are very good.

There you are. I don't know if I have made myself clear, but this is how it is.

To be clearer, we may say that prayer is always formulated in words; but the words may have different values according to the state in which they are formulated. Prayer is a formulated thing and one may aspire. But it is difficult to pray without praying to someone. For instance, those who have a conception of the universe from which they have more or less driven out the idea of the Divine (there are many people of this kind; this idea troubles them — the idea that there is someone who knows all, can do everything and who is so formidably greater than they that there can be no comparison; that's a bit troublesome for their *amour-propre*; so they try to make a world without the Divine), these people evidently cannot pray, for to whom would they pray? Unless they pray to themselves, which is not the custom! But one can aspire for something without having any faith in the Divine. There are people who do not believe in the existence of a God, but who have faith in progress. They have the idea that the world is in constant progress and that this progress will go on indefinitely without stopping, towards an ever greater betterment. Well, these people can have a very great aspiration for progress, and they don't even need any idea of a divine existence for that. Aspiration necessarily implies a faith but not necessarily faith in a divine being; whilst prayer cannot exist if it is not addressed to a divine being. And pray to

## 8 July 1953

what? One does not pray to something that has no personality! One prays to someone who can hear us. If there is nobody to hear us, how could one pray? Hence, if one prays, this means that, even when one doesn't acknowledge it, one has faith in somebody infinitely higher than us, infinitely more powerful, who can change our destiny and change us also, if one prays so as to be heard. That is the essential difference.

So the more intellectual people admit aspiration and say that prayer is something inferior. The mystics tell you that aspiration is all very well but if you want to be really heard and want the Divine to listen to you, you must pray, and pray with the simplicity of a child, a perfect candour, that is, a perfect trust: "I need this or that (whether it be a moral need or a physical or material need), well, I ask You for it, give it to me." Or else: "You have given me what I asked of You, You have made me realise concretely those experiences which were unknown to me and are now marvels I can attain at will; yes, I am infinitely grateful to You and I offer a prayer of thanksgiving to sing Your praise and thank You for Your intervention." It is like that. To aspire it is not necessary to direct the aspiration to someone, towards someone. One has an aspiration for a certain state of being, for knowledge, for a realisation, a state of consciousness; one aspires for something, but it is not necessarily a prayer; prayer is something additional.

Prayer is a personal thing, addressed to a personal being, that is, to something — a force or a being — who can hear you and answer you. Otherwise you can't ask for anything. Do you understand?

*When somebody has an ill-will against a person, how does this will act upon that person?*

It is the same thing. Through a formation, a mental formation. When somebody is very ill-willed and wants to harm you, his will is expressed more or less; at times he does not dare to acknowledge this to himself for he would feel ashamed, but that may come spontaneously. Or else, it may be as with malicious people, something shut up very deep in the consciousness, all the time there, like that, stirring up their spite; and then there are violent people who wish that a calamity may befall those who have caused them some so-called harm or have displeased them for some reason or other.... Anyway, that is it, it belongs to the field of formation; and it is so strong that if you just pass by someone who has a manifest ill-will, you may suddenly feel very uneasy.

Now, if you have a little knowledge and consciousness, you can become aware of the reason, and then, when one realises the reason, there is only one thing to do, just this (*gesture*), as one brushes off a fly. Flies are very troublesome and come back again and again; and evil formations — take care! — have the same habit as flies. You brush flies away, they return, you brush them away again, again they return. They think it is a game. Have you never remarked, flies take this as a game? truly, even as they are sent away, they return. Only, if at a particular moment you become angry, you get into a temper and do this (*gesture*), even if you do not touch it, the fly will not come back. It feels it. Try, you will see.

But a bad thought is a bad act. There are people who do not know it, but truly a bad thought is a bad act and if one thinks and wishes harm to someone, well, one is responsible for the misfortunes that come upon him just as much as though one had acted. But the unfortunate thing is that this is not recognised and that never does one intervene in the bad thoughts of people.... There are even people who take great pleasure in inciting the bad thoughts of others. I have known such people (unfortunately far too many), when they have something unpleasant to say to somebody, they never miss the opportunity of telling him: "You know, somebody said that about you", and also: "You know, that other person said this about you." And thus they create as much harm as they think of. And this they do at times simply through stupidity, most often through vanity, in order to show off that they know something. But at bottom, in the consciousness, there is what is called mischief-making — something that enjoys creating disorder, misunderstandings, disputes among people, unpleasant situations, and feels at ease amidst these. There are many people with a very sharp tongue. It is called in French "une langue de vipère", a viperish tongue. This is their great amusement. And they do much, much, much harm. But even without speaking, if one has a strong thought and thinks ill of people, one does a bad deed.

*Why is there ill-will?*

My child, it is as though you asked me why there is inconscience, ignorance, darkness in the nature! It is the why of the world you are asking me! Why is the world like this and not otherwise?... There are people who have written volumes on the subject. And each one explains it in his own way and that changes nothing, in fact. You may ask me: Why is there ill-will? Why is there ignorance? Why is there stupidity? Why is there wickedness? Why is there all the evil? Why is the world not a very charming place?... All the philosophers explain it to you, each in his own way. The materialists explain it in their way, the scientists explain it in their way, but nobody in all that can find the means of getting out of it! and after all, the one thing that's truly important is, it would be just (you ask me: Why is there ill-will?) it would be to find the way so that there may no longer be any ill-will. That would be worth the trouble. If you tell me: Why is there suffering, why is there misery?... What can that do to you, this why, unless it be a means of finding a remedy? But I don't believe it would, for (we have said that here) if you seek for the why, you will find within yourself simply all sorts of explanations which will be more or less useless and will lead you nowhere.

The fact is that it *is* so, isn't it? and the second fact is that one doesn't want it thus, and the third is to find the means that it may no longer exist. That is our problem. The world is not as we think it ought to be. There are lots of things in the world which we do not approve of. Well, there are people who like what they call "knowledge" very much and begin to inquire why it is like that. In a way this is very well, but as I said, it would be much more important to find out what to do so that it may be otherwise. This is exactly the problem the Buddha put to himself. He sat under a tree, it is said, until he found the solution. But his solution is not very good, for when you tell me: "The world is bad", well, his solution is: "Do away with the world." — "For whose benefit?" as Sri Aurobindo has written somewhere. Then the world will no longer be bad, for it will not exist! But what is the use of its no longer being bad, since it will not exist? It is very simple logic. It is like those who want the whole world to return to its Origin; and so Sri Aurobindo answers: "You will be the all-powerful master of something that no longer exists, an emperor without an empire or a king without a kingdom", that's all.... It is one solution. But there are other better ones. I believe we have found better ones.

Some say that ill-will comes from ignorance (that was exactly what the Buddha claimed) and that if ignorance disappeared there would no longer be any ill-will. There are others who say that ill-will comes from division, separation, that if the universe were not cut off from its Origin there would be no ill-will. Others still say that it is ill-will which is the cause of everything, of separation and ignorance; and so there arises the problem: Whence does it come, this ill-will? If it were at the origin of everything, it was then *in* the origin of everything. And there we are altogether at a loss, my children! We could speculate upon this for years, we shall never get out of it. And so those who push it so far finish by telling you: Ill-will doesn't exist, it is an illusion. And that's simply because they stop midway in their reasoning, for if they went a little farther they might say: Perhaps it is a human invention, this ill-will.... That is possible!

8 July 1953

*Animals don't have ill-will, do they?*

I do not think so. I can't say for sure since I don't know all the animal species, but I have heard things which to us seem monstrosities, yet are not at all instances of ill-will. For example, take the world of insects; of all the animal species it is this which most contains the sense of what we call wickedness — and what may be called ill-will, but it could very well be that this is our consciousness applied to their movements which sees a movement of wickedness or ill-will.... There are insects whose larvae can live only on a living being. They can feed only on a living being; dead flesh does not nourish these. So the parent insect that is going to lay its eggs (which will change into larvae) begins by stinging a nervous centre of another insect or small lower animal which it paralyses, and after that gently lays its eggs inside in such a way that when the eggs are hatched the larvae feed on that paralysed but not dead animal. It is Machiavellian, isn't it? Evidently it is not the result of reasoning, it is an instinct. Can this be called ill-will? Is this ill-will?... It is simply the instinct of procreation.

Perhaps, if we say that these insects are moved by the spirit of the species which in itself is conscious and has a conscious will, we can then say that all these imaginations (I give you this one instance, but there are any number of them as terrible, as monstrous for our human consciousness), all these beings, fashioners, who have created these insects must be frightful beings (don't you think so?) and have a perverse and diabolical imagination. It is quite possible, for indeed it is said that the origin of the insect species is a vital origin, that the fashioners are those of a vital type, that is, beings who not only symbolise but represent and live upon the ill-will in the world. These are very conscious of their ill-will, and it is deliberate. The ill-will of men is usually only a kind of reflection — an imitation or a reflection — of the will of the beings of the vital, a will clearly hostile to creation, a will to make things as painful, as ugly, as sorrowful, as monstrous as possible. It is said that it is these who have created insects, and so the insect species would perhaps be... But they do not wilfully represent evil, you understand, they are moved by an unconscious instinct. They do not do evil intentionally. They do it because it is in their nature. What I call ill-will is truly the will to do evil for the sake of doing evil, destroying for the sake of destroying, harming for harming's sake and taking pleasure in the fact of doing evil. That really is ill-will. Egoism, I do believe, begins with the birth of mind. I can't tell for certain, for always new things are being found. But what I have seen of the animal species, specially of the higher animals, may be the instinct of preservation, may be violence, obscure and brutal reactions, but is that truly what is called ill-will?... It is possible. If someone were to tell me a story he has witnessed which proves the opposite, I am ready to admit it but for the time being — I haven't seen it. All that I know of animals is their instinct which pushes them into action, but they don't have that perversity that's in the human mind. I believe it is with this kind of mental functioning and under the direct influence of the vital that man has become an ill-willed being. The Titans are ill-willed beings but the Titans are beings of the vital world manifested in the forces of Nature: they want to do evil for the pleasure of doing it, to destroy for the pleasure of destroying.

People always speak about the wickedness of cats, for instance, playing with the mouse before eating it. That's an example given to children; but I have seen cats. I know what they do. It is not at all true. They don't do this at all through malice. Usually it happens like this: the mother-cat hunts for the little ones and catches a mouse. If it were to give the mouse immediately to the kittens to eat, they wouldn't be able to eat it, for it is hard, tough, and they don't have the capacity to eat such hard, tough flesh. Besides, it is also bad when it is like that. So they play with it (they seem to be playing with it), they toss it about, roll it, catch it, let it run, run after it, until it is very nicely softened. And then, when it is well softened, ready for eating, and the meat already worked upon, then they give it to the little ones who can now eat it. But certainly they don't go and play with the mouse for the pleasure of playing! They hunt first, you see, and then prepare the dinner. They have neither furnace nor fire to cook and soften the thing. They must prepare it and make it ready for eating.

But it is also said that the first expression of love in living beings is the desire to devour. One wants to absorb, desires to devour. There is one instance which would seem to prove that this is not altogether false — that is when the tiger catches its prey or the snake its victim, it happens that both the tiger's and the snake's victims give themselves up in a kind of delight of being eaten. An experience is narrated of a man who was in the bush with his friends and had lagged behind and was caught by a tiger, a man-eater. The others came back when they saw that he was missing. They saw the tracks. They ran after him, just in time to prevent the tiger's eating him. When he came to himself a little, they told him he must have had a frightful experience. He said: "No, just imagine, I don't know what happened to me, as soon as that tiger caught me and while it was dragging me along, I felt an intense love for it and a great desire to be eaten by it!"

This is quite true, it is not an invention. It is a true story.

Well, I have seen with my own eyes.... I believe I have already narrated this to you — the story of the little rabbit which had been put in a python's cage. It was in the cage in the *Jardin des Plantes* in Paris. It was the breakfast day. I happened to be there. The cage was opened, the little white rabbit put inside. It was a pretty little white rabbit and it immediately fled to the other end of the cage and trembled like anything. It was horrible to see this, for it knew very well what was happening, it had felt the snake, it knew very well. The serpent was simply coiled up on its mat. It seemed to be asleep, and very quietly it stretched out its neck and head, and then began looking at the rabbit. It looked at it without stirring — just looked at it. I saw the rabbit which at first stopped trembling; it no longer was afraid. It was quite doubled up and it began to recover. And then I saw it lift its head, open its eyes wide, and look at the snake, and slowly, very slowly it went forward towards it till it was just at the right distance. Then the snake with a single leap — without any disturbance, without even uncoiling itself, just remaining where it was, you understand — hop! it took it. And then it began rolling it, preparing it for its dinner. It was not in order to play with it. It prepared the thing. It crushed all its bones nicely, made them crack; then it smeared it with a kind of gluey substance to make it quite slippy. And when it was all quite ready, it began swallowing it slowly, comfortably.... But it didn't have to disturb itself, it didn't have to make the least movement, except the last swift one just to catch it when it was right in front. It was the other creature that had come to it.

There you are. Indeed there are many things in Nature. There is this, there is perhaps ill-will also. But I am not quite sure that it is not one of those presents that mental activity has given to man... as soon as he was separated from his instinct and wanted to act independently....

*What exactly is instinct?*

It is the consciousness of Nature. Nature is conscious of its action, but this is not an individual consciousness. There is an instinct of the species. Some have said that there were even "spirits of the species", conscious beings for each species. Instinct depends on the way Nature works, and Nature is a conscious force which knows what it wants, does it in its own way, knowing where it is going and its roads: it chooses them itself. For man this appears incoherent, for his own consciousness is too narrow (he can't see the whole well enough; when one sees only the small details of things or little fragments, one can't understand at all), but Nature has a plan, it has a conscious will, it is altogether a conscious entity — it can't be called a being, for it is not in the

# 8 July 1953

same proportion. When we speak of a being with our human consciousness, we immediately imagine a human being, perhaps a little larger or much larger, but still functioning always in the same way. That is why I don't call it a being, but it is a conscious entity, a conscious will doing things consciously, deliberately, and having formidable forces at its disposal.

It is also said that the forces of Nature are blind and violent. But it is not at all that! It is man in his relative proportion with Nature who judges like that. Wait a little, let us take this example. When there is an earthquake, many islands are engulfed and millions of people killed. People say: "This Nature is monstrous." From the human point of view this Nature is monstrous. What has it done? It has wrought a cataclysm. But just think how in jumping or running or doing something or other, you get a good knock and turn black and blue. It is the same thing for our cells as an earthquake; you destroy a huge number of cells! It is a question of proportion. For us, our little consciousness, ever so little, this appears something formidable but after all it is quite simply a contusion somewhere upon earth (not even in the universe). We are speaking only of the earth. What is it? Nothing at all, just a tiny little plaything in the universe. If we speak of this universe, then the disappearance of the worlds — these are just contusions. It is nothing.

One must, if one can, widen one's consciousness.

I knew somebody who wanted to widen his consciousness; he said he had found a way, it was to lie flat on his back at night, out-of-doors, and look at the stars and try to identify himself with them, and go away deep into an immense world, and so lose completely all sense of proportion, of the order of the earth and all its little things, and become vast as the sky — you couldn't say as vast as the universe, for we see only a tiny bit of it, but vast as the sky with all the stars. And so, you know, the little impurities fall off for the time being, and one understands things on a very vast scale. It is a good exercise.

Both are good exercises. Try to compare them, you'll see:

you are walking on a street, there is an army of ants going from one nest to another (you do not look down, you are talking with someone); very negligently you put one foot and then the other, and you crush hundreds of ants without even being aware of it. If you were an ant, you would say: "What a wicked and beastly force!" You are just walking. You have not paid attention. But suppose there are beings of this kind for whom we are just tiny little ants. They put one foot and then the other and millions of people are killed. They are not even aware of it! They have not done it on purpose. They were just walking along, that's all. The only difference you could make (and yet I am not quite sure), the only difference between the ant and man is that man is able to think of what happens to him, and perhaps the ant is not conscious of it? I don't know at all. I don't guarantee it. *Voilà.*

# 15 July 1953

*"Each man has some fad or one preferred shibboleth or another, each thinks that he is free from this or that prejudice from which others suffer and is willing to regard such notions as quite false; but he imagines that his is not like theirs, it is for him the truth, the real truth. An attachment to a rule of the mind is an indication of a blindness still hiding somewhere."*

*Questions and Answers 1929 (19 May)*

*Are superstitions mental rules?*

No, not rules but mental formations. Generally a superstition originates in an experience. For instance, there is a certain superstition in Europe, and you are told: "Never walk under a ladder, it will bring you ill-luck." It is probable that someone walked under a ladder and the ladder slipped and fell upon him, and the story starts off like that. It can happen that this is a repeated experience, for, in fact, if a ladder is badly placed and you pass underneath it could fall at that very moment, and that would bring ill-luck! There are innumerable superstitions of this kind. They depend upon the countries, besides; these things are quite local and one may even find contradictory superstitions in different countries. In certain countries if you see a black cat, it is a sign that a catastrophe will come. In others if you see a black cat, it means that something very fine will happen! If you put things together you will come to the conclusion that nothing at all will happen to you! It is like that. Almost all superstitions are the result of an experience that is quite local, occasional, exceptional, which has been raised into a mental principle. It is a mental formation, it is not a rule.

Now, there are other instances, as for example a large

number of religious rules which are founded solely on hygienic principles, on medical knowledge, and have been raised into religious principles, for that was the only way to make people observe them. If you are not told that "God wants" that you should do this or that, you would not do it, the majority of men ordinarily do not do it. For instance, that very simple thing — washing your hands before eating; in countries where the civilisation is not quite scientific, some people discovered that in truth it was probably more hygienic to wash the hands first! If they had not made a religious rule, if they hadn't said that "God wanted" that a man wash his hands before eating, otherwise it would be an offence against Him, people would have said: "Oh, why? No, not today, tomorrow. I have no time, I am in a hurry!" But in this way there is that constant fear at the back of their minds that something bad will happen to them due to God's anger. This too is a superstition, a big superstition.

They do things because they are told to do them. There is an entire class of religion — for instance the Chaldean religion — which forbids the eating of pork. They say it is altogether impure and that you will become impure if you eat it. The truth is that in these countries (for they are hot countries), pig's flesh is full of little worms which one takes in with the meat, even if it is cooked. It has to be cooked over an extremely long time to kill the worms. And so the little worms resist ordinary cooking and settle in your stomach or intestines, and then there they flourish and at times even end up by killing you or, in any case, by making you ill. These worms breed specially in this kind of meat. Now, if all this is explained to people, they do not understand; they haven't any medical, scientific or hygienic ideas and this does not at all interest them: "Ah, but this meat is not expensive, it is sold cheap! We'll see what happens." What will happen is that after a while they will have terrible pains in their intestines, and then they will grow thinner and thinner and eat more and more, quite uselessly; they will not know what has happened; they will be simply eaten up by the worms. But if they are told: "Don't do

15 July 1953

this, God will be furious and will punish you", that is enough. They won't do it.

Another question?

*"Someone has said that when you open the door to Yoga, you are confronted by a multitude of obstacles. Is this true?*

*"It is not an absolute rule; and much depends upon the person. Adverse conditions come to many as a test for the weak points in their nature. The indispensable basis for Yoga, which must be well established before you can walk freely on the path, is equanimity. Naturally, from that point of view, all disturbances are tests which you have to pass. But they are necessary too in order to break down the limits which your mental constructions have built around you and which prevent your opening to the Light and the Truth."*

Questions and Answers 1929 (19 May)

*When we come to the spiritual life with an aspiration, can the adverse forces attack us?*

Everybody, without exception.

*Even though they look very nice?*

Sometimes, yes. Sometimes these are the most dangerous.

*But how can we know?*

Ah! The easiest way, when you have a Guru, is to go and ask him. It is within the reach of everyone. It is enough to have faith in one's Guru, to go and find him and ask him; he will tell you, for he indeed knows.

If you do not have a Guru, then it is a little more difficult, because these forces are very clever; they do not put on a look of catastrophe and misery and wickedness, for you will immediately find it out and will not let yourself be taken in; generally they come in the garb of a friend. If you are very sincere, soon you notice some little indications, like small suggestions that satisfy your vanity or awaken in you doubts or make you a bit unconscious of what exactly is to be done — very tiny things. If you are very sincere, you see through them; particularly if you are alert enough not to allow yourself to be deceived by compliments or attempts that encourage you in these satisfactions of *amour-propre*. Things that give just a little encouragement to your vanity — that is the surest sign; something that makes you think: "After all, I am not so bad. All that I do, I do well. My attempt is very praiseworthy. My sincerity is above all reproach, etc." You become more and more self-satisfied and then there you may be sure. But even there, it does not always take these forms. There are other things, depending upon the persons. For some it is this; for others, they awaken ideas of grandeur: "If I continue in this way I shall become a great Yogi. I shall have great powers. I shall do much fine work. How nicely I am going to serve the Divine, how happy he will be with me!" It is very dangerous. The very opposite thing may happen: "After all, perhaps I am good for nothing. Is it worth while my making any effort? Nothing will come out of this effort. Am I capable of the spiritual life? Probably I shall never do anything, I am giving up tangible things for the sake of an unrealisable dream. And what am I after all? A grain of dust. Is it worth my making an effort to find the Divine? Probably I shall find nothing at all and all my efforts are futile." That is even much more dangerous. I could cite hundreds of examples like that.

There is only one thing that can truly save you, it is to have a contact, even the slightest, with your psychic being — to have felt the *solidity* of that contact. Then whatever comes to you

**15 July 1953**

from this person or that circumstance you place in front of that and see whether it is all right or not. Even if you are satisfied — in every way — even if you say to yourself: "At last I have found the friend I wanted to have. I am in the best circumstances of my life, etc.", then put that before this little contact with your psychic being, you will see whether it keeps its bright colour or suddenly there comes a little uneasiness, not much, nothing making a great noise, but just a little uneasiness. You are no longer so sure that it was as you thought! Then you know: yes, it is that small voice which one must listen to always. It is that which is the truth and the other can't trouble you any longer.

If you come to the spiritual life with a sincere aspiration, sometimes an avalanche of unpleasant things falls upon you: you quarrel with your best friends, your family kicks you out of the house, you lose what you thought you had gained.... I knew someone who had come to India with a great aspiration and after a very long effort towards knowledge and even towards Yoga. That was long long ago. At that time, people used to put on watch-chains and trinkets. This gentleman had a golden pencil which his grandmother had given him to which he was attached as the most precious thing in the world. It was fixed to his chain. When he landed at one of these ports — at Pondicherry or perhaps elsewhere in India or at Colombo, I believe it was at Colombo — they used to get into small boats and the boats took you ashore. And so this gentleman had to jump from the gangway of the ship into the boat. He missed his step, somehow got back his balance, but he made a sudden movement and the little gold pencil dropped into the sea and went straight down into the depths. He was at first very much aggrieved, but he told himself: "Why, that is the effect of India: I am freed from my attachments...." It is for very sincere people that the thing takes such a form. Fundamentally, the avalanche of troubles is always for sincere people. Those who are not sincere receive things with the most beautiful bright colours just to deceive them, and then in the end to enable them to find out that they are mistaken! But when someone has big troubles, it proves that he has reached a certain degree of sincerity.

> *Here you say: "When you come to the Divine, you must abandon all mental conceptions; but, instead of doing that, you throw your conceptions upon the Divine and want the Divine to obey them."*
>
> Questions and Answers 1929 (19 May)

Yes, everyone. All the while, constantly. If the Divine is not as you understand him, well, that is not the Divine. If he does not do what you want, if he does not act as you think he should, if he has not the character you lend him, it is not the Divine: "I recognise you as the Divine if you do exactly what I want you to do!" Naturally, people are not sincere enough to admit that, but it is so. I could give you millions of examples — not hundreds, but millions. And there is not a single one among you who does not do this unconsciously. It is a rule, you know; one says: "Yes, I am quite ready to surrender to the Divine and do his will, to accept his presence and his action, but *on condition* that it is like this or like that, that he thinks like that, feels like that, acts like that, etc." At the first opportunity I shall show you a little example dangling before your eyes. That will not fail. It will come one of these days. Quite soon. *Voilà.*

> *"The power of money is at present under the influence or in the hands of the forces and beings of the vital world. It is because of this influence that you never see money going in any considerable amount to the cause of Truth. Always it goes astray, because it is in the clutch of the hostile forces and one of the principal means by which they keep their grip upon the earth. The hold of the hostile forces upon money-power is powerfully, completely and thoroughly organised and to extract anything out of this compact organisation is a most difficult task. Each*

*time that you try to draw a little of this money away from its present custodians, you have to undertake a fierce battle."*

Questions and Answers 1929 (12 May)

*What is the money situation now? Have these beings still a great power over money?*

Yes, it continues. It continues, it is no better. Besides, the conditions to be fulfilled are not fulfilled.[1] So you can't expect that it would be better. Even this very morning, I was complaining (but "I was complaining" is just a way of speaking, it is to make myself understood), I was telling myself: to do what we want to do we need a great deal of money — a great deal, you understand, not just a little — and then I said to myself: still, it is not that money is lacking; there is a lot of money in the world. There are even people who have so much that they do not know what to do with it. But it will never come to their mind to give it for the divine Work.... They can't say that they do not know, for one has always the means to know if one wants to know. When the idea comes to you: "I want to make the best use of my money" (and the best use, not only from the viewpoint that this gentleman or lady conceives as being useful), well, one can always find out. Generally (there are exceptions), generally these people who have a lot of money put one condition: it must bring them at least some satisfaction. There must be some merit — they give, but they must get something. If they are not business people and do not give their money to gain more, if they are, for example, philanthropists who wish to give money to help humanity make progress, they always wish, more or less consciously (but generally very consciously) they always wish, that it should bring them fame, a kind of satisfaction of

---

[1] In a former talk (of 10 March 1951) Mother had said that the condition to be fulfilled for obtaining power over money was to become master of the sex impulse in human beings.

their *amour-propre*. They give money for founding a school: the school will bear their name. They build a monument somewhere: it must be mentioned that Mr. So-and-so has donated the money and so on.... There was a time when I was building Golconde,[2] there were people who approached me or sent others to me to say: "I am quite willing to give you so much or so much, but you must place in one of the rooms a marble tablet on which is written: "This room has been built by the gift of Mr. So-and-so." Then, I said: "I am sorry. I can make marble tablets for you but I'll pave the basement with them!" It is like that.

There are exceptions, as there are exceptions to all rules; however I cannot say that money goes spontaneously, freely, without effort there where useful things will be done most. No. The maximum of goodwill is to give money for something which one understands well (which is also easy to understand), to build a hospital, for example, or to open a crèche for little children. These are all works of goodwill that men understand. But if they are told that we want to change the human consciousness, we want to create a new world, oh! the first thing they say is: "Pardon me! Do not speak of God, for if it is God who is doing the work, well, it is God who will give you the means for it and you have no need of our help." I have heard people saying: "If you represent the Divine upon earth you can do whatever you like; there is no need for us to give you anything." And how many among you are free from that idea (an aftertaste of that idea): the Divine is all-powerful, therefore, the Divine can do whatever he likes?

That is the first argument, that is the theory. The Divine is all-powerful, he can do whatever he likes; therefore he does not need anybody's help. And if you push your idea sufficiently far, you will see that if the Divine is truly all-powerful in this world and does always whatever he wants, well, I tell you, he

---

[2] One of the guest-houses of the Ashram.

## 15 July 1953

is the greatest monster in the universe! Because One who is all-powerful and makes the world such as it is, looking with a smile at people suffering and miserable, and finding that all right, I would call a monster. It was the kind of thing I used to think about when I was five. I used to tell myself: "It is not possible, what is taught there is not true!" Now, as you have a little more philosophical mind, I shall teach you how to come out of the difficulty. But, first of all, you must understand that that idea is a childish idea. I simply call on your common sense. You make of your Divine a person, because that way you understand him better. You make of him a person. And then this person has organised something (the earth, it is too big, it is difficult to understand — take anything else) and then this thing the Divine has organised with the full power to do exactly as he likes. And in this thing — that he has made with the full power to do as he likes — there is ignorance, stupidity, bad will, fear, jealousy, pride, wickedness, and also suffering, illness, grief, all the pains; and a set of people who cannot say that they have perhaps more than a few minutes of happiness in the whole day and the rest of it is a neutral condition, passing by like a thing that's dead — and you call that a creation!... I call it something like a hell! And one who would make that deliberately and not only make it but look at it and say: "Ah! it is very good", as it is narrated in some religious books, that after having made the world such as it is, the seventh day he looked at it and was extremely satisfied with his work and he rested.... Well, that never! I do not call that God. Or otherwise, follow Anatole France and say that God is a demiurge and the most frightful of all beings.

But there is a way out of the difficulty. (*To a child*) Do you know it, you? Yes, yes, you know it! You will see all these conceptions and this idea that you have are based upon one thing, an entity that you call God and a world that you call his creation, and you believe these are two different things, one having made the other and the other being under the first, being the expression of what the first has made. Well, that is the initial error. If you could feel deeply that there is no division between that something you call God and this something you call his creation, if you said: "It is exactly the same thing" and if you could feel that what you call God (perhaps it is only a word), what you call God suffers when you suffer, he does not know when you do not know; and that it is through this creation, little by little, step by step, that he finds himself again, unites with himself, is realising himself, expressing himself, and it is not at all something he wanted in an arbitrary way or made like an autocrat, but that it is the growing expression, developing more and more, of a consciousness that is objectifying itself to itself.... Then there is no other thing but the sense of a collective advancing towards a more total realisation, a self-awareness of knowledge-consciousness — no other thing but that, a progressive self-awareness of knowledge-consciousness in a total unity which will reproduce integrally the First Consciousness.

That changes the problem.

Only, it is a little difficult to understand and one must make a little more progress. Instead of being like a little child that kneels down, joins its hands and says: "My God, I pray to Thee, make me a good child so that I may never hurt my mother...." That of course is very easy and indeed I cannot say that it is bad. It is very good. Only there are children with whom these things do not go, because they say: "Why should I ask You to make me good? You should make me good without there being any need of my asking You for it. Otherwise You are not nice!" It is very good when one has a simple heart and does not think much, but when one begins to think, it becomes more difficult. But if you had by your side someone to tell you: instead of that, instead of lighting a candle and kneeling down before it with your hands folded, light a flame in your heart and then have a great aspiration towards "something more beautiful, more true, more noble, better than all that I know. I ask that from tomorrow I begin to know all these things, all that I cannot do I begin to do and every day a little more." And then, if you throw yourself out a little, if, for

**15 July 1953**

one reason or another, you were put in the presence of much misery in the world, if you have friends who are unhappy or relatives who suffer or you meet any kind of difficulties, then you ask that the whole consciousness might be raised *all together* towards that perfection which must manifest and that all this ignorance that has made the world so unhappy might be changed into an enlightened knowledge and all this bad will be illumined and transformed into benevolence. And then as far as one can, as far as one understands, one wishes it with all one's heart; and indeed that can take the form of a prayer and one can ask — ask of what? — ask of that which knows, ask of that which can, ask of all that is greater and stronger than oneself, to help so that it may be thus. And how beautiful those prayers would be!

My children, in five years I shall take with you a study course of spiritual life. I give you five years to prepare yourselves; what I am telling you now is just a little of the kind, as one would light a small candle to give you an idea of what light is. But I want you all to see that we do not repeat and say over and over again indefinitely all that nonsense which is uttered every time one turns towards something other than the ordinary life. Even as I have spoken here, in this book, of the confusion that is made between asceticism and the spiritual life,[3] well, one day I shall

---

[3] "Take, for example, the universal superstition, prevalent all over the world, that asceticism and spirituality are one and the same thing. If you describe someone as a spiritual man or a spiritual woman, people at once think of one who does not eat or sits all day without moving, one who lives in a hut in great poverty, one who has given away all he had and keeps nothing for himself. This is the picture that immediately arises in the minds of ninety-nine people out of a hundred, when you speak of a spiritual man; the one proof of spirituality for them is poverty and abstinence from everything that is pleasant or comfortable. This is a mental construction which must be thrown down if you are to be free to see and follow the spiritual truth.... Once it is gone, you find something that is much higher than your narrow ascetic rule, a complete openness that leaves the being free. If you are to get something, you accept it, and if you are to give up the very same thing, you with an equal willingness leave it. Things come and you take them up; things go and you let them pass, with the same smile of equanimity in the taking or the leaving."

*Questions and Answers 1929 (19 May)*

## Questions and Answers 1953

speak to you of the confusion made between what one calls God and what I call the Divine. This will be later on.

It is 9.20 — time to wind up.

Next time we shall speak of health and illness and I shall confound all those who are attached by iron chains to their illness and who do not want to let it go! I shall give them scissors to cut their chains.

## 22 July 1953

*"There are two factors that have to be considered in the matter [the causes of illness]. There is what comes from outside and there is what comes from your inner condition. Your inner condition becomes a cause of illness when there is a resistance or revolt in it or when there is some part in you that does not respond to the protection; or even there may be something there that almost willingly and wilfully calls in the adverse forces. It is enough if there is a slight movement of this kind in you; the hostile forces are at once upon you and their attack takes often the form of illness."*

Questions and Answers 1929 (19 May)

*"Some part in you that does not respond to the protection." What does this mean, Mother?*

I have already explained it to you. What is it that you do not understand?

*I have understood the sense of the words, but I do not understand why it is so.*

Because I said "some part of the being"? You understand very well, don't you, what "being under protection" means? You understand also "going out of the protection"? If you do something contrary, for example, if you are under the protection of the Divine and for a moment you have a thought of doubt or ill-will or revolt, immediately you go out of the protection. So the protection acts around you to prevent adverse forces from coming upon you or an accident from happening, that is to say, even if you lose consciousness, because of the protection even your lack of consciousness will not produce a bad result immediately. But if you go out of the protection and are not all the time vigilant, then either you will be attacked by the adverse forces or an accident will happen.

*But those who are not conscious?*

Those who are not conscious? But there, too, I have said that I was not speaking of ordinary people. I am not speaking of ordinary people, they are not under a special protection. Ordinary people are under ordinary conditions. They have no special protection watching over them. I am not saying all this for them. They follow all the ordinary laws of life and you cannot explain things to them in the same way.... You were thinking of everybody, that it was so for everybody? It is only for people who do yoga, it is not for everybody.

*Can one get ill through fear?*

Yes. I knew someone who was so full of fear that he got cholera! There was cholera in the next house and he got so frightened that he caught the illness and without any other reason, there was no other reason for his catching it: it was through sheer fright. And it is a very common thing; in an epidemic, it is so in the majority of cases. It is through fear that the door is opened and you catch the illness. Those who have no fear can go about freely and generally they catch nothing. But still as I have said there,[1] you may have no fear in the mind, you may have no fear even in the vital, but who has no fear in the body?... Very few.

A strict discipline is needed to cure the body of fear. The cells themselves tremble. It is only by discipline, by yoga that one can overcome this fear. But it is a fact that one can catch anything through fear, even invite an accident. And, you see,

---

[1] *Questions and Answers 1929 (19 May).*

**22 July 1953**

from a certain point of view everything is contagious. I knew a person who got a wound through the kind of fear that he felt seeing someone else's wound. He really got it.

*What is the difference between mental, vital and physical fear?*

If you are conscious of the movement of your mind, the movement of your vital and the movement of your physical, you know it.

The mental is very simple: it is thoughts. You begin thinking, for example, there is this illness and this illness is very contagious, perhaps you are going to catch it, and if you catch it, it is going to be a terrible affair and what is to be done so as not to catch it?... So the mind begins to tremble: what is going to happen tomorrow? etc.

The vital, you feel it. You feel it in your sensations. All at once you feel hot, you feel cold, you perspire or all kinds of unpleasant things happen. And then you feel your heart beating fast and suddenly you have fever and then the circulation stops and you become cold.

Physically, well... When you do not any longer have the other two fears, you can become aware of the physical fear. Generally, the other two are much more conscious. They hide the physical fear from you. But when you have no longer any mental or vital fear, then you become aware of it. It is a curious little vibration that gets into your cells and they begin shivering that way. But the cells are not like a heart beating very fast. It is in the very cells: they tremble with just a slight quivering. And it is very difficult to control this. Yet it can be controlled.

I am sure that most of you have felt this as, for example, when one does an exercise which is not done often or does it for the first time; these are tiny little vibrations which seize you in all the cells. And then naturally, you lose your full control over the movement. The body does not answer to the Force any more. When you want to put your will to do something, that brings about a kind of resistance and incapacity in the body. Only, you are not aware of it usually because your attention is drawn more to the mental apprehension or to the kind of vital recoil which is very apparent in the consciousness, whereas you are not so very conscious of the resistance produced in the body. Generally in all sports (athletics and all competitions), a certain incident occurs: you must have noticed with your friends that some do much better than usual, while others who usually do well are almost incapacitated at that moment. They do much worse. Well, this depends on those small vibrations. Because you lose your full control. Your will has no longer the full control over the body, for it vibrates and answers to forces other than yours.... Naturally I am not speaking of those whose head is in a whirl or whose vital is altogether upset. Nothing can be done with these, it is better that they don't try. But I mean those who have some control over themselves, who undergo the training, to be sure, but at the time of the competition, cannot do as well as usual; it depends on a lack of receptivity in the body which gets this little tremor in the cells of which you are not conscious but which acts as an obstruction. That prevents it from receiving the Force fully.

*Are illnesses tests in the Yoga?*

Tests? Not at all.

You are given an illness purposely to make you progress? Surely it is not like that. That is, you may turn the thing round and say that there are people whose aspiration is so constant, whose goodwill so total that whatever happens to them they take as a trial on the path to make progress. I knew people who, whenever they fell ill, took that as a proof of the Divine Grace to help them to progress. They told themselves: it is a good sign, I am going to find out the cause of my illness and I shall make the necessary progress. I knew a few of this kind and they moved on magnificently. There are others, on the contrary, who, far from making use of the thing, let themselves fall flat on the ground. So much the worse for them. But the true attitude when one is ill, is to say: "There is something that is not all right; I am going to see what it is." You must never think that the Divine has purposely sent an illness, for that would truly be a very undesirable Divine!

*Even so, there are microbes in water?*

These people are in such a physical, mental, and vital condition that they are liable to catch an illness, even without drinking water, I assure you! Their whole being is a constant disharmony, their whole physical being. I do not mean inwardly, they are perhaps all right there, but those who are all right resist everything.

And I have seen just the contrary. I have seen in this country, here, village people who had only such water as was no longer water to drink, it was mere mud, I have seen it with my own eyes. It was yellowish mud in which cows had bathed and done all the rest and people had waded through it after walking on the roads. They threw their rubbish and everything was in it. And then I saw these people. They entered it, it was, as I said, yellowish mud and there at the end there was a little bit of water — it was not water, it was yellowish, you know — they bent over, collected this water in their palms and drank it. And there were some who did not even allow it to settle. Some knew what to put in it, the herbs needed to make it settle, and if one leaves it sufficiently long it becomes a little clearer. But there were some who knew nothing at all and drank it as it was. And I came to learn that there was just then an epidemic of cholera all round and I said: "There are still people living in that village with that kind of water?" I was told: "We do not have a single case of cholera...." They had become immune, they were habituated. But if there had been a single person who had caught it by chance, probably all would have been dead; for then fear would enter and with fear in them there would be no more resistance, for they were poor miserable things. But it is the moral conditions of these people that are terrible, more than the physical conditions — the moral conditions.

There are sadhus, you know, who accept the conditions of a dirty life through saintliness. They never wash themselves, they have nothing about them that hygiene demands. They live in a truly dirty condition — and they are free from all illness. Probably because they have faith and they do so purposely. Their morale is magnificent.... I am speaking of sincere people and not those who pretend. They have faith. They do not think of their body, they think of the life of their soul. They have no illness. There are some who come to a state in which an arm or a leg or any part of the body has become completely stiff due to their ascetic posture. They cannot move any more; anybody else would die under such conditions; they continue to live because they have faith and they do it purposely, because it is a thing they have imposed on themselves.

Therefore, the moral condition is much more important than the physical. If you were in surroundings where everyone was tidy and then you remained three days without taking a bath, you would fall ill. This is not to say that you should not take a bath! Because we do not want to be sadhus, we want to be yogis. It is not the same thing. And we want the body to take part in the yoga. So we must do whatever is necessary to keep it fit. However, this is only to tell you that the moral condition is much more important than the physical.

Besides, these people, by their asceticism, wilfully spoil their body, torture themselves, yet if it was someone else who did the same thing, people would shout, protest, declare he is a monster. But one does it by one's own choice. And one bears it very well because it is imposed on one's own self and one feels a kind of glory in having done something very "remarkable", through one's aspiration for the divine life!

No other questions?

### 22 July 1953

Well, now, I told you the other day that I would speak to you of illness; I thought of it today and have made notes.... For you may tell me there are microbes, and that there are people who have no thought of illness and catch it all the same; but thinking is not the only factor, not by any means. Still, I shall try to explain to you now the notes I have made. (*Mother looks at a paper.*)

I have told you first of all that all illness without any exception — without exception — is the expression of a break in equilibrium. But there are many kinds of breaks in equilibrium.... First, I am speaking only of the body, I am not speaking of the nervous illnesses of the vital or of mental illnesses. We shall see that later on. We are speaking only of this poor little body. And I say that all illnesses, all, whatever they may be (I would add even accidents) come from a break in equilibrium. That is, if all your organs, all the members and parts of your body are in harmony with one another, you are in perfect health. But if there is the slightest imbalance anywhere, immediately you get either just a little ill or quite ill, even very badly ill, or else an accident occurs. That always happens whenever there is an inner imbalance.

But then, to the equilibrium of the body, you must add the equilibrium of the vital and the mind. For you to be able to do all kinds of things with immunity, without any accident happening to you, you must have a triple equilibrium — mental, vital, physical — and not only in each of the parts, but also in the three parts in their mutual relations.... If you have done a little mathematics, you should have been taught how many combinations that makes and what a difficult thing it means! There lies the key to the problem. For the combinations are innumerable, and consequently the causes of illness too are innumerable, the causes of accidents also are innumerable. Still, we are going to try to classify them so that we may understand.

First of all, from the point of view of the body — just the body — there are two kinds of disequilibrium: functional and organic. I do not know if you are aware of the difference between the two; but you have organs and then you have all the parts of your body: nerves, muscles, bones and all the rest. Now, if an organ by itself is in disequilibrium, it is an organic disequilibrium, and you are told: that organ is ill or perhaps it is badly formed or it is not normal or an accident has occurred to it. But it is the organ that is ill. But the organ may be in a very good condition, all your organs may be in a very good condition, but there is still an illness as they do not function properly: there is a lack of balance in the functioning. You may have a very good stomach, but suddenly something happens to it and it does not function properly; or the body may also be excellent, but something happens to it and it does not work properly any more. Then you have an illness due to functional imbalance not organic imbalance.

Generally, illnesses due to functional imbalance are cured much more quickly and easily than the others. The others become a little more serious. Sometimes they become very grave. So there are already two domains to see and know, but if you have a little knowledge of your body and the habit of observing its working, you can know what kind of imbalance yours is.

Most often when you are young and leading a normal life, the imbalance is purely functional. There are only a few poor people who for one reason or other have had an accident or imbalance before their birth, these carry with them something that is much more difficult to cure (not that it is incurable; in theory, there is nothing incurable), but it becomes more difficult.

Good. Now what are the causes of this imbalance, whatever it may be? As I told you just now, the causes are innumerable; because, first of all, there are all the inner causes, that is, those personal to you, and then all the external causes, those that come to you from outside. That makes two major categories.

The internal causes:

We said: you have a brain, lungs, a heart, a stomach, a liver, etc. If each one does its duty and works normally and if

## 22 July 1953

all move together in harmony at a given moment and in the right way (note that it would be very complicated if you were obliged to think of all that, and I am afraid things would not go right all the time! Fortunately, it does not need our conscious thinking), admitting however they are in good harmony with one another, good friends, in perfect agreement, and each one fulfilling its task, its movement at the right time, in tune with the rest, neither too soon nor too late, neither too fast nor too slow, indeed, every one going all right, then you are marvellously well! Suppose now that one of them, for some reason or other, happens to be in a bad mood: it does not work with the necessary energy, at the required moment it goes awhile on strike. Do not believe that it alone will fall ill: the whole system will go wrong and you will feel altogether unwell. And if, unfortunately, there is a vital imbalance, that is, a disappointment or too violent an emotion or too strong a passion or something else upsetting your vital, that comes in addition. And if furthermore your thoughts roam about and you begin to have dark ideas and formulate frightful things and make catastrophic formations, then after that you are sure to fall ill altogether.... You see the complication, don't you, just a tiny thing can go the wrong way and thus through an inner contagion can lead to something very serious. So what is important is to control things immediately. One must be conscious, conscious of the working of one's organs, aware of the one that does not behave very well, telling it immediately what is to be done to set itself right. What is needed (I shall explain it to you later on) is to give them a lesson as one does to little children. When they begin indulging in unhealthy fancies (indeed it is then the occasion to say it) you must tell them: no, it is not like that the work is to be done, it is the other way! Suppose for example, your heart begins to throb madly; then you must make it calm, you tell it that this is not the way to act, and at the same time (solely to help it) you take in long very regular rhythmic breaths, that is, the lung becomes the mentor of the heart and teaches it how to work properly. And so on. I could give you countless examples.

Good. We say then that there is an imbalance between the different parts of the being, disharmony in their working. That is what I have just told you. And then there are internal conflicts. These are quarrels. There are internal quarrels among the different parts of yourself. Supposing there is an organ (it happens very often) that needs rest and there is another that wants action, and both at the same time. How are you going to manage it? They begin to quarrel. If you do what one wants, the other protests! And so you have to find a middle term to put them in harmony. And then, at times, if you add to the physical the vital and mental (I do not speak of the speculative mind or the independent vital, I am speaking of the mental and vital parts of the *body*, because there is a physical vital and a physical mind; there is a physical mind and this physical mind is the worst of all, it is that which goes on all the time and you have the utmost difficulty in stopping it: it goes on and on and on); well, if there is a dispute between them, between the mind, the vital and the physical, you have a battlefield, and this battlefield can become the cause of all possible illnesses. They fight violently. One wants something, the other does not, they quarrel and you are in a kind of internal whirlwind. That can give you fever — you do get it usually — or else you are seized by an inner shivering and you have no longer any control. For the most important of all causes for bodily illness is that the body begins to get restless; it trembles and the trembling increases more and more, more and more and you feel that you will never be able to reestablish the balance, it eludes you. Then in that case you must know what the dispute is about, the reason of the dispute and find out how to reconcile the people within you.

All these are functional imbalances.

There are other kinds of imbalance and they are more or less a part of what you were saying just now. There is an aspiration within you (I am now speaking of people who do yoga or at any rate know what the spiritual life is and try to walk on the path), within you there is a part of the being — either mental or vital or sometimes even physical — that has understood well, has much aspiration, its special aptitudes, that receives the forces well and is making good progress. And then there are others that cannot, others still that don't want to (that of course is very bad), but there are yet others that want to very much but cannot, do not have the capacity, are not ready. So there is something that rises upward and something that does not move. That causes a terrible imbalance. And usually this translates itself into some illness or other, for you are in such a state of inner tension between something that cannot or something that clings, that does not want to move and something else that wants to: that produces a frightful unease and the result usually is an illness.

Now there is the opposite, almost the opposite, that is, the whole being goes ahead, progresses, advances in an increasing equilibrium and achieves remarkable progress; you have the feeling you are in a wonderfully favourable state, everything is going on well, you are sure; and you see yourself already gloriously well on the way.... Crack! an illness. Then you say: "How is it? I was in such a good condition and now I have fallen ill! It is not fair." But this happens because you are not completely conscious. There was a small part in the being that did not want to move. Usually it is something in the vital; sometimes it is a tiny mental formation that does not agree to follow; sometimes it is simply something in the body which is quite inert or has not the slightest intention of moving, that wants things to remain always as they are. It pulls backward, separates itself wilfully, and naturally, even if it is quite small, it brings about such an imbalance in the being that you fall ill. And then you say to yourself: "It is truly a pity, I was going on so well, it is not fair! Truly God is not kind!... When I was making so much progress, He ought to have prevented me from becoming ill!"... It is like that.

Now, there is still another thing. You do the yoga according to your capacity. You have been told: "Open yourself, you will receive the Force." You have been told: "Have faith, be of goodwill and you will be protected." And indeed you are bathed in the Consciousness, bathed in the Force, bathed in the Protection and to the extent you have faith and open yourself, you receive all that, and it helps you in keeping fit and in rejecting the little inner disturbances and re-establishing order when these come, in protecting yourself against small attacks or accidents which might have happened. But if somewhere in your being — either in your body or even in your vital or mind, either in several parts or even in a single one — there is an incapacity to receive the descending Force, this acts like a grain of sand in a machine. You know, a fine machine working quite well with everything going all right, and you put into it just a little sand (nothing much, only a grain of sand), suddenly everything is damaged and the machine stops. Well, just a little lack of receptivity somewhere, something that is unable to receive the Force, that is completely shut up (when one looks at it, it becomes as it were a little dark spot somewhere, a tiny thing hard as a stone: the Force cannot enter into it, it refuses to receive it — either it cannot or it will not) and immediately that produces a great imbalance; and this thing that was moving upward, that was blooming so wonderfully, finds itself sick, and sometimes just when you were in the normal equilibrium; you were in good health, everything was going on well, you had nothing to complain about. One day when you grasped a new idea, received a new impulse, when you had a great aspiration and received a great force and had a marvellous experience, a beautiful experience opening to you inner doors, giving you a knowledge you did not have before; then you were sure that everything was going to be all right.... The next day, you are taken ill. So you say: "Still that? It is impossible! That should not happen." But it was quite simply what I have just said: a grain of sand. There was something that could not receive; immediately it brings about a disequilibrium. Even though very small it is enough, and you fall ill.

## 22 July 1953

You see there are reasons! — many reasons, numberless reasons. For all these things combine in an extraordinarily complex way, and in order to know, in order to be able to cure an illness, one must find out its cause, not its microbe. For it happens that (excuse me, I hope there are no doctors here!), it happens that when microbes are there, they find out magnificent remedies to kill the microbes, but these remedies cure some and make others much more ill! Nobody knows why.... Perhaps I know why. Because the illness had another cause than the purely physical one; there was another. The first was only an outer expression of a different disorder, and unless you touched that, discovered that disorder, never would you be able to prevent the illness from coming. And to discover the disorder, you must have an extensive occult knowledge and also a deep knowledge of all the inner workings of each one.

Thus we have seen in brief, very rapidly all the internal causes. Now there are external causes that come and bring complications.

If you were in a perfectly harmonious environment where everything was full of a total and perfect goodwill, then evidently you could lay the blame only on yourself. But the difficulties that are within are also without. You can, to a certain extent, establish an inner equilibrium, but you live in surroundings full of imbalance. Unless you shut yourself up in an ivory tower (which is not only difficult but not always recommendable), you are obliged to receive what comes from outside. You give and you receive; you breathe in and absorb. So there is a mixture and that is why one can say that all is contagious, for you live in a state of ceaseless vibrations. You give out your vibrations and receive also the vibrations of others, and these vibrations are of a very complex kind. There are still (we shall say for simplifying the language) mental vibrations, vital vibrations, physical vibrations and many others. You give, you receive; you give, you receive. It is a perpetual play. Even granting that there is no bad will, there is necessarily contagion. And as I was saying just now, all is contagious, everything. You are looking at the effect of an accident: you absorb a certain vibration. And if you are over-sensitive and, over and above that, you have fear or disgust (which is the same thing, disgust is only a moral expression of a physical fear), the accident can be translated physically in your body. Naturally you will be told that it is persons in a state of nervous imbalance who have such reactions. It is not quite that. They are persons with an ultra-suprasensitive vital, that is all. And it is not always a proof of inferiority, on the contrary! For as you progress spiritually, a certain hypersensitiveness of nerves occurs and if your self-control does not increase along with your sensibility, all kinds of untoward things may happen to you.

But that is not the only thing.

Unhappily there is much bad will in the world, and among the different kinds of bad will there is the small type that comes from ignorance and stupidity, there is the big type that comes from wickedness and there is the formidable one that is the result of anti-divine forces. So, all that is in the atmosphere (I am not telling you this to frighten you, for it is well understood that one should fear nothing — but it is there all the same) and these things attack you, sometimes intentionally, sometimes unintentionally. Unintentionally, through other people: others are attacked, they don't know, they pass it on without even being aware of it. They are the first victims. They pass the illness to others. But there are wilful attacks. We were speaking the other day of mental formations and of wicked people who make mental formations to harm you, make them wilfully to do harm. And then there are others who go still a step further.

There is a misguided, perverted occultism which is called black magic, it is a thing one must never touch. But unfortunately, there are people who touch it through pure wickedness. You must not believe it is an illusion, a superstition; it is real. There are people who know how to do magic and do it, and with their magic they obtain altogether detestable results.... It is understood of course that when you have no fear and remain

## 22 July 1953

under protection, you are sheltered. But there is a "when", there is a condition, and then if the condition is not always fulfilled, very unpleasant things may happen. So long as you are in a state full of strength, full of purity — that is, in a state of invincibility, if anybody does anything against you, that falls back upon him automatically, as when you throw a tennis-ball against the wall, it comes back to you; the thing comes back to them exactly in the same way, sometimes with a greater force, and they are punished by the very thing through which they sinned. But naturally it all depends on the person against whom the magic is done, on his inner force and purity.... These things I have known, many cases like this. And in such cases, in order to resist, one must be, as I said, a warrior in the vital, that is, a spiritual fighter in the vital. All who do yoga sincerely must become that, and when they do become that, they are altogether sheltered. But one of the conditions for becoming it is never to have bad will or a bad thought towards others. For if you have a bad feeling or bad will or a bad thought, you come down to their level and when you are on the same level with them, well, you may receive blows from them.

Now, without going to that extreme, there are in the physical atmosphere, the earth-atmosphere, numerous small entities which you do not see, for your sight is too limited, but which move about in your atmosphere. Some of them are quite nice, others very wicked. Generally these little entities are produced by the disintegration of vital beings — they pullulate — and these form quite an unpleasant mass. There are some which do very fine things. I believe I narrated to you the story of the little beings who tugged at my sari to tell me that the milk was about to boil and that I had to go and see that it did not boil over. But all of them are not so good. Some of them like to play ugly little tricks, wicked little pranks. And so most often it is they who are behind an accident. They like little accidents, they like the whole whirl of forces that gather round an accident: a mass of people, you know, it is very amusing! And then that gives them their food, because, in reality, they feed upon human vitality thrown out of the body by emotions and excitements. So they say: just a small accident, it is quite nice, many accidents!...

And then if there is a group of such small entities, they may clash with one another, because among themselves they do not have a very peaceful life: clashing with one another, fighting, destroying, demolishing each other. And that is the origin of microbes. They are forces of disintegration. But they continue to be alive even in their divided forms and this is the origin of germs and microbes. Therefore most microbes have behind them a bad will and that is what makes them so dangerous. And unless one knows the quality and kind of bad will and is capable of acting upon it, there is a ninety-nine per cent chance of not finding the true and total remedy. The microbe is a very material expression of something living in a subtle physical world and that is why these very microbes (as I have said there) [2] that are always around you, within you, for years together do not make you ill and then suddenly they make you fall ill.

There is another reason. The origin of the microbes and their support lie in a disharmony, in the being's receptivity to the adverse force. I will tell you a story. I do not know whether I have already told it to you, but I am going to tell you now for it will give you an illustration.

I was in Japan. It was at the beginning of January 1919. Anyway, it was the time when a terrible flu raged there in the whole of Japan, which killed hundreds of thousands of people. It was one of those epidemics the like of which is rarely seen. In Tokyo, every day there were hundreds and hundreds of new cases. The disease appeared to take this turn: it lasted three days and on the third day the patient died. And people died in such large numbers that they could not even be cremated, you understand, it was impossible, there were too many of them. Or otherwise, if one did not die on the third day, at the end of

---

[2] *Questions and Answers 1929 (19 May).*

seven days one was altogether cured; a little exhausted but all the same completely cured. There was a panic in the town, for epidemics are very rare in Japan. They are a very clean people, very careful and with a fine morale. Illnesses are very rare. But still this came, it came as a catastrophe. There was a terrible fear. For example, people were seen walking about in the streets with a mask on the nose, a mask to purify the air they were breathing, so that it might not be full of the microbes of the illness. It was a common fear.... Now, it so happened I was living with someone who never ceased troubling me: "But what is this disease? What is there behind this disease?" What I was doing, you know, was simply to cover myself with my force, my protection so as not to catch it and I did not think of it any more and continued doing my work. Nothing happened and I was not thinking of it. But constantly I heard: "What is this? Oh, I would like to know what is there behind this illness. But could you not tell me what this illness is, why it is there?" etc. One day I was called to the other end of the town by a young woman whom I knew and who wished to introduce me to some friends and show me certain things. I do not remember now what exactly was the matter, but anyway I had to cross the whole town in a tram-car. And I was in the tram and seeing these people with masks on their noses, and then there was in the atmosphere this constant fear, and so there came a suggestion to me; I began to ask myself: "Truly, what is this illness? What is there behind this illness? What are the forces that are in this illness?" I came to the house, I passed an hour there and I returned. And I returned with a terrible fever. I had caught it. It came to you thus, without preparation, instantaneously. Illnesses, generally illnesses from germs and microbes take a few days in the system: they come, there is a little battle inside; you win or you lose, if you lose you catch the illness, it is not complicated. But there, you just receive a letter, open the envelope, hop! puff! The next minute you have the fever. Well, that evening I had a terrible fever. The doctor was called (it was not I who called him), the doctor was called and he told me: "I must absolutely give you this medicine." It was one of the best medicines for the fever, he had just a little (all their stocks were exhausted, everyone was taking it); he said: "I have still a few packets, I shall give you some" — "I beg of you, do not give it to me, I won't take it. Keep it for someone who has faith in it and will take it." He was quite disgusted: "It was no use my coming here." So I said: "Perhaps it was no use!" And I remained in my bed, with my fever, a violent fever. All the while I was asking myself: "What is this illness? Why is it there? What is there behind it?... " At the end of the second day, as I was lying all alone, I saw clearly a being, with a part of the head cut off, in a military uniform (or the remains of a military uniform) approaching me and suddenly flinging himself upon my chest, with that half a head to suck my force. I took a good look, then realised that I was about to die. He was drawing all my life out (for I must tell you that people were dying of pneumonia in three days). I was completely nailed to the bed, without movement, in a deep trance. I could no longer stir and he was pulling. I thought: now it is the end. Then I called on my occult power, I gave a big fight and I succeeded in turning him back so that he could not stay there any longer. And I woke up.

But I had seen. And I had learnt, I had understood that the illness originated from beings who had been thrown out of their bodies. I had seen this during the First Great War, towards its end, when people used to live in trenches and were killed by bombardment. They were in perfect health, altogether healthy and in a second they were thrown out of their bodies, not conscious that they were dead. They did not know they hadn't a body any more and they tried to find in others the life they could not find in themselves. That is, they were turned into so many countless vampires. And they vampirised upon men. And then over and above that, there was a decomposition of the vital forces of people who fell ill and died. One lived in a kind of sticky and thick cloud made up of all that. And so those who took in this cloud fell ill and usually got cured, but those

## 22 July 1953

who were attacked by a being of that kind invariably died, they could not resist. I know how much knowledge and force were necessary for me to resist. It was irresistible. That is, if they were attacked by a being who was a centre of this whirl of bad forces, they died. And there must have been many of these, a very great number. I saw all that and I understood.

When someone came to see me, I asked to be left alone, I lay quietly in my bed and I passed two or three days absolutely quiet, in concentration, with my consciousness. Subsequently, a friend of ours (a Japanese, a very good friend) came and told me: "Ah! you were ill? So what I thought was true.... Just imagine for the last two or three days, there hasn't been a single new case of illness in the town and most of the people who were ill have been cured and the number of deaths has become almost negligible, and now it is all over. The illness is wholly under control." Then I narrated what had happened to me and he went and narrated it to everybody. They even published articles about it in the papers.

Well, consciousness, to be sure, is more effective than packets of medicine!... The condition was critical. Just imagine, there were entire villages where everyone had died. There was a village in Japan, not very big, but still with more than a hundred people, and it happened, due to an extraordinary chance, that one of the villagers was to receive a letter (the postman went there only if there was a letter; naturally, it was a village far in the countryside); so he went to the countryside; there was a snowfall; the whole village was under snow... and there was not a living person. It was exactly so. It was that kind of epidemic. And Tokyo was also like that; but Tokyo was a big town and things did not happen in the same fashion. And it was in this way the epidemic ended. That is my story.

Now this brings us naturally to the cure. All that is very well, we now have the knowledge; so, how to prevent illnesses from coming, first of all, and when the illness does occur, how to cure it?

One may try ordinary means and sometimes that succeeds. It is usually when the body is convinced that it has been given the conditions under which it must be all right; it takes the resolution that it must be all right and it is cured. But if your body has not the will, the resolution to get cured, you may try whatever you like, it won't be cured. This also I know by experience. For I knew people who could be cured in five minutes, even of a disease considered very serious, and I knew people who had no fatal illness, but cherished it with such persistence that it did become fatal. It was impossible to persuade their body to let go their illness.

And it is here that one must be very careful and look at oneself with great discrimination to discover the small part in oneself that — how to put it? — takes pleasure in being ill. Oh! there are many reasons. There are people who are ill out of spite, there are people who are ill out of hate, there are people who are ill through despair, there are people... And these are not formidable movements: it is quite a small movement in the being: one is vexed and says: "You will see what is going to happen, you will see the consequences of what he has done to me! Let it come! I am going to be ill." One does not say it openly to oneself, for one would scold oneself, but there is something somewhere that thinks in that way.

So there are two things you have to do when you have discovered the disorder, big or small — the disharmony. Firstly, we said that this disharmony creates a kind of tremor and a lack of peace in the physical being, in the body. It is a kind of fever. Even if it is not a fever in general, there is localised fever; there are people who get restless. So the first thing to do is to quieten oneself, bring peace, calm, relaxation, with a total confidence, in this little corner (not necessarily in the whole body). Afterwards you see what is the cause of the disorder. You look. Of course, there are many, but still you try to find out approximately the cause of this disorder, and through the pressure of light and knowledge and spiritual force you re-establish the harmony, the

## 22 July 1953

proper functioning. And if the ailing part is receptive, if it does not offer any obstinate resistance, you can be cured in a few seconds.

It is not always the case. Sometimes there is, as I have said, a bad will: you are more or less on strike, at least you want the illness to have its consequences. So, that takes a little more time. However, if you do not happen to be particularly ill-willed, after some time the Force acts: after a few minutes or hours or at the most some days you are cured.

Now, in the case of special attacks of adverse forces, the thing gets complicated, because you have not only to deal with the will of the body (note that I do not admit the argument of those who say: "But as for myself I do not want to be ill!", for your consciousness always says that it does not want to be ill, one must be half-crazy to say, "I want to be ill"; but it is not your consciousness that wants to be ill, it is some part of your body or at the most, a fragment of the vital that has gone wrong and wishes to be ill, and unless you observe with a good deal of attention you do not notice it). But I say that the situation gets complicated if behind this there is an attack, a pressure from adverse forces who really want to harm you. You may have opened the door through spiritual error, through a movement of vanity, of anger, of hatred or of violence; even if it is merely a movement that comes and goes, that can open the door. There are always germs watching and only waiting for an occasion. That is why one should be very careful. Anyhow, for some reason or other, the influence has pierced through the shell of protection and acts there encouraging the illness to become as bad as it can be. In that case the first means is not quite sufficient. Then you have to add something; you must add the Force of spiritual purification which is such an absolutely perfectly constructive force that nothing that's in the least destructive can survive there. If you have this Force at your disposal or if you can ask for it and get it, you direct it on the spot and the adverse force usually runs away immediately, for if it happens to be in the midst of this Force it gets dissolved, it disappears; for no force of disintegration can survive within this Force; therefore disintegration disappears and with it that also disappears. It can be changed into a constructive force, that is possible, or it may be simply dissolved and reduced to nothing. And with that not only is the illness cured, but all possibility of its return is also eliminated. You are cured of the illness once for all, it never comes back. There you are.

Now, all that is seen on the whole; on the details could be written books and books. I have given you only general explanations.

*With the causes you have told us about, one should be always ill!*

But in ordinary life, most of the time, people are almost always ill — except a few who escape for reasons of a different order that we shall explain one day. There are very few people who are not more or less ill all the while. But even in ordinary life, if within you there is trust, goodwill, a kind of certitude, this kind of inner confidence, oh! as there is in most children perhaps (I do not know, for, after all, those we see here are fairly exceptional), however, there is a trust in life, they are young and they have the feeling that the whole life is before them. Very few things are behind, everything is in front. So that gives them a kind of self-confidence, that pulls them out.

Otherwise, I do not know, in the ordinary life I have known very few people who did not complain of having at least some physical ailment which they carried always with them.... You know perhaps that play of Jules Romains, *Doctor Knock*, in which he says that a healthy man is a sick fellow who is unaware. It is usually true. When you are sufficiently busy not to be all the while occupied with yourself, you do not notice it, but it is there.

# 29 July 1953

*Mother, you told us one day that all that happens to us has been decided in advance. What does that mean?*

This is but a way of speaking. This happens because to express a thing I can't be saying all the words at the same time, can I? I am obliged to say them one after another. Otherwise, if all the words were spoken at the same time, it would make a big noise and nobody would understand anything! Well, when you try to explain the universe, you do as you would when you speak. You say one thing after another, but to tell the truth, you must say everything at one go. Now, how can that be done?... Indeed, since you repeat it to me very likely I must have said that somewhere.... I must have said the contrary also! But if you put it in this way, that everything that happens has been decided in advance, then with the consciousness of time that you have now, it is as if you said: yesterday it was decided what would happen today; and this year it is decided what will happen next year. It is in this way that the thing is translated in your consciousness — naturally, because it is thus that we see, think, understand and above all speak and express ourselves. But it is not like that.

There are people who have perceived this unreality so strongly that they have felt there was no reason why they could not go back instead of going forward, for backward, forward, the present, everything that we express in this way exists all at the same time. It is on different levels. If I tell you: "What is happening to you had been decided in advance", I could also say: "What is happening here, has already happened elsewhere", that would be equally true, and equally false, because it is impossible to express this in words.

I am going to give you an example which perhaps will make you understand. I do not remember exactly when it happened;

it must have been some time in the year 1920 probably (perhaps earlier, perhaps in 1914-1915, but I don't think so, it was some time in the year 1920). One day — every day I used to meditate with Sri Aurobindo: he used to sit on one side of a table and I on the other, on the veranda — and one day in this way, in meditation, I entered (how to put it?... ), I went up very high, entered very deep or came out of myself (well, whatever one may say does not express what happened, these are merely ways of speaking), I reached a place or a state of consciousness from which I told Sri Aurobindo just casually and quite simply: "India is free." It was in 1920. Then he put to me a question: "How?" And I answered him: "Without any fight, without a battle, without a revolution. The English themselves will leave, for the condition of the world will be such that they won't be able to do anything else except go away."

It was *done*. I spoke in the future when he asked me the question, but there where I had seen, I said, India *is* free, it was a fact. Now, India was not free at that time: it was 1920. Yet it was there, it had been done. And it happened in 1947. That is to say, from the external physical point of view I saw it twenty-seven years in advance. But it had been done.

*Could you see Pakistan?*

No, for the freedom could have come about without Pakistan. Indeed, if they had listened to Sri Aurobindo there would have been no Pakistan.

Well, externally it seems to take time, but in fact it is like that.

*If you see some catastrophe coming, can you, Mother, by your effort change it?*

That depends upon the nature of the event. There are many things.... That depends also upon the level from which one sees.

## 29 July 1953

There is a plane where there are all the possibilities, and on that level, as there are all the possibilities, there is the possibility also of changing these possibilities. If a catastrophe is foreseen in that plane, one can have the power of preventing it also. In other cases, even though one is forewarned, one has no action upon the event. And yet there, it depends on the level from where one sees.

A case of this kind was reported to me once where the very seeing of a thing prevented it from happening. An American gentleman had arrived at one of those big American hotels where there are lifts (you do not go down a staircase, you take a lift to go up or come down); now, early in the morning just before getting up, he had a dream which he remembered well: he had seen a boy dressed as a lift-boy and making the same movement a lift-boy makes directing you to get in. He was there. And then, at the end of the movement, instead of a lift, there was a hearse! — that is to say, that kind of carriage... oh! you must have seen some here now and then, to carry the dead to the cemetery; when they are not burnt, they are carried on a bier with black draperies, etc. So there was such a carriage, a hearse for carrying the dead. And the boy was signing to him to get into the carriage. When he came out of his room, the boy was there with the lift to take him down: exactly the same boy, the same face, the same dress, the same gesture. He remembered the hearse — he did not get into the lift. He said: "No, no!" and he walked down. And before he reached the groundfloor, he heard a terrible noise and the lift had crashed down to the ground and all who were in it were killed. It was because of the dream that he had not got in, for he had understood.

Therefore in such a case when you have the vision, you can avert the catastrophe.

There are other cases, as I said, when you are simply forewarned. You are forewarned. In reality, it is to help you to prepare within for what must come, so that you may take the right inner attitude to face the event. It is like a lesson telling you: "This is what it must teach you." You cannot change the thing, but you can change your attitude and your inner reaction. Instead of having a bad reaction, a wrong attitude towards the experience that occurs, you have a good reaction, a good attitude, and you derive as much benefit as possible out of what has happened.

In either case, it depends absolutely on the plane on which you see. When you have control over your nights and are conscious of your sleep and your dreams or of your visions, you also see the difference between the two; you can distinguish the difference: what is given to you as a warning so that you may intervene and what is given to you as an intimation so that you may take the right attitude towards what is going to happen. It is always a lesson, but it is not always the same lesson. At times you can act with your will; at times you must learn the inner lesson which the incident is about to give you so that you may be ready for the event to have a fully favourable consequence. The same thing holds for everything that you see, there are hundreds of different varieties of visions and dreams and each one brings you the lesson it has to bring.

For example, when people are taken ill or when they are caught in an accident. Well, whether I see it myself or come to know of it from outside through someone's telling me about it — in every case it is not the same. There are cases when I am informed and I see that it is for intervening and I have the full power to change the consequence, that is, to cure the sick person. There are cases where I see I am not to intervene. For instance, it is time for the person to quit his body: he will leave the body. But knowing this, I must do for the person and for his environment what has to be done for the event to have the maximum beneficial effect or the minimum adverse effect — it depends on the circumstances.

There are events appertaining to a universal necessity and those one cannot change. There are events still in the balance which can be decided either way. The whole thing is to have a

## 29 July 1953

perception that's not only clear-sighted but also quite impartial and impersonal, without even the shadow of a shadow of preference. Then, when one is in that perfect state — it can't be said, of neutrality, it is not neutrality: it is a state of consciousness which is immobile like a mirror — then one can see within it the quality of the thing that's happening, one can see the things that have been decided so that they cannot be altered and those that are still in the balance and can be changed.

To tell the truth, for each event the situation is different. There are some that can be changed completely, reversed altogether; there are some that are capable of undergoing quite a considerable change; there are others that can suffer only a slight modification — a slight modification but one that has a considerable consequence; and there are some that are inescapable; they are so because they are so; if you tried to oppose, you would break your head against a wall and that would serve no purpose. The whole thing is to have this perspicacity, know to which domain the event belongs and not will any other thing than what *must be*.

I could give hundreds of instances of different cases.

A thing seems to have been completely determined: it is *going* to be so. But you have within you a will that surges up, a flame that is kindled, a great aspiration that is in harmony with a higher Will and you force it upon the event. And then a kind of combination takes place: what had to happen will happen, but along with something else which comes at the same time and changes the nature of the former. For events of importance to the earth, this happens very often. For example, when an entire set of movements, circumstances, combinations of forces bring about an absolute necessity of war, one can, by calling in another force, change the extent and the consequences, and sometimes even the nature of the war, but one is not able to avert it. I could give you examples of this kind, of a very general nature.

I told you the other day with regard to the "spirit" of death, what can be done, through an inner action, to prevent Death from coming to someone's house; but then it goes to another's. You cannot deprive Death of what is its due. I have explained this to you. There are other cases where one might say in a somewhat childish way: "Death was not yet informed", and so you can take away from it its booty without any consequences. But that does not always happen. There are cases when one does that. But put in this way it sounds childish like a fairy tale. Yet, it corresponds to something in the setting of the circumstances: it depends on the way the circumstances move.

What I would like to bring home to you is that the problem is extremely complicated and subtle, and that at times the direction of the movement can be altered a little; at other times, the movement can be reversed; and at still others just the consequences and the inner attitude with regard to the movement alone can be changed. And naturally men see all these things in a too simplified way and translate all this by their prayer to God: they say, in one case, "God has given me what I asked from him", in another case, "He has refused me." And so, that's that. That is how they understand and it is sheer stupidity. To know how it happens, you must have a general, collective consciousness, at least as wide as the earth. That is the minimum. To understand truly one must have a universal consciousness. Then you can understand. For, I have said it somewhere in what I was reading today; I have said that all things are interdependent and there is neither any "beginning" nor any "end". Where do you put the beginning?[1] ... To understand that, you

---

[1] "If you look from one plane of consciousness, the individual will appear to you as if he were not only an instrument and recorder, but a creator. But look from another and higher plane of consciousness with a wider view of things and you will see that this is only an appearance. In the workings of the universe whatever happens is the result of all that has happened before. How do you propose to separate one being from the integral play of the manifestation or one movement from the whole mass of movements? Where are you going to put the origin of a thing or its beginning? The whole play is a rigidly connected chain; one link merges imperceptibly into another. Nothing can be taken out of the chain and explained by itself as if it were its own source and beginning."
*Questions and Answers 1929 (26 May)*

## 29 July 1953

have to go beyond the earth-bound consciousness, you have to enter a universal consciousness. Then you will be able to understand.

But we are compelled — I am repeating what I said at the beginning — we are compelled to say things one after another. We say: "When the universe began... When the creation began.... it begins in that way.... This happened and then that happened and then this took place and then that took place.... " We say one thing after another, and to say the truth, it is not really like that at all! From a certain point of view, it is foolishness, but we cannot do otherwise. I cannot say all the words at the same time. So it is the state of our consciousness and the means at our disposal for expressing ourselves which make us say things that are stupid from the point of view of the absolute knowledge. But it is an approximation. Our stupidity is an approximation and becomes less stupid when we become aware that it happens only because we cannot express ourselves otherwise. We are obliged to say things in succession, but they are a single whole.

And for most people it is not merely a question of saying but of knowing. They know things only one after another, feel them still more thus, live them yet more so. But there is a consciousness in which one knows all at the same time, understands all at the same time, can express all at the same time and can live wholly at the same time. But how to do it? Here it is not like that!

And so, you see, what one tries to do is to bring the two modes of consciousness as near each other as one is able to, so that even while living externally in the way we are compelled to do (because the physical world is like that and our physical consciousness is like that), we may be able at the same time to join the other Consciousness so closely that while doing things according to the material law and in the material way, in our consciousness we may not lose sight of the fact that it is only an approximation, a translation, and that it is not the Thing itself.

> *Mother, I do not understand the question put here: "If our will is only an expression or echo of the universal Will, where is the place of individual initiative? Is the individual only an instrument to register universal movements? Has he no power of creation or origination?"*
> Questions and Answers 1929 (26 May)

Ah! Nor do I. When these questions were put to me, I had the utmost difficulty in answering them, for they were altogether outside my understanding of things. Here precisely, when I read the question, I felt like telling you: "I am very sorry, but the person who put the question had a terribly confused thought and consciousness, she was mixing up everything." For there are three things mixed up here.

First of all, I do not know who told her that our will is only an expression or echo of the universal Will.... Perhaps I had said somewhere before that there is only *one* Will and it is translated or rather deformed in the individual consciousness and this Will is taken as one's own will. I must have said something like that, and that our will becomes truly our own will by the fact that it separates itself from the initial universal Will and it is so deformed that it no longer resembles that Will at all. So, it must be that which worked in her head and she asked whether our will was only the expression or echo of the universal Will.

What place does there remain then for individual initiative... that is to say, what can the individual do? Can he say, "It is I who have decided? It is I, I have decided that?" Then the second question; but here I do not understand at all: "Is the individual merely an instrument for recording universal movements?" What does that mean? I do not understand quite well what was meant by that. An instrument for recording? A gramophone, probably, yes, for recording universal movements.... There are very few people who are capable of recording universal movements, to start with. Generally, they record only the movements

### 29 July 1953

of their small surrounding, themselves and what's around them. And then, a third idea is added to that: "Has he no power of creation?" This is yet another thing. But I answered (perhaps at that time I understood better what she meant than I do now!), I answered, for I speak of the three things in the text that follows. I said that only when the individual rises in his consciousness up to the highest Consciousness which is the origin of all things, where is the origin of all things, can he become a creator. That is to say, if he is identified with the creative Consciousness, he *is* naturally and he becomes the creative Consciousness. If he identifies himself, he is identified.[2]

So, what was it that was troubling you in the question? What did you not understand?

*The whole question.*

The whole question? And now, do you understand?... Not quite? I told you that you did not understand because it was muddled up; in one question three different ideas were included. So naturally it created a confusion. But taken separately they are what I explained to you just now, most probably; that is to say, one has this altogether ignorant and obliterated consciousness and is convinced that he is the cause and effect, the origin and result of himself, separate from all others, separate with a limited power to act upon others and a little greater capacity to be set in movement by others or to react to others' influence. That is how people think usually, something like that, isn't that so? How do you feel, you? What effect do you have upon yourself? And you? And you?...

You have never thought about it? You have never looked

---

[2] "If a being were able to create in that way a thought or feeling or action or anything else, he would be the creator of the world.... He can initiate a movement only by identifying himself with the conscious Power which is the ultimate source of all movements."
*Questions and Answers 1929 (26 May)*

into yourself to see what effect you exercise upon yourself? Never thought over it? No? How do you feel? Nobody will tell me? Come, you tell me that. Never tried to understand how you feel? Yes? No? How strange! Never sought to understand how, for example, decisions take place in you? From where do they come? What makes you decide one thing rather than another? And what is the relation between a decision of yours and your action? And to what extent do you have the freedom of choice between one thing and another? And how far do you feel you are able to, you are free to do this or that or that other or nothing at all?... You have pondered over that? Yes? Is there any one among the students who has thought over it? No? Nobody put the question to himself? You? You?...

*Even if one thinks over it, perhaps one is not able to answer!*

One cannot explain?

*No.*

It is difficult to explain? Even this simple little thing, to see where in your consciousness the wills that come from outside meet your will (which you call yours, which comes from within), at what place the two join together and to what extent the one from outside acts upon that from within and the one from within acts upon that from outside? You have never tried to find this out? It has never seemed to you unbearable that a will from outside should have an action upon your will? No?

*I do not know.*

Oh! I am putting very difficult problems! But, my children, I was preoccupied with that when I was a child of five!... So I thought you must have been preoccupied with it since a long time.

**29 July 1953**

*In oneself, there are contradictory wills.*

Yes, many. That is one of the very first discoveries. There is one part which wants things this way; and then at another moment, another way, and a third time, one wants still another thing! Besides, there is even this: something that wants and another which says no. So? But it is exactly that which has to be found if you wish in the least to organise yourself. Why not project yourself upon a screen, as in the cinema, and then look at yourself moving on it? How interesting it is!

This is the first step.

You project yourself on the screen and then observe and see all that is moving there and how it moves and what happens. You make a little diagram, it becomes so interesting then. And then, after a while, when you are quite accustomed to seeing, you can go one step further and take a decision. Or even a still greater step: you organise — arrange, take up all that, put each thing in its place, organise in such a way that you begin to have a straight movement with an inner meaning. And then you become conscious of your direction and are able to say: "Very well, it will be thus; my life will develop in that way, because that is the logic of my being. Now, I have arranged all that within me, each thing has been put in its place, and so naturally a central orientation is forming. I am following this orientation. One step more and I know what will happen to me for I myself am deciding it...." I do not know, I am telling you this; to me it seemed terribly interesting, the most interesting thing in the world. There was nothing, no other thing that interested me more than that.

This happened to me.... I was five or six or seven years old (at seven the thing became quite serious) and I had a father who loved the circus, and he came and told me: "Come with me, I am going to the circus on Sunday." I said: "No, I am doing something much more interesting than going to the circus!" Or again, young friends invited me to attend a meeting where we were to play together, enjoy together: "No, I enjoy here much more...." And it was quite sincere. It was not a pose: for me, it was like this, it was true. There was nothing in the world more enjoyable than that.

And I am so convinced that anybody who does it in that way, with the same freshness and sincerity, will obtain exhilarating results.... To put all that on a screen in front of yourself and look at what is happening. And the first step is to know all that is happening and then you must not try to shut your eyes when something does not appear pleasant to you! You must keep them wide open and put each thing in that way before the screen. Then you make quite an interesting discovery. And then the next step is to begin saying: "Since all that is happening within me, why should I not put this thing in this way and then that thing in that way and then this other in this way and thus wouldn't I be doing something logical that has a meaning? Why should I not remove that thing which stands obstructing the way, these conflicting wills? Why? And what does that represent in the being? Why is it there? If it were put there, would it not help instead of harming me?" And so on.

And little by little, little by little, you see clearer and then you see why you are made like that, what is the thing you have got to do — that for which *you are born*. And then, quite naturally, since all is organised for this thing to come, the path becomes straight and you can say beforehand: "It is in this way that it will happen." And when things come from outside to try and upset all that, you are able to say: "No, I accept this, for it helps; I reject that, for that harms." And then, after a few years, you curb yourself as you curb a horse: you do whatever you like, in the way you like and you go wherever you like.

It seems to me this is worth the trouble. I believe it is the most interesting thing.

*Mother, what is this little screen?*

## 29 July 1953

This screen? It is the psychic consciousness.

*And this play?*[3]

Play? It is the play of the central consciousness. It is precisely the consciousness that is at the origin of the psychic being. And then there you have to take only a tiny step to find out how this psychic consciousness should reflect and translate the one supreme Consciousness. And there the matter ends. This last step becomes very easy.

But it is the secret that's discovered at the end. And when it is discovered, there is no more fighting, for the battle has already been fought and everything arranged; so it is in one single movement and in a way as simple, as natural and as straight as possible that the thing happens, without any reaction.

I think that is what the sages of the past meant when they said: "Know thyself." Not anything else. But then, instead of going in there as if with a bandage on your eyes, and knocking your nose or forehead against something hard to find out that it is hard or that it is a wall or a closed door or an obstruction or some bad will; instead of all that, there is no need of years of experience and all kinds of misfortune and more or less unpleasant circumstances, in order to learn to know oneself: you do the work quietly, as I said.

When I did that, there was no cinema, so I could not compare what I was doing with the cinema — it was not yet there, but it is exactly like projecting on the screen what is inside,

---

[3] "In the universal play there are some, the majority, who are ignorant instruments; they are actors who are moved about like puppets, knowing nothing. There are others who are conscious, and these act their part, knowing that it is a play. And there are some who have the full knowledge of the universal movement and are identified with it and with the one Divine Consciousness and yet consent to act as though they were something separate, a division of the whole. There are many intermediary stages between that ignorance and this full knowledge, many ways of participating in the play."
*Questions and Answers 1929 (26 May)*

objectifying it. And a screen that's all white, quite smooth, that does not deform. If the screen were not quite smooth and very white, your image would be all hazy, you would not be able to see anything. Well, it is the same thing. The screen must be very white, quite smooth, quite clean, quite pure. Then one sees things as they are.

You must have a great deal of sincerity, a little courage and perseverance and then a sort of mental curiosity, you understand, curious, seeking to know, interested, wanting to learn. To love to learn: that, one must have in one's nature. Not to be able to bear standing before something grey, all hazy, in which nothing is seen clearly and which gives you quite an unpleasant feeling, for you do not know where you begin and where you end, what is yours and what is not yours and what is settled and what is not settled — what is this pulp-like thing you call yourself in which things get intermingled and act upon one another without even your being aware of it? You ask yourself: "But why have I done this?" You know nothing about it. "And why have I felt that?" You don't know that, either. And then, you are thrown into a world outside that is only fog and you are thrown into a world inside that is also for you another kind of fog, still more impenetrable, in which you live, like a cork thrown upon the waters and the waves carry it away or cast it into the air, and it drops and rolls on. That is quite an unpleasant state. I do not know, but to me it appears unpleasant.

To see clearly, to see one's way, where one is going, why one is going there, how one is to go there and what one is going to do and what is the kind of relation with others... But that is a problem so wonderfully interesting — it is interesting — and you can always discover things every minute! You can never have finished your work.

There is a time, there is a certain state of consciousness when you have the feeling that you are in that condition with all the weight of the world lying heavy upon you and besides you are going in blinkers and do not know where you are going,

*29 July 1953*

but there is something which is pushing you. And that is truly a very unpleasant condition. And there is another moment when one draws oneself up and is able to see what is there above, and one becomes it; then one looks at the world as though from the top of a very very high mountain and one sees all that is happening below; then one can choose one's way and follow it. That is a more pleasant condition. This then is truly the truth, you are upon earth *for that*, surely. All individual beings and all the little concentrations of consciousness were created to do this work. It is the very reason for existence: to be able to become fully conscious of a certain sum of vibrations representing an individual being and put order therein and find one's way and follow the way.

And so, as men do not know it and do not do it, life comes and gives them a blow here: "Oh! that hurts", then a blow there: "Ah! that's hurting me." And the thing goes on like that and all the time it is like that. And all the time they are getting pain somewhere. They suffer, they cry, they groan. But it is simply due to that reason, there is no other: it is that they have not done that little work. If, when they were quite young, there had been someone to teach them to do the work and they had done it without losing time, they could have gone through life gloriously and instead of suffering they would have been all-powerful masters of their destiny.

This is not to say that necessarily all things would become pleasant. It is not at all that. But your reaction towards things becomes the true reaction and instead of suffering, you learn; instead of being miserable, you go forward and progress.

After all, I believe it is for this that you are here — so that there is someone who can tell you: "There, well, try that. It is worth trying." Indeed, this should be said when children are quite young. For unless it be awakened in their consciousness, they won't understand. Yet it can be done even with a very young brain, for at five one doesn't have a very big brain; you have particularly the feeling that there are gaps, that many things should be known but are not known. The brain has not yet been formed. There is the consciousness there, fully conscious, luminous, clear-sighted, all is there; but there are gaps, and when one tries to draw anything out of it, it does not come through. That is what happens when one is quite young. But if one continues little by little, little by little, the ideas are organised as they arrive, and instead of being a chaos which must be put into order afterwards, it gets organised as it takes shape. It is a great advantage.

Anyway, you are all still very young. You can try. Try for five minutes every day — not more — looking at yourself, seeing what happens there, within. It is so interesting!

# 5 August 1953

*Does the psychic being always progress?*

There are in the psychic being two very different kinds of progress: one consisting in its formation, building and organisation. For the psychic starts by being only a kind of tiny divine spark inside the being and out of this spark will emerge progressively an independent conscious being having its own action and will. The psychic being at its origin is only a spark of the divine consciousness and it is through successive lives that it builds up a conscious individuality. It is a progress similar to that of a growing child. It is a thing in the making. For a long time, in most human beings the psychic is a being in the making. It is not a fully individualised, fully conscious being and master of itself and it needs all its rebirths, one after another, in order to build itself and become fully conscious.

But this sort of progress has an end. There comes a time when the being is fully developed, fully individualised, fully master of itself and its destiny. When this being or one of these psychic beings at that state, takes birth in a human being, that makes a very great difference: the human being, so to say, is born free. He is not tied to circumstances, to surroundings, to his origin and atavism, like ordinary people. He comes into the world with the purpose of doing something, with a work to carry out, a mission to fulfil. From this point of view his progress in growth has come to an end, that is, it is not indispensable for him to take birth again in a body. Till then rebirth is a necessity, for it is through rebirth that he grows; it is in the physical life and in a physical body that he gradually develops and becomes a fully conscious being. But once he is fully formed, he is free, in this sense that he can take birth or not, at will. So there, one kind of progress stops.

But if this fully formed being wants to become an instrument of work for the Divine, if instead of retiring to repose in a psychic bliss, in its own domain, he chooses to be a worker upon earth to help in the fulfilment of the Divine Work, then he has a fresh progress to make, a progress in the capacity for work, for organisation of his work and for expression of the Divine Will. So there is a time when the thing changes. So long as he remains in the world, so long as he chooses to work for the Divine, he will progress. Only if he withdraws into the psychic world and refuses to continue doing the Divine Work or renounces it, can he remain in a static condition outside all progress, because, as I have told you, only upon earth is there progress, only in the physical world; it is not acquired everywhere. In the psychic world there is a kind of blissful repose. One remains what one is, without any movement.

*But for those who are not conscious of their psychic?*

They are compelled to progress whether they want it or not.

The psychic being itself progresses in them and they are not conscious of it. But they themselves are compelled to progress. That is to say, they follow a curve. They follow an ascent in life. It is the same progress as that of the growing child; there comes a time when it is at the summit of its growth and then, unless it changes the plane of progress, unless the purely physical progress turns into a mental progress, a psychic progress, a spiritual progress, it goes down the curve and then there will be a decomposition and it will not exist any longer.

It is just because progress is not constant and perpetual in the physical world that there is a growth, an apogee, a decline and a decomposition. For anything that does not advance, falls back; all that does not progress, regresses.

So this is just what happens physically. The physical world has not learnt how to progress indefinitely; it arrives at a certain point, then it is either tired of progressing or is not capable

*5 August 1953*

of progressing in the present constitution, but in any case it stops progressing and after a time decomposes. Those who lead a purely physical life reach a kind of summit, then they slide down very quickly. But now, with the general collective human progress, there is behind the physical progress a vital progress and a mental progress, so that the mental progress can go on for a very long time, even after the physical progress has come to a stop, and through this mental progress one keeps up a kind of ascent long after the physical has ceased to progress.

And then there are those who do yoga, who become conscious of their psychic being, are united with it, participate in its life; these, indeed, progress till the last breath of their life. And they do not stop even after death, when they have left their body under the plea that the body cannot last any longer: they continue to progress.

It is the incapacity of the body to transform itself, to continue progressing that causes it to regress and in the end become more and more open to the inner disequilibrium until one day that becomes strong enough to bring about a total imbalance and it can no longer regain its balance and health. We shall see that next week. It is only in the pure spiritual life — that which is outside all physical and terrestrial existence, including the mental — that there is no progress. You reach a static state and are outside all movements of progress. But at the same time you are outside the manifestation also. When you reach that state, you no longer belong to the manifestation, you go out of the manifested world. One must go out of the manifested world in order to go out of all progress, because the two are identical: manifestation means progress and progress means manifestation.

*Many men think and write through inspiration. From where does it come?*

Many! That is indeed a wonderful thing. I did not think there have been so many.... So?

*Poets, when they write poems...*

Ah! Inspirations come from very many different places. There are inspirations that may be very material, there are inspirations that may be vital, there are inspirations that come from all kinds of mental planes, and there are very, very rare inspirations that come from the higher mind or from a still higher region. All inspirations do not come from the same place. Hence, to be inspired does not necessarily mean that one is a higher being.... One may be inspired also to do and say many stupid things!

*What does "inspired" mean?*

It means receiving something which is beyond you, which was not within you; to open yourself to an influence which is outside your individual conscious being.

Indeed, one can have also an inspiration to commit a murder! In countries where they decapitate murderers, cut off their heads, this causes a very brutal death which throws out the vital being, not allowing it the time to decompose for coming out of the body; the vital being is violently thrown out of the body, with all its impulses; and generally it goes and lodges itself in one of those present there, men half horrified, half with a kind of unhealthy curiosity. That makes the opening and it enters within. Statistics have proved that most young murderers admit that the impulse came to them when they were present at the death of another murderer. It was an "inspiration", but of a detestable kind.

Fundamentally it is a moment of openness to something which was not within your personal consciousness, which comes from outside and rushes into you and makes you do something. This is the widest formula that can be given.

Now, generally, when people say: "Oh! he is an inspired poet", it means he has received something from high above and

5 August 1953

expressed it in a remarkable manner. But one should rather say that his inspiration is of a high quality.

*Does it not come, Mother, whenever one wants it?*

Whenever one wants it? Generally not, for one does not know the mechanism of one's being and cannot open the doors at will.

It is a thing that can be done. It is one of the earliest things that you are taught to do in Yoga: to open the door whenever one wants. It is the result of meditation or concentration or aspiration: all these processes are followed to open the door somewhere.

And generally you try to open it precisely towards the highest thing, not towards anything whatever. For the other kind of receptivity people unfortunately always have.... It is impossible to be altogether shut up in an ivory tower — besides, I believe it would not be very favourable, it would be impossible to progress if one were completely shut up in oneself. One would be able only to rearrange whatever was in oneself. Just imagine you were like a closed globe, altogether closed, that there was no communication with outside — you put out nothing, you receive nothing, you are shut up — you have a few elements of consciousness, movements, vibrations (call them what you like), all that is contained as within a ball, along with your consciousness also. You have no relation with things outside, you are conscious only of yourself. What can you do?... Change the organisation within; that you can do, you can do many things by changing this organisation. But it is confined to that. It is a kind of inner progress, but there is no true progress in relation to the forces outside oneself. You would find yourself extremely limited after a time, you would be tired of yourself: turning and turning again, turning and turning again the elements inside — not very pleasant.

But all the while you externalise yourself and all the while you bring back something from this externalisation; it is like something porous: a force goes out and then a force comes in. There are pulsations like that. And this is why it is so important to choose the environment in which one lives, because there is constantly a kind of interchange between what you give and what you receive. People who throw themselves out a great deal in activity, receive more. But they receive on the same level, the level of their activity. Children, for example, who are younger, who always move about, always shout and romp and jump (very rarely do they keep quiet, except while asleep, and perhaps not even so), well, they spend much and they receive much, and generally it is the physical and vital energy that is spent and it is physical and vital energies that are received. They recuperate a good part of what they spend. So there, it is very important for them to be in surroundings where they can, after they have spent or while they are spending, recover something that is at least equal in quality to theirs, that is not of an inferior quality.

When you no longer have this generosity in your movements, you receive much less and this is one of the reasons — one of the chief reasons — why physical progress stops. It is because you become thrifty, you try not to waste; the mind intervenes: "Take care, don't tire yourself, don't do too much, etc." The mind intervenes and physical receptivity diminishes a great deal. Finally, you do not grow any more — by growing reasonable, you stop growing altogether!

But receptivity opens to other levels. Those who live in a world of desires and passions, increase their vital receptivity so much at times that it reaches proportions very unpleasant to themselves and to their surroundings. And then there are those who live in the mental consciousness; their mental receptivity grows very much. All who create mentally, study and live in mental activity, if the mental activity is constant, can progress indefinitely. Mind in the human being does not stop functioning even when the physical instrument has deteriorated. It may no longer manifest its intelligence materially, if there is a lesion in the brain, for example, but the mind itself, independently

## 5 August 1953

of the instrument, nothing can prevent from progressing, from continuing to grow. It is a being that lasts infinitely longer than the physical. It is still young when physically one is already old. Only when you do not take enough care to keep your brain in a good state, only if accidents occur and there are lesions then you can no longer express yourself. But the mind in itself continues to grow. And those who have a sufficient physical balance, for example, those who have not gone to excesses of any kind, who have never maltreated their body, who have never poisoned themselves like most people — who have never smoked, drunk alcohol and so on — keep their brain in a relatively good condition and they can progress, even in their expression, till the end of their life. It is only if in the last years of their life they make a kind of withdrawal within themselves, that they lose their power of expression. But the mind goes on progressing.

The vital is by nature immortal. But it is not organised, and in its normal state, it is over-excited, full of contradictory passions and impulses. So with all that it destroys itself. But otherwise the elements continue to exist. A desire, a passion is a very living thing and continues to live for a very long time, even independently of the being who... undergoes them, I might say, rather than creates them, because they are things that one undergoes, that rush upon you from outside like a storm that seizes you and carries you away, unless you keep very calm like that, very still, very quiet, as though one were clinging to something solid and immobile in oneself, allowing the storm to pass over when it begins to blow — it blows, but one must not stir, one must not let oneself tremble or shiver or shake; one must remain altogether immobile and know that these are passing storms. And when the storm has blown over, it passes and goes away; then one can heave a deep breath and resume one's normal balance; and there has been only a minimum destruction. In such cases, generally, things turn out well in the end.

But those who are like a piece of cork on water and rush about in all directions and do not succeed in recovering their poise and watching themselves, are liable to any occurrence. They may be drawn into a whirlpool all of a sudden and lo! engulfed. And there remains nothing.

That's all?

*There are people who do foolish things...*

Yes.

*And they know they are doing so, but their mind does not justify them, it gives no support, no excuse, no reasoning or explanation. What is this state?*[1]

What is this state? People who know that they are doing foolish things, who are conscious, but who are not able to refrain from them, because their mind does not have enough strength to check them?...

But the mind never has sufficient strength to check them! For the mind is an instrument made to see all things from all sides. Then how can you expect to have a will strong enough to resist an impulse when the mind looks at it first from this side and then from that side? And then it says: "After all, it is like that and why should it not be like that?" And so, where is your will?...

As I said there,[1] it always finds a way to explain everything, justify everything and give admirable reasons for all things.

It is only the psychic being that has the strength to intervene. If your mind is in contact with your psychic being, if it receives the influence of the psychic being, then it is strong enough to organise the resistance. It knows what the true thing is and

---

[1] "This physical mind is usually in a kind of alliance with the lower vital consciousness and its movements; when the lower vital manifests certain desires and impulses, the more material mind comes to its aid and justifies and supports them with specious explanations and reasonings and excuses."

*Questions and Answers 1929 (26 May)*

## 5 August 1953

what the false; and knowing what the true thing is, if it has the goodwill, it will organise the resistance, give battle and gain the victory. But that is the only condition: it must be in contact with the psychic being.

For even the most beautiful theories, even if one knows mentally many things and holds admirable principles, that is not sufficiently strong to create a will capable of resisting an impulse. At one time you are quite determined, you have decided that it would be thus — for example, that you would not do such a thing: it is settled, you will not do it — but how is it that suddenly (you do not know how or why nor what has happened), you have not decided anything at all! And then you immediately find in yourself an excellent reason for doing the thing.... Among others, there is a certain kind of excuse which is always given: "Well, if I do it this time, at least I shall be convinced that it is very bad and I shall do it no longer and this will be the last time." It is the prettiest excuse one always gives to oneself: "This is the last time I am doing it. This time, I am doing it to understand perfectly that it is bad and that it must not be done and I shall not do it any more. This is the last time." Every time, it is the last time! and you begin again.

Of course there are some who have less clear ideas and who say to themselves: "After all, why don't I want to do it? These are theories, they are principles that might not be true. If I have this impulse, what is it that tells me that this impulse is not better than a theory?... " It is not for them the last time. It is something they accept as quite natural.

Between these two extremes there are all the possibilities. But the most dangerous of all is to say: "Well, I am doing it once more this time, that will purify me of this. Afterwards I shall no longer do it." Now the purification is never enough!

It happens only when you have decided: "Well, this time, I am going to try not to do it, and I shall not do it, I shall apply all my strength and I shall not do it." Even if you have just a little success, it is much. Not a big success, but just a small success, a very partial success: you do not carry out what you yearn to do; but the yearning, the desire, the passion is still there and that produces whirls within, but outside you resist, "I shall not do it, I shall not move; even if I have to bind myself hand and foot, I shall not do it." It is a partial success — but it is a great victory because, due to this, next time you will be able to do a little more. That is to say, instead of holding all the violent passions within yourself, you can begin calming them a little; and you will calm them slowly at first, with difficulty. They will remain long, they will come back, they will trouble you, vex you, produce in you a great disgust, all that, but if you resist well and say: "No, I shall carry out nothing; whatever the cost, I shall not carry out anything; I will stay like a rock", then little by little, little by little, that thins out, thins out and you begin to learn the second attitude: "Now I want my consciousness to be above those things. There will still be many battles but if my consciousness stands above that, little by little there will come a time when this will return no longer." And then there is a time when you feel that you are absolutely free: you do not even perceive it, and then that is all. It may take a long time, it may come soon: that depends on the strength of character, on the sincerity of the aspiration. But even for people who have just a little sincerity, if they subject themselves to this process, they succeed. It takes time. They succeed in the first item: in not expressing. All forces upon earth tend towards expressing themselves. These forces come with the object of manifesting themselves and if you place a barrier and refuse expression, they may try to beat against the barrier for a time, but in the end, they will tire themselves out and not being manifested, they will withdraw and leave you quiet.

So you must never say: "I shall first purify my thought, purify my body, purify my vital and then later I shall purify my action." That is the normal order, but it never succeeds. The effective order is to begin from the outside: "The very first thing is that I do not do it, and afterwards, I desire it no longer and

5 August 1953

next I close my doors completely to all impulses: they no longer exist for me, I am now outside all that." This is the true order, the order that is effective. First, not to do it. And then you will no longer desire and after that it will go out of your consciousness completely.

*When the psychic is about to enter into the world, does it choose in advance the form it is going to take?*

It is an interesting question. That depends. As I have just told you, there are psychic beings who are in the making, on the way to progress; these generally, right at the outset, cannot choose much, but when they have arrived at a certain degree of growth and of consciousness (generally while they are still in a physical body and have had a certain amount of experience), they decide at that time what their next field of experience will be like.

I can give you some rather external examples. For instance, a psychic being needed to have the experience of mastery, of power in order to know the reactions and how it is possible to turn all these movements towards the Divine: to learn what a life of power may teach you. It took birth in a king or a queen. These enjoyed some power and during that time they had their experiences; they reached the end of the field of experience. Now, they know what they wanted to know, they are about to go, they are going to leave their body that's now become useless, and they are going to prepare for the next experience. Well, at that time, when the psychic being is still in the body and has noted what it has learnt, it decides for the next occasion. And sometimes it is a movement of action and reaction: because it has studied one entire field, it needs to study the opposite field. And very often it chooses a very different life from the one it had. So before leaving, it says: "Next time, it is in this domain that I shall take birth.... " Suppose, for example, the psychic has reached a stage of growth when it would like to have the chance of working on the physical body to make it capable of coming consciously into contact with the Divine and of transforming it. Now, it is about to leave the body in which it had authority, power, activity, the body it has used for its growth; it says: "Next time I shall take birth in a neutral environment, neither low nor high, where it will not be necessary (how to put it?) to have a highly external life, where one will have neither great power nor great misery — altogether neutral, as you know, the life in between." It chooses that. It returns to its own psychic world for the necessary rest, for assimilation of the experience gained, for preparation of the future experience. It naturally remembers its choice and, before coming down once more, when it has finished its assimilation, when it is time to return, to come down upon earth, it cannot, from that domain, see material things as we see them, you know: they appear to it in another form. But still the differences can be foreseen: the differences of environment, differences of activity in the environment are clearly seen, quite perceptible. It can have a vision that is total or global. It can choose. At times it chooses the country; when it wants a certain kind of education, civilisation, influence, it can choose its country beforehand. Sometimes it can't, sometimes it chooses only its environment and the kind of life it will lead. And then from up there, before it comes down, it looks for the kind of vibrations it wants; it sees them very clearly. It is as though it was aiming at the place where it is going to drop. But it is an approximation because of the fact that another condition is necessary: not only its choice but also a receptivity from below and an aspiration. There must be someone in the environment it has chosen, generally the mother (sometimes both the parents, but the most indispensable is the mother), she must have an aspiration or a receptivity, something sufficiently passive and open or a conscious aspiration towards something higher. And that kindles for the psychic being a little light. In the mass representing for it the environment in which it wants to be born, if under the influence of its own projected will a small light is kindled, then it knows that it is there it must go.

It is necessary, it is this that makes the difference in months

## 5 August 1953

or days, perhaps, not so much perhaps in years; however, this creates an uncertainty, and that is why it cannot foretell the exact date: "On that date, that day, at that hour I shall take birth." It needs to find someone receptive. When it sees that, it rushes down. But what happens is something like an image: it is not exactly that, but something very similar. It throws itself down into an unconsciousness, because the physical world, even human consciousness whatever it may be, is very unconscious in comparison with the psychic consciousness. So it rushes into an unconsciousness. It is as though it fell head foremost. That stuns it. And so generally, apart from some very very rare exceptions, for a long time it does not know. It does not know any longer where it is nor what it is doing nor why it is there, nothing at all. It finds a great difficulty in expressing itself, especially through a baby that has no brain, naturally; it is only the embryo of a brain which is hardly formed and it does not have the elements for manifesting itself. So it is very rare for a child to manifest immediately the exceptional being it contains.... That happens. Such things we have heard being narrated. It happens, but generally some time is needed. Only slowly it awakens from its stupor and becomes aware that it is there for some reason and by choice. And usually this coincides with the intensive mental education which shuts you completely from the psychic consciousness. So a mass of circumstances, happenings of all kinds, emotions, all sorts of things are necessary to open the inner doors so that one might begin to remember that after all one has come from another world and one has come for a precise reason.

Otherwise, if all went normally, it could very quickly have a connection, very quickly. If it had the luck to find someone possessing a little knowledge, and instead of falling into a world of ignorance, it fell upon a little bit of knowledge, everything would be done quite quickly.

But the psychic will and psychic growth escape completely all common notions of justice, of reward and punishment as men understand them. There are religions, there are philosophies that tell you all kinds of stories, which are simply the application of notions of human justice to the invisible world, and so these are stupidities. For it is not at all like that truly; the notion of reward and punishment as man understands it is an absurdity. That does not apply at all, not at all to the inner realities. So once you enter the true spiritual world, all that becomes really stupidities. For things are not at all like that.

A large number of people come and tell me: "What then have I done in my previous life to be now in such difficult conditions, with such misfortunes happening to me?" And most often I am obliged to tell them: "But don't you see that it is a blessing upon you, a grace! And perhaps in your previous life you have asked for it so that you could make a greater progress...." These ideas are quite current: "Oh! I am ill. Oh! my body is in a bad condition, what have I done? What crime have I committed in the other life so that in this... " This is all childishness.

So there you are. *Au revoir*, my children.

# 12 August 1953

*How do you know the character of a man by looking at his eyes?*

Not only by looking at his eyes. I know the character of a man through self-identification. And then outwardly, if you want, the eyes are like doors or windows: there are some which are open, so one enters within, goes very deep inside, and one may see everything that happens there. There are others which are partly open, partly closed; others still have a veil, a kind of curtain; and then there are others which are fastened, locked up, doors closed so well that they cannot be opened. Indeed, this is already an indication, it gives an indication of the strength of the inner life, the sincerity and transparency of the being. And so, through these doors that are open I enter and identify myself with the person within. And I see what he sees, understand what he understands, think what he thinks, and I could do what he does (but usually I refrain from that!) and in this way I get to know what people are like. And it doesn't need much time; it goes very fast. It can even be done through a photograph, but not so well. A photograph captures only a moment, a minute of somebody; if there were many photographs... But still, even with a photograph, by going a little deeper one can have a fairly clear idea. But *all* knowledge is knowledge by identification. That is, one must become that which one wants to know. One may surmise, imagine, deduce, one may reason, but one does not know.

*So it is something difficult for human beings?*

No, why?
One can learn how to identify oneself. One must learn. It is

indispensable if one wants to get out of one's ego. For so long as one is shut up in one's ego, one can't make any progress.

*How can it be done?*

There are many processes. I'll tell you one.

When I was in Paris, I used to go to many places where there were gatherings of all kinds, people making all sorts of researches, spiritual (so-called spiritual), occult researches, etc. And once I was invited to meet a young lady (I believe she was Swedish) who had found a process of knowledge, exactly a process for learning. And so she explained it to us. We were three or four (her French was not very good but she was quite sure of herself!); she said: "It's like this, you take an object or make a sign on a blackboard or take a drawing — that is not important — take whatever is most convenient for you. Suppose, for instance, that I draw for you... (she had a blackboard) I draw a design." She drew a kind of half-geometric design. "Now, you sit in front of the design and concentrate all your attention upon it — upon that design which is there. You concentrate, concentrate without letting anything else enter your consciousness — except that. Your eyes are fixed on the drawing and don't move at all. You are as it were hypnotised by the drawing. You look (and so she sat there, looking), you look, look, look.... I don't know, it takes more or less time, but still for one who is used to it, it goes pretty fast. You look, look, look, you *become* that drawing you are looking at. Nothing else exists in the world any longer except the drawing, and then, suddenly, you pass to the other side; and when you pass to the other side you enter a new consciousness, and you know."

We had a good laugh, for it was amusing. But it is quite true, it is an excellent method to practise. Naturally, instead of taking a drawing or any object, you may take, for instance, an idea, a few words. You have a problem preoccupying you, you don't know the solution of the problem; well, you objectify

**12 August 1953**

your problem in your mind, put it in the most precise, exact, succinct terms possible, and then concentrate, make an effort; you concentrate only on the words, and if possible on the idea they represent, that is, upon your problem — you concentrate, concentrate, concentrate until nothing else exists but that. And it is true that, all of a sudden, you have the feeling of something opening, and one is on the other side. The other side of what?... It means that you have opened a door of your consciousness, and instantaneously you have the solution of your problem.

It is an excellent method of learning "how" to identify oneself.

For instance, you are with someone. This person tells you something, you tell him the contrary (as it usually happens, simply through a spirit of contradiction) and you begin arguing. Naturally, you will never come to any point, except a quarrel if you are ill-natured. But instead of doing that, instead of remaining in your own ideas or your own words, if you tell yourself: "Wait a little, I am going to try and see why he said that to me. Yes, why did he tell me that?" And you concentrate: "Why, why, why?" You stand there, just like that, trying. The other person continues speaking, doesn't he? — and is very happy too, for you don't contradict him any longer! He talks profusely and is sure he has convinced you. Then you concentrate more and more on what he is saying, and with the feeling that gradually, through his words, you are entering his mind. When you enter his head, suddenly you enter into his way of thinking, and next, just imagine, you understand why he is speaking to you thus! And then, if you have a fairly swift intelligence and put what you have just come to understand alongside what you had known before, you have the two ways together, and so can find the truth reconciling both. And here you have truly made progress. And this is the best way of widening one's thought.

If you are beginning an argument, keep quiet immediately, instantaneously. You must be silent, say nothing at all, and then try to see the thing as the other person sees it — that won't make you forget your own way of seeing it, not at all! but you will be able to put both of them together. And you will truly have made progress, a real progress.

It is the same for everything. In all that you do together with others, if you do not agree, take it as a divine Grace, a marvellous opportunity given you to make a progress. And it is simple: instead of being on this side, you are on the other; instead of looking at yourself, you enter the other person and look. You must have just a little bit of imagination, a little more control over your thoughts, over your movements. But that is not very difficult. When you have tried it out a little, after a while you find it very easy.

You must not just look and then make a mental effort, telling yourself: "Why is it like this and like that? Why does he do that? Why does he say that?" You will never arrive at anything. You won't understand, you will imagine all kinds of explanations which will be worthless and teach you nothing at all except to tell yourself: "That person is stupid or else wicked" — things that lead nowhere. On the other hand, if you only make that little movement, and instead of looking at him as an object quite alien to you, you try to enter within, you enter within, into that little head that's before you, and then, suddenly, you find yourself on the other side, you look at yourself and understand quite well what he is saying — everything is clear, the why, the how, the reason, the feeling which is behind the whole thing.... It is an experiment you have the opportunity of making a hundred times a day.

At first you won't succeed very well, but if you persist, you will end up by succeeding admirably. This adds a lot of interest to life. And besides it is a work which really makes you progress, for it makes you come out of that little armour of yours in which you are nicely shut up, in which you knock against everything. You have seen moths knocking against the light, haven't you?... Everyone's consciousness is like that, it goes along knocking here, knocking there, for these are things foreign

**12 August 1953**

to it. But instead of knocking about, one enters within, then it begins to become a part of oneself. One widens oneself, breathes freely, has enough space to move in, one doesn't knock against anything, one enters, penetrates, understands. And one lives in many places at the same time. It is very interesting, one does it automatically.

For instance, when you are reading a book that interests you very much, a wonderful novel full of exciting adventures, when you are completely absorbed in the story, at times you forget your class-hour or even dinner-time or your bed-time. You are completely absorbed in what you are reading. Well, this is a phenomenon of self-identification. And if you do it with a certain perfection, you succeed in understanding ahead what is going to happen. There is a moment when, being fully absorbed in the story, you come to know (without trying to look for it) towards what end the author is leading you, how he is going to unfold his story and come to his conclusion. For you have identified yourself with the creative thought of the author. You do it more or less perfectly, without knowing that you are doing it, but these are phenomena of self-identification.

There are, in Paris, theatres of the third or fourth rank where sensational dramas are performed. These are suburban theatres. They are not for intellectuals but for the masses, and all the elements are always extremely dramatic, moving. Well, those who go there are mostly very simple people and forget completely that they are in a theatre. They identify themselves with the drama. And so, things like this happen: on the stage there is the traitor hiding behind the door, and the hero comes along, not aware naturally that the traitor is hiding there and he is going to be killed. Now, there are people sitting up there (in what is called the gallery), right up in the theatre, who shout: "Look out, he is there!" (*Laughter*) It has not happened just once, it happens hundreds of times, spontaneously. I had seen a play of this kind called *Le Bossu*, I believe; anyway it was quite a sensational drama and it was being played at the *Théâtre de la*

221

## Questions and Answers 1953

*Porte Saint-Martin.* In this play there was a room. On the stage a large room could be seen and at its side a small room and... I don't remember the story now, but in the small room there was a button which could be pressed, and by pressing the button the ceiling of the bigger room could be brought down on those who were there so as to crush them inexorably!... And a warning had been given, people had already spoken about it, passed on the word. And now there was a traitor who had hidden himself in the little room and he knew the trick of the button, and then there was the hero who came in with other people, and they started arguing; and everyone knew that the ceiling was going to come down.... I didn't say anything, I remembered I was in the theatre, I was waiting to see how the author was going to get out of this situation to save his hero (for it was evident he couldn't kill him off like that before everybody!). But the others were not at all in the same state. Well, there were spectators who shouted, really shouted: "Look out, mind the ceiling!" That's how it was.

These are phenomena of self-identification. Only, they are involuntary. And this is also one of the methods used today to cure nervous diseases. When someone cannot sleep, cannot be restful because he is too excited and nervous and his nerves are ill and weakened by excessive agitation, he is told to sit in front of an aquarium, for instance — an aquarium, that's very lovely, isn't it? — before an aquarium with pretty little fish in it, goldfish; just to sit there, settle down in an easy-chair and try not to think of anything (particularly not of his troubles) and look at the fish. So he looks at the fish, moving around, coming and going, swimming, gliding, turning, meeting, crossing, chasing one another indefinitely, and also the water flowing slowly and the passing fish. After a while he lives the life of fishes: he comes and goes, swims, glides, plays. And at the end of the hour his nerves are in a perfect state and he is completely restful!

But the condition is that one must not think of one's troubles, simply watch the fish.

## 12 August 1953

*Can the Divine be attained in this way?*

Do you understand, the only way of knowing the Divine is by identifying oneself with Him. There is no other, there is only one, one single way. Hence, once you are master of this method of identification, you can identify yourself. So you choose your object for identification, you want to identify yourself with the Divine. But so long as you do not know how to identify yourself, a hundred and one things will always come across your path, pulling you here, pulling you there, scattering you, and you will not be able to identify yourself with Him. But if you have learnt how to identify yourself, then you have only to orientate the identification, place it where you want it, and then hold on there until you get a result. It will come very fast if you are master of your power of identification. Yes, it will come very quickly. Ramakrishna used to say that the time could vary between three days, three hours and three minutes. Three days for very slow people, three hours for those who were a little swifter, three minutes for those who are used to it.

*Three days for very slow people?*

For very slow people, yes. He was asked: "How long does it take one to get identified with the Divine?" that was his answer.

*And that means three days without doing anything?*

No, not without doing anything. It is not necessary to do nothing simply in order to be identified with the Divine. Evidently you cannot remain seated motionless for three days without doing anything; it would mean you had already attained an extraordinary degree of perfection if you could do that — forget all your needs and remain motionless for three days. No, it is not that he means; the thought must be concentrated solely on the Divine. And he did it before that person, to show him, prove to him that what he was saying was true. That did not take him more than three minutes.

But it is just that, what hinders the experience is the absence of the practice of concentration, and also the absence of one-pointedness, singleness of purpose, of will. One "wants" it for a minute, two minutes, ten minutes, a quarter of an hour, an hour, and afterwards, one wants many other things.... One "thinks" about it for a few seconds, and after that thinks of a thousand other things. So naturally in this way you could take an eternity. For indeed, in this you cannot add up; if it could be accumulated like grains of sand, if with every thought you give to the Divine you deposit a little grain of sand somewhere after a time this would make a mountain. But it is not like that, it does not remain. It has no result. It does not accumulate, you cannot go on adding, cannot progress quantitatively — you can progress in intensity, progress qualitatively. Yes, you can learn within yourself how to do it; but what you have done counts only in this way. It does not get accumulated like grains of sand on a dune. Else it would be enough to become quite clever and tell yourself: "Well, I shall give at least a dozen thoughts to the Divine every day." And then, by little bits like that, after some time one has a little hill....

Well, my children, it will soon be ten o'clock. But if someone has a very interesting question... You? Ask.

*I have a question.*

Very interesting?

*It is interesting for me. It is said that there are people who are very intelligent, and others who are foolish. Why?*

Why? But, my child, there are all kinds of things in Nature! No two things are identical. All the possibilities exist in Nature:

**12 August 1953**

everything you can imagine and a hundred million times more. So you notice that there are intelligent people and again others who are not. And then there are others still who are unbalanced. And yet, your observations cover a very narrow field. But you can tell yourself that all this exists and hundreds of thousands of millions of other things also exist, and that no two things are alike in the world. And I don't think there is anything one can imagine which doesn't exist somewhere. This is exactly what amuses Nature most — she tries out everything, does everything, makes everything, undoes everything, and she makes all possible combinations and goes on changing them, re-handling them, remaking them, and it is a perpetual movement of all the possibilities following one another, clashing, intermingling, combining and falling apart. No two moments of terrestrial life are alike; and for how long has the earth existed?... Very well-informed people will perhaps tell you approximately. And for how long will it yet live? They will perhaps tell you that also: figures with many zeros, so many zeros that you won't be able to read them. But it won't ever be the same thing twice over nor will there be two similar moments. If you find things looking alike, that is only an appearance. There are no two things alike, and no two identical moments. And all this goes back so far that you cannot count. And it goes so far in front that you cannot count. And it will never be twice the same thing. So, you can't ask me why this exists and why that exists!... You wanted to ask me why? Nature has much more imagination than you, you know! She imagines new things all the time. It must be so for it is changing all the time and all combinations are always new. Not two seconds in the universe are identical. She has a great deal of imagination. Have you never thought about that?... Do you ever really have two similar moments? No. You know very well that you are not today what you were yesterday and you won't be tomorrow what you are today... and that if you went back only... say, ten years, you wouldn't recognise yourself at all any longer! You don't know even what you used to think about, granting that you thought about anything!

So, there is no problem. All that you can do is to try and investigate the field of experience given to you which is extremely limited, to see all the possibilities. And you could begin noting them; you would see that it would make a huge volume immediately, simply in that tiny little field of experience which is yours!

And what are you?... One second in Eternity!
*Voilà!*

# 19 August 1953

*"The movement of love is not limited to human beings and it is perhaps less distorted in other worlds than in the human. Look at the flowers and trees. When the sun sets and all becomes silent, sit down for a moment and put yourself into communion with nature, you will feel rising from the earth, from below the roots of the trees, and mounting upward and coursing through their fibres, up to the highest outstretching branches, the aspiration of an intense love and longing, — a longing for something that brings light and gives happiness, for the light that is gone and they wish to have back again. There is a yearning so pure and intense that if you can feel the movement in the trees, your own being too will go up in an ardent prayer for the peace and light and love that are unmanifested here."*

Questions and Answers 1929 (2 June)

*The trees aspire for the light. What is this light?*

The sun, my child. Have you never seen leaves closing up when night comes, as soon as the sun dips below the horizon?

*Can trees have an aspiration for something else?*

Something else means what? What are the possible openings for a tree?

*To become a man?*

A man? But they know nothing about man! As man aspires to be a god?... I knew animals which aspired to become human beings, but they were living with human beings. Cats and dogs, for example, which lived in a close intimacy with human beings, truly had an aspiration. I had a cat which was very, very unhappy for being a cat, it wanted to be a man. It had an untimely death. It used to meditate, it certainly did a kind of sadhana of its own, and when it left, even a portion of its vital being reincarnated in a human being. The little psychic element that was at the centre of the being went directly into a man, but even what was conscious in the vital of the cat went into a human being. But these are rather exceptional cases.

*You say that perhaps stones also feel love?*[1]

It is possible.

*Can it be known?*

One can feel it. There is a certain state of consciousness in which one perceives this divine Love wherever it is found, and one does not feel so great a difference between creatures as it appears physically. There is much more aspiration than one would think in things we call inanimate. Much more. There is also in stones a kind of spontaneous sense of what is higher, more noble, more pure, and though they cannot express it in any way, they feel it, and this affects them differently.

Even in things, even in objects, even in stones, there is a strange receptivity which comes from this Presence. There are stones — if you know how to do it — that can accumulate forces. They can accumulate forces, keep them and transmit them. One

---

[1] "Love is universal and eternal; it is always manifesting itself and always identical in its essence. And it is a Divine Force; for the distortions we see in its apparent workings belong to its instruments. Love does not manifest in human beings alone; it is everywhere. Its movement is there in plants, perhaps in the very stones; in the animals it is easy to detect its presence."

*Questions and Answers 1929 (2 June)*

### 19 August 1953

can take stones (what are called precious stones) and concentrate forces into them and they keep them. And these forces irradiate slowly, very gradually. But if one knows how to do it one can accumulate such a quantity as would last, so to speak, indefinitely.

*Are these forces of any use when they come out from the stones?*

Certainly, yes! The stone can preserve the force almost indefinitely. There are those stones which can serve as a link, there are stones which can serve as a battery. There are stones which can hold a force for protection. That indeed is remarkable, my child. One can accumulate in a stone (particularly in amethysts) a force for protection, and the force truly protects the one who wears the stone. It is very interesting, I have experienced it. I knew someone who had a stone of this kind, charged with the power of protection, and it was wonderful when he wore it.... There are stones which can be used to foretell events. Some people know how to read in these stones events which are going to happen. Stones can carry messages. Naturally, this requires an ability on both sides: on one side, a sufficiently strong power of concentration; on the other, a power to see and read directly, without using very precise words either. Consequently, because they can serve as batteries, it means that they carry within them the source of the force itself, otherwise they wouldn't be receptive. It is a force of this kind that is at the origin of crystallisations, as in rock-crystals, for instance, which form such magnificent patterns, with such a complete harmony, and that comes from one thing alone, this Presence at the centre. Now, one doesn't see because one has no inner sensibility, but once one has the direct perception of the forces of love behind things, one sees that they are the same everywhere. Even in constructed things: one can come to understand what they say.

*Anything else?*

# Questions and Answers 1953

*Mother, when flowers are brought to you, how do you give them a significance?*

To the flowers? But it's in the same way, by entering into contact with the nature of the flower, its inner truth. Then one knows what it represents.

*Mother, one day you said you would tell us the difference between what you call "the Divine" and we call "God".*

Oh! but I told you that it would be later, several years later. I said that you had to be sufficiently old. I even said what age. I don't now remember which, but the brain must be a little more ready to be able to follow.

*"All the deformations of this great and divine Power come from the obscurity and ignorance and selfishness of the limited instrument. Love, the eternal force, has no clinging, no desire, no hunger for possession, no self-regarding attachment; it is, in its pure movement, the seeking for union of the self with the Divine, a seeking absolute and regardless of all other things. Love divine gives itself and asks for nothing. What human beings have made of it, we do not need to say; they have turned it into an ugly and repulsive thing. And yet even in human beings the first contact of love does bring down something of its purer substance; they become capable for a moment of forgetting themselves, for a moment its divine touch awakens and magnifies all that is fine and beautiful. But afterwards there comes to the surface the human nature, full of its impure demands, asking for something in exchange, bartering what it gives, clamouring for its own inferior satisfactions, distorting and soiling what was divine."*

*Questions and Answers 1929 (2 June)*

### 19 August 1953

*Why do human beings always want to have something in exchange for what they give?*

Because they are shut up in themselves.

They sense their limitation and think that in order to grow, increase and even survive, they need to take things from outside, for they live in the consciousness of their personal limitation. So, for them, what they give makes a hole and this hole must be filled up by receiving something!... Naturally, this is a mistake. And the truth is that if instead of being shut up in the narrow limits of their little person, they could so widen their consciousness as to be able not only to identify themselves with others in their narrow limits, but to come out of these limits, pass beyond, spread out everywhere, unite with the one Consciousness and become all things, then, at that moment the narrow limits will vanish, but not before. And as long as one senses the narrow limits, one wants to take, for one fears to lose. One spends and wants to replenish. It is due to that, my child. For if one were spread out in all things, if all the vibrations which come and go expressed the need to merge into everything, to widen oneself, grow, not by remaining within one's limits but coming out of them, and finally to be identified with everything, one would no longer have anything to lose for one would have everything. Only, one doesn't know this. And so, as one doesn't know, one can't do it. One tries to take, accumulate, accumulate, accumulate, but that is impossible, one can't accumulate. One must identify oneself. And then, the little bit one gives, one wants to get back: one gives a good thought, one expects some recognition; one gives a little affection, one expects it from others... for one doesn't have the ability to become the good thought in everything, one doesn't have the ability to be the affection, the tender love in all things. One feels just like that, all cut up and limited, and fears to lose everything, fears to lose what one has because one would be impoverished. On the other hand, if one were able to identify oneself, one would no longer need to pull. The more one spreads out, the more one has. The more one gets identified, the more one becomes. And then, instead of taking, one gives. And the more one gives, the more one grows.

But for this, one must be able to come out of the limits of one's little ego. One must be identified with the Force, identified with the Vibration instead of being identified with one's ego.

It is very difficult, but one can succeed.

*Why do they say that it is easier to do bad things than good ones?*

They say so, but it is not always true, and it depends on people. I knew people (not many, but still... ) for whom it was impossible to do anything bad. Everything in their nature revolted at the idea of doing harm; the spontaneous movement was completely against this. But this is rare. Still, it does exist.

This happens because the world as it is at present is still largely under the influence of the adverse forces, particularly the vital force which is dynamic and generally makes you act. This force is largely under the influence of the adverse vital, that is, forces which like to hurt, destroy, damage. That kind of will to spoil things: when one sees something beautiful, instead of admiring, loving, being happy, wishing that it grows and progresses (which is the true divine movement), one feels a sort of anger, rage, one wants to destroy, one wants to damage. This is the movement of the adverse forces. Unfortunately, this is quite spontaneous in many people, and even in children... the instinct to destroy and spoil. Well, it is the presence of the adverse forces. And these are forces which come directly from the vital world and incarnate on earth in human consciousness, and at times also in animal consciousness. It is the hatred for things beautiful, for what is pure, what is good, what is true. It is the hatred of the divine Presence. And naturally, with this hatred, the will to destroy and damage, to spoil, mar, deform,

**19 August 1953**

disfigure. One step more and it is the will to inflict suffering. And all this is the influence of the adverse forces, which acts quite spontaneously in the inconscient, in the subconscient, in half-consciousness. It is only the pure and luminous consciousness which can oppose this and prevent it from acting. But the state of the world is such that this is a constant battle. Very few people can escape from this hold. Everyone generally has a tiny little corner in him — at times quite small, at times bigger, sometimes quite unconscious, sometimes a little conscious, sometimes superbly, completely conscious — which likes destroying, likes spoiling. And the state of the world is such that when one gives way to that, one is helped by an onrush of forces which lie waiting for the opportunity, waiting for the moment to be able to manifest, which need human collaboration to be able to manifest and seek it. As soon as the opportunity comes, they rush forth, throwing out a formidable amount of energy. And so one feels stronger as soon as one begins to do evil. That is why it is easier, whilst if one wants to react, refuses to become the instrument of these forces, one must fight hard, be very strong, very straight, very pure, very sincere, and above all, not egoistic. One must not turn round upon oneself, and must never be afraid. And this is not easy. That is, the world is in such a state that in order never to be moved by the adverse forces — the forces of darkness, destruction, wickedness, hatred — one must be a hero, a true hero, who is not afraid of blows and fears nothing, who never turns round upon himself and doesn't have that kind of self-pity which is so despicable a thing. That is why... in order not to do evil, think evil, wish evil, never, under any circumstances, one must be a hero.... It is not always easy to be a hero. The days one is tired, the days one wants to rest, not to make any effort, one slips, everything slips down. It is terribly slippery. It is more slippery than a children's toboggan. One slides down, down like that, down in a whirlwind. And it is only when one is right at the bottom that one realises that one has come down. Then one must climb back. That is not always comfortable.

But for one who has faith in the Divine Grace, the return to the Light becomes easy.[2]

---

[2] This last sentence was added by Mother in September 1969 when this talk was published for the first time.

# 26 August 1953

*"Love is a supreme force which the Eternal Consciousness sent down from itself into an obscure and darkened world that it might bring back that world and its beings to the Divine. The material world in its darkness and ignorance had forgotten the Divine. Love came into the darkness; it awakened all that lay there asleep; it whispered, opening the ears that were sealed: 'There is something worth waking to, worth living for, and it is love!' And with the awakening to love there entered into the world the possibility of coming back to the Divine. The creation moves upward through love towards the Divine and in answer there leans downward to meet the creation the Divine Love and Grace."*

Questions and Answers 1929 (2 June)

*Where does love come from?*

Where does love come from? From the source of the universe.

Besides, I say that there. That's what I say. I say that love is a supreme force which the Eternal Consciousness has emanated in order to send it into the world. Love comes from that. (*Mother takes the* Bulletin *of August 1953 and reads a passage from "The Four Austerities and the Four Liberations".*) This answers the question:

*"Love is, in its essence, the joy of identity: it finds its supreme expression in the bliss of union. Between the two there are all the phases of its universal manifestation."*

First, it is the joy of identity. Something must be there already which can become conscious of the identity, and that precisely is love. Then comes the manifestation of love. And in its supreme form, that is, when it returns to its source crossing all the phases of its manifestation, it becomes the bliss of union. For the feeling of union comes as a consequence of the feeling of separation. The passage through the whole manifested universe gives the feeling of separation from the Origin; and the return to the Origin is the bliss of union, that is, the two things that were separated are united once again. And it is still Love; it is Love after the great circuit of the manifestation. When it returns to its Origin, it becomes the bliss of union. (*Mother continues reading the passage from "The Four Austerities"*):

> *"At the beginning of this manifestation, Love is, in the purity of its origin, composed of two movements, two complementary poles of the impulsion towards complete fusion. On one side, it is the supreme power of attraction and on the other the irresistible need of absolute self-giving. No other movement can do better in throwing a bridge over the abyss that was dug in the individual being when its consciousness separated from its origin and became inconscience.*
>
> *"What was projected into space had to be brought back to itself without, however, destroying the universe so created. Therefore Love burst forth, the irresistible power of union.*
>
> *"It has been soaring over darkness and inconscience; it has scattered itself, pulverised itself in the bosom of unfathomed night. And from that moment began the awakening and the ascent, the slow formation of matter and its endless progression."*

That is the answer to your question. That is, no matter how high you may climb back, at the Origin you will find love. But not what men call love.

## 26 August 1953

*Mother, what kind of love is that which says, "If you love me, I shall love you"?*

If you love me, I shall love you? That's exactly the way men speak: "If you love me, I love you, if you don't love me, I don't love you." This is just the most human expression of love. And it goes still farther, they apply it also to their relation with the Divine. They say to the Divine: "If you do what I want, I shall say that you love me, and I shall love you. But if you don't do what I want, then I won't think at all that you love me, and I certainly will not love you."

That's how it is. That means that it becomes commercial.

*But "If you don't love me, I shall love you"?*

That begins to be better!

And what is better still is not to ask oneself whether one is loved or not, one should be absolutely indifferent to that. And that begins to be true love: one loves because one loves, not at all because one receives a response to one's love or because the other person loves you. All those conditions — that is not love. One loves because one cannot do otherwise but love. One loves because one loves. One doesn't care at all about what will happen; one is perfectly satisfied with the feeling of one's love. One loves because one loves.

All the rest is bargaining, it is not love.

And, moreover, one thing is certain: the moment one enters true love, one doesn't even put the question any longer. It seems altogether childish and ridiculous and insignificant to ask this question. One has the complete plenitude of joy and realisation the moment one enters true love and one doesn't at all need any kind of response. One *is* love, that's all. And one has the plenitude of the satisfaction of love. There is no need at all of any reciprocity.

I tell you, so long as there is this calculation in the mind or the feelings and sensations, so long as there is some calculation, more or less acknowledged, it is bargaining, it is not love.

You can't manage to understand?... I hope it will come one day!

All the rest is exactly what men have made of love. And besides it is not very pretty and leads to all kinds of things which are still less pretty, like jealousy, for instance, or envy, and in violent natures it goes as far as hatred. The small beginning is this: the need, when one loves, that what one loves or the person one loves should know that he is loved. But in the relation with the Divine: one loves the Divine but insists that the Divine should know that one loves Him! That's the beginning of the fall. The real thing one does not even think about. It doesn't even slightly touch the mind.

One doesn't think: one loves, that's all. One loves and is in the plenitude of love and the intense joy of love, and then, that's all.

It is a long, long, long way to go from what men call "love" to true love — a long way.

I am not even speaking here about all the repulsive forms it takes in the ordinary human consciousness; I am telling you about the best conditions, about love in its best form, even the most disinterested. I don't know, if you question human beings, I would like to know very much the percentage of those who don't even care for reciprocity. Simply that. Not those who say: "If you love me, I love you", that indeed is at the very bottom of the ladder, right at the bottom, almost in the pit.... There is a still lower rung: "Love me and then I shall see if I love you." There you have to deal with altogether disgusting folk. I am speaking only of the need of reciprocity: that is the first step of the descending scale.

However, you will understand this one day. You are still very young.

*What kind of love do animals have for men?*

## 26 August 1953

It is almost the same as that of rather unintellectual men for the Divine. It is made of admiration, trust and a sense of security. Admiration: it seems to you something really very beautiful. And it is not reasoned out: an admiration from the heart, so to speak, spontaneous. For instance, dogs have this in a very high degree. And then, trust — naturally this is sometimes mixed with other things: with the feeling of some need and dependence, for it is that person who will give me to eat when I am hungry, give me shelter when it is rough weather, who will look after me. This is not the most beautiful side. And then, unfortunately, it gets mixed up (and I believe — I consider it entirely man's fault) with a kind of fear; a feeling of dependence and a kind of fear of something which is much stronger, much more conscious, much more... which can harm you, and you have no strength to defend yourself. It is a pity, but I believe it is altogether man's fault.

But if men really deserved the love of animals, it would be made of a feeling of wonder and of the sense of security. It is something very fine, this sense of security; something that's able to protect you, to give you all that you need, and near which you can always find shelter.

Animals have an altogether rudimentary mind. They are not tormented by incessant thoughts like human beings. For example, they feel a spontaneous gratitude for an act of kindness towards them, whilst men, ninety-eight times out of a hundred, begin to reason and ask themselves what interest one could have in being good. This is one of the great miseries of mental activity. Animals are free from this and when you are kind to them they are grateful to you, spontaneously. And they have trust. So their love is made of that, and it turns into a very strong attachment, an irresistible need to be near you.

There is something else. If the master is really a good one and the animal faithful, there is an exchange of psychic and vital forces, an exchange which becomes for the animal something wonderful, giving it an intense joy. When they like to be quite close to you in that way, when you hold them, it is that they vibrate internally. The force one gives them — the strength of affection, of tenderness, protection, all that — they feel it, and it creates a deep attachment in them. Even fairly easily, in some of the higher animals like dogs, elephants, and even horses, it creates quite a remarkable need for devotion (which indeed is not thwarted by all the reasonings and arguments of the mind), which is spontaneous and very pure in its essence, something that's very beautiful.

The working of the mind in man in its rudimentary form, its first manifestation has spoilt many things which were much finer before.

Naturally, if man rises to a higher level and makes good use of his intelligence, then things can take on a much greater value. But between the two, there is a passage where man makes the most vulgar and low use of his intelligence; he makes it an instrument for calculation, domination, deception, and there it becomes very ugly. I have known in my life animals I considered much higher than a large number of men, for that sordid calculation, that wish to cheat and profit was precisely not there in them. There are others that catch it — through contact with man they catch it — but there are those who don't have it.

The unselfish movement, uncalculating, is one of the most beautiful forms of psychic consciousness in the world. But the higher one rises in the scale of mental activity, the rarer it becomes. For with intelligence come all the skill and cleverness, and corruption, calculation. For instance, when a rose blossoms it does so spontaneously, for the joy of being beautiful, smelling sweet, expressing all its joy of living, and it does not calculate, it has nothing to gain out of it: it does so spontaneously, in the joy of being and living. Take a human being, well, apart from a very few exceptions, the moment his mind is active he tries to get some advantage out of his beauty and cleverness; he wants it to bring him something, either men's admiration or even much more sordid gains yet. Consequently, from the psychic point of view, the rose is better than human beings.

**26 August 1953**

Only, if you climb a rung higher and consciously do what the rose does unconsciously, then it is much more beautiful. But it must be the same thing: a spontaneous flowering of beauty, uncalculating, simply for the joy of being. Little children have this at times (at times, not always). Unfortunately, under the influence of their parents and the environment, they learn to be calculating when yet very young.

But this kind of wish to gain by what one has or does is truly one of the ugliest things in the world. And it is one of the most widespread and it has become so widespread, that it is almost spontaneous in man. Nothing can turn its back on the divine love more totally than that, that wish to calculate and profit.

*Do flowers love?*

This is their form of love, this blossoming. Certainly, when one sees a rose opening to the sun, it is like a need to give its beauty. Only, for us, it is almost unintelligible, for they do not think about what they do. A human being always associates with everything he does this ability to see himself doing it, that is, to think about himself, think of himself doing it. Man knows that he is doing something. Animals don't think. It is not at all the same form of love. And flowers, so to speak, are not conscious: it is a spontaneous movement, not a consciousness that is conscious of itself, not at all. But it is a great Force which acts through all that, the great universal Consciousness and the great Force of universal love which makes all things blossom in beauty.

That is what I have written there also (*Mother resumes reading "The Four Austerities"*):

> "*Is it not love, under an erring and obscure form, that is associated with all the impulsions of the physical and vital nature as the push towards every movement and every grouping and which has become quite visible in the plant world?*"

You know, crystals which are formed in matter already obey a movement of love; but this becomes quite perceptible in the vegetable kingdom, in the tree and plant. It is the need to grow to get more light. All these trees which are always growing higher — always growing, the smaller ones trying to catch up with the taller, the taller ones trying to climb yet higher; you put two plants side by side, they both try to find an orientation that gives them the maximum light possible — that is the need to grow to get more air, more light, more space (*Mother continues reading*):

> "*In the flower it is the gift of beauty and fragrance in a loving efflorescence. And in the animal is it not there behind hunger and thirst, the need for appropriation, expansion, procreation, in brief, behind all desire, whether conscious or not? and, among the higher orders, in the self-sacrificing devotion of the female for her young ones?*"

... which in human beings becomes maternal love. The only difference is that it is conscious of itself. And in animals it is often even purer than in human beings. There are instances of the devotion, care, self-forgetfulness of animals for their young, which are absolutely wonderful. Only, it is spontaneous, not thought out, not reflected upon; the animal does not think about what it is doing. Man thinks. At times this spoils the movement (at times — most often), sometimes it can give it a higher worth but that is rare. There is less spontaneity in man's movements than in an animal's.

I had a puss, the first time it had its kittens it did not want to move from there. It did not eat, did not satisfy any call of nature. It remained there, stuck to her kittens, shielding them, feeding them; it was so afraid that something would happen to them. And that was quite unthought out, spontaneous. It refused to move, so frightened it was that some harm might come to them

## 26 August 1953

— just through instinct. And then, when they were bigger, the trouble it took to educate them — it was marvellous. And what patience! And how it taught them to jump from wall to wall, to catch their food; how, with what care, it repeated once, ten times, a hundred times if necessary. It was never tired until the little one had done what it wanted. An extraordinary education. It taught them how to skirt houses following the edge of walls, how to walk so as not to fall, what had to be done when there was much space between one wall and another, in order to cross over. The little ones were quite afraid when they saw the gap and refused to jump because they were frightened (it was not too far for them, but there was the gap and they did not dare) and then the mother jumped, it went over to the other side, it called them: come, come along. They did not move, they were trembling. It jumped back and then gave them a speech, it gave them little blows with its paw and licked them, and yet they did not move. It jumped. I saw it do this for over half an hour. But after half an hour it found that they had learnt enough, so it went behind the one it evidently considered the most ready, the most capable, and gave it a hard knock with its head. Then the little one, instinctively, jumped. Once it had jumped, it jumped again and again and again....

There are few mothers who have this patience. *Voilà*, my children. That's all? Nothing more?... Good night.

# 2 September 1953

*"All religions have each the same story to tell. The occasion for its birth is the coming of a great Teacher of the world. He comes and reveals and is the incarnation of a Divine Truth. But men seize upon it, trade upon it, make an almost political organisation out of it. The religion is equipped by them with a government and policy and laws, with its creeds and dogmas, its rules and regulations, its rites and ceremonies all binding upon its adherents, all absolute and inviolable. Like the State, it too administers rewards to the loyal and assigns punishments for those that revolt or go astray, for the heretic and the renegade.*

*"The first and principal article of these established and formal religions runs always, 'Mine is the supreme, the only truth, all others are in falsehood or inferior'....*

*"This attitude is natural to the religious mind; but it is just that which makes religion stand in the way of the spiritual life. The articles and dogmas of a religion are mind-made things and, if you cling to them and shut yourself up in a code of life made out for you, you do not know and cannot know the truth of the spirit that lies beyond all codes and dogmas, wide and large and free. When you stop at a religious creed and tie yourself in it, taking it for the only truth in the world, you stop the advance and widening of your inner soul."*

Questions and Answers 1929 (9 June)

*If someone follows a religion and has a good capacity, can he go farther and reach identification with the Divine?*

2 September 1953

It is impossible.

Religion is always a limitation for the spirit.

If a man has a spiritual life independently of his mental formations and the set limits in which he lives, then this spiritual life makes him, so to say, cross the religious principles and enter something higher. But his consecration must come from within and not be formal. If it comes exclusively from the form, then the limitation is so great that he cannot go farther.

There are people who have necessarily to come out of their religion if they do not want to be halted in their progress. But those who have practically no mental activity, who do not ask themselves any questions, who have only an intense devotion in their heart and an urge to give themselves to something that is infinitely greater, for these it does not matter whether they have a religion or don't. It is all the same. But if one is attached to forms, one can never go any farther.

It is difficult to go so far unless the mind is free and dwells in the light. It is one of the fairly indispensable conditions (although not absolutely indispensable). However, there are people who have no mental power and accept any dogma whatever without discussion; they feel that nothing can prevent them from having this inner urge which will put them in contact with the Divine. But generally they do not have a mental life: it is very much restricted.

*Do castes have any importance in the spiritual life?*

Castes? What has that got to do with spiritual life? Absolutely nothing. It is merely a social organisation, that is all.

*It is said that the Brahmins are more advanced for serving the Divine?*

They say many things.

Spiritual life does not depend upon these considerations, not at all. Certain social virtues depend upon them and solely because there exist in some environments special traditions of education and a particular education is better than others. But that is all.

As for the question of not mixing blood, it is a subject for discussion. Because, for example, if you take the various kinds of dogs (excuse me, I do not mean to make an improper comparison), still, the dog belonging to its kind of breed, when great care is taken to keep the type pure, to prevent any mixture, becomes more and more stupid, whilst the street-dog, product of mixed breed and sometimes a horror from the physical point of view — it is hideous, made of one kind crossed with another — is generally much superior from the point of view of intelligence. So even in these cases one cannot say.... Marriages in small communities, made within the caste, where no mixture is allowed, end usually in a gradual, progressive decline of intelligence in the group. It is not a selection, rather the contrary. New admixtures are always necessary to bring forth new types capable of manifesting progress.... From the social point of view, this is quite defensible, and it is very convenient and simple: it gives frames allowing precisely an easier organisation but that is all the worth it has.

But I believe it is the same for the caste as for the country. Each caste is convinced that it alone holds the maximum progress possible! And when you hear people speaking, even those who are outcastes are full of contempt for the others and believe themselves superior.

> *"One who holds a particular faith, or who has found out some truth, is disposed to think that he alone has found the Truth, whole and entire. This is human nature. A mixture of falsehood seems necessary for human beings to stand on their legs and move on their way. If the vision of the Truth were sud-*

# 2 September 1953

*denly given to them they would be crushed under the weight."*

Questions and Answers 1929 (9 June)

*Are men advancing more and more towards the Divine?*

It is difficult to say. Logically the whole creation must advance more and more towards the Divine, because it is its ultimate goal. But in fact it is a peculiar movement, for one takes three steps forward and two backward; one takes two steps forward and one sideways! So, it will take very long to arrive at the goal. It looks like that.

There is a great difference between the general principle, the theory seen in its totality over the millenniums, without taking any account of the number of years (not years, I say millenniums, thousands of centuries), a great difference between that and the practical facts. It can be said that the whole creation is moving towards union with its Creator, but there is the fact, first of all, that the whole evolutionary movement is a spiral movement. And in this spiral there are innumerable points, and at each point a progress in the vertical line is achieved. But one has to make a whole round in order to come back once more to the same point, but at a slightly higher level.... And so, all the time you spend doing other things, reaching other points, the first one is as it were forgotten. In human history that is translated in this way:

There is a wonderful civilisation with all kinds of extraordinary productions, from the scientific point of view, the artistic point of view, even the political, organisational and social point of view. There were fine civilisations like those which have left a kind of occult memory of a continent that might have linked India with Africa, for example, of which no trace remains (unless some human races be the remnants of that civilisation). There are civilisations like that which disappear suddenly and then a whole history, full of darkness, unconsciousness, ignorance, of altogether primitive races which seem so close to animals that one asks whether there is really any difference. And so there is a big hole in the darkness, passing through all kinds of disorders. Then all of a sudden there emerges to the top, and to a greater height still, with greater virtues, a greater realisation... as though all those hours in the night, of work in the night had prepared Matter so that it might express something higher. Then again another darkness, an oblivion: the earth becomes again barbarous, obscure, ignorant, painful. And suddenly some thousands of years later, a new civilisation comes....

So if you look at that from below, you ask yourself: "Where is the progress?" Because always it disappears, collapses or it rots, is ruined completely — and is forgotten. And mankind becomes once again something very ordinary, amorphous, grovelling in a half-obscurity. And then yet once more suddenly there is an illumination. And while one is in the midst of the illumination one says, "Now, we have it, it is the right thing, now we must not fall again...."

So far there has always been a relapse.

It has to be seen.

*Will there be a fall once again?*

That, my child, I have not said. I have said nothing, I said: "We shall see."

In reality, I believe it depends somewhat upon each one of us and on our aspiration. If everyone does all that is needed and the maximum he can do, there is a chance of arriving at a stabilised stage where the upward movement will go on without the need to destroy anything in order to begin again.

It is not indispensable, but it has always been so till now, and indeed, I don't know if Nature does not take great pleasure in it....

It happens we are obliged to take our support on what Nature has done, because it is she who has been at work till

## 2 September 1953

now. But at the same time we do not approve of her ways of working. So, that produces a small inner conflict (in the family, if I may say so!); but it makes things somewhat difficult, because she does not like her way of being to be disturbed. And yet, if one goes on doing as she wants, then it will always be the same story, always there will have to be this disappearing and beginning again, for it is her play. Hence one must be able to prevent her from destroying. But if by chance a good way is found to get her interested and make her collaborate, then with her collaboration it would be possible to succeed.

In reality, all that is needed is to make her understand that things can be done in another way than hers.

And then since she possesses (as you see) a wonderful ingenuity and a truly fantastic imagination.... You have only to look at animals or to photograph them. If you look at that and compare the little mouse with the giraffe or the elephant with the cat, all those animals that were once there and all the animals that still have extraordinary and grotesque forms — what an imagination, what a tremendous imagination! If you had to create all the animals that are on earth, you would have found it rather difficult! Now that you see them, it appears to you quite natural.... I saw the other day a picture representing simply a giraffe picking fruits from far up a tree. I said: "One must have an imagination to find that, an animal having a neck long enough to reach the top of a tree so that it may eat the fruit!" It is wonderful. And everything is like that. It appears to us quite natural because we have always lived with it, but one must truly have a genius....

So, the person who has genius and at the same time the power to realise whatever she imagines, does not like very much people meddling in her affairs! She says: "Are you capable of doing what I do?"

You must convince her that you don't want to upset anything she is doing, but that you wish simply to bring in something more. To convince her there is only one way: to do it. So long as it is an aspiration, she smiles, she looks on, she says: "Let us see, let us see, what are you going to do?"

But when it will have been done, I believe, she will say: "It is all right."

So there is only one way, it is to do it.

# 9 September 1953

*"Each time that something of the Divine Truth and the Divine Force comes down to manifest upon earth, some change is effected in the earth's atmosphere. In the descent, those who are receptive are awakened to some inspiration from it, some touch, some beginning of sight. If they were capable of holding and expressing rightly what they receive, they would say, 'A great force has come down; I am in contact with it and what I understand of it, I will tell you.' But most of them are not capable of that, because they have small minds. They get illumined, possessed, as it were, and cry, 'I have the Divine Truth, I possess it whole and entire....'*

*"One Divine Consciousness is here working through all these beings, preparing its way through all these manifestations. At this day it is here at work upon earth more powerfully than it has ever been before. There are some who receive its touch in some way, or to some degree; but what they receive they distort, they make their own thing out of it. Others feel the touch but cannot bear the force and go mad under the pressure. But some have the capacity to receive and the strength to bear, and it is they who will become the vessels of the full knowledge, the chosen instruments and agents."*

Questions and Answers 1929 (9 June)

*How does the divine Force choose the instrument in which it wants to manifest itself?*

Through affinity. For the quality, the nature of the consciousness is visible in the divine domain. It has a special vibration, a special light and this can be perceived. And so, when there is an affinity (sometimes merely an affinity, sometimes an identity, depending on the being's degree of perfection), the Force goes there. Those who are still in the course of formation but whose psychic being is sufficiently developed are seen, their vibrations are seen, the being that is there is seen and accordingly the degree of manifestation is determined, the exact line of manifestation, the importance and conditions of the manifestation. All that is included in the inner vision.

*But it may happen that the instrument does not understand, for the man in whom the Force is manifested sometimes loses his head and is unable to contain the Force?*

That may happen, everything is possible. But generally... I told you this the other day, when I spoke of the rebirth of psychic beings, I told you that from their domain they see a certain vibration, a certain light and they know that it is there that they must go. But when they drop down, most of the time they drop into unconsciousness and lose their faculties, at least for the moment. In the end they will come to themselves. But it takes time to recover, it comes as one progresses, through successive illuminations.

*Between the vital being and the mental, which progresses faster generally?*

That depends on people. It is the vital in those who have a stronger vital and the mental in those who have a stronger mental being. You mean in the same person? That depends absolutely on which one is more active and more strong. In what way? In each person the combination is different, so one cannot make a general rule and say how it must be. One can say that in certain types of cases, it is like this, and in certain others it is like that.

But to tell the truth, I do not believe that much progress

## 9 September 1953

can be made if the two do not agree, if one pulls one way and the other another. It will always be difficult. And generally it is better if the mind is converted first, for it is the mind that must have the power to organise the other parts of the being.

(*Mother stops and suddenly looks at the disciples.*) Someone here has just sent a mental formation that... has taken, if you like, the shape of a blue paper on which something was written. It dropped down whirling, and dropped upon one of you. So I would like to know if anyone has all of a sudden received some sensational answer?... Nobody?... I could not spot who it was among you, for it fell twirling .... So much the worse. But it dropped upon one of you. It was some blue paper, it took the form of a blue paper and there was a very interesting answer upon it. Nobody received anything? Didn't some idea all of a sudden enter your head? Didn't it?

(*Nobody answers*)

*If the vital is not converted and if the mind is convinced?*

Well, you pass your life in disputing with yourself! One draws you to one side and the other tries to be your good mentor but you don't listen to it. So you feel as though pulled from all sides. You know what you ought to do and you do not do it. You know what ought not to be done and you do it. And because you do stupid things, you feel sorry. So there are two things, you are unhappy for two reasons: first of all, because of the stupid things you have done, and then due to the regret they bring. It is a somewhat painful situation....

*Can't the vital be converted?*

Convert the vital? Surely one can. It is a difficult task, but it can be done. If it could not be done, then there would be no hope. But generally the mind is not sufficient. For, I have known very many people who could see very clearly, understand very well, were mentally thoroughly convinced, could even describe to you and tell you extraordinary things, could easily give excellent lessons to others, but their vital was up to all sorts of tricks and would not listen at all to all that. It said, "It is all the same to me, say what you may; as for myself, I go my own way!"

It is only when contact with the psychic has been established that this can convert anything at all — even the worst criminal — in a moment. These are those "illuminations" which seize you and turn you inside out completely. After that, all goes well. There may be slight difficulties of adjustment, but still things go well.

But the mind is a big preacher, that is its nature: it gives speeches, sermons, as it is done in the churches. So the vital usually gets impatient and answers the mind, not very politely: "You are a nuisance! what you say is very good for you, but for me it won't do." Or, at the best, when the mind is gifted with especially remarkable capacities and the vital is of a little higher kind, it may say: "Oh! how beautiful it is, what you tell me (sometimes this happens), but you see, I, I am unable to do it; it is very beautiful, but it is beyond my capacity."

But this vital is a curious creature. It is a being of passion, enthusiasm and naturally of desire; but, for example, it is quite capable of getting enthusiastic over something beautiful, of admiring, sensing anything greater and nobler than itself. And if really anything very beautiful occurs in the being, if there is a movement having an exceptional value, well, it may get enthusiastic and it is capable of giving itself with complete devotion — with a generosity that is not found, for example, in the mental domain nor in the physical. It has that fullness in action that comes precisely from its capacity to get enthused and throw itself wholly without reserve into what it does. Heroes are always people who have a strong vital, and when the vital is enthused over something, it is no longer a reasonable being but a warrior; it is wholly in its action and can perform exceptional

9 September 1953

things because it does not calculate, does not reason, does not say "One must take precautions, one must not do this, must not do that." It is not prudent, it flares up, as people say, it gives itself totally. Therefore, it can do magnificent things if it is guided in the right way.

A converted vital is an all-powerful instrument. And sometimes it gets converted by something exceptionally beautiful, morally or materially. When it witnesses, for example, a scene of total self-abnegation, of uncalculating self-giving — one of those things so exceedingly rare but splendidly beautiful — it can be carried away by it, it can be seized by an ambition to do the same thing. It begins by an ambition, it ends with a consecration.

There is only one thing the vital abhors; it is a dull life, monotonous, grey, tasteless, spiritless. Faced with that, it goes to sleep, falls into inertia. It likes extremely violent things, it is true; it can be extremely wicked, extremely cruel, extremely generous, extremely good and extremely heroic. It always goes to extremes and can be on one side or the other, yes, as the current flows.

And this vital, if you place it in a bad environment, it will imitate the bad environment and do bad things with violence and to an extreme degree. If you place it in the presence of something wonderfully beautiful, generous, great, noble, divine, it can be carried away with that also, forget everything else and give itself wholly. It will give itself more completely than any other part of the being, for it does not calculate. It follows its passion and enthusiasm. When it has desires, its desires are violent, arbitrary, and it does not at all take into account the good or bad of others; it doesn't care the least bit. But when it gives itself to something beautiful, it does not calculate either, it will give itself entirely without knowing whether it will do good or harm to it. It is a very precious instrument.

It is like a horse of pure breed: if it lets itself be directed, then it will win all the races, everywhere it will come first. If it is untamed, it will trample people and cause havoc and break its own legs or back! It is like that. The one thing to know is to which side it will turn. It loves exceptional things — exceptionally bad or exceptionally good, it loves the exceptional. It does not like ordinary life. It becomes dull, it becomes half inert. And if it is shut up in a corner and told: "Keep quiet there", it will remain there and become more and more like something crumbling away, and finally just like a mummy: there is no more life in it, it is dried up. And one will no longer have the strength to do what one wants to do. One will have fine ideas, excellent intentions, but one won't have the energy to execute them.

So do not wail if you have a powerful vital, but you must have strong reins and hold them quite firmly. Then things go well.

*Does depression come from the vital?*

Oh, yes. All your troubles, depression, discouragement, disgust, fury, all, all come from the vital. It is that which turns love into hate, it is that which induces the spirit of vengeance, rancour, bad will, the urge to destroy and to harm. It is that which discourages you when things are difficult and not to its liking. And it has an extraordinary capacity for going on strike! When it is not satisfied, it hides in a corner and does not budge. And then you have no more energy, no more strength, you have no courage left. Your will is like... like a withering plant. All resentment, disgust, fury, all despair, grief, anger — all that comes from this gentleman. For it is energy in action.

Therefore, it depends on which side it turns. And I tell you, it has a very strong habit of going on strike. That is its most powerful weapon: "Ah! you are not doing what I want, well, I am not going to move, I shall sham dead." And it does that for the least reason. It has a very bad character; it is very touchy and it is very spiteful — yes, it is very ill-natured. For I believe it is very conscious of its power and it feels clearly that if it gives

## 9 September 1953

itself wholly, there is nothing that will resist the momentum of its force. And like all people who have a weight in the balance, the vital also bargains: "I shall give you my energy, but you must do what I want. If you do not give me what I ask for, well, I withdraw my energy." And you will be flat as a pancake. And it is true, it happens like that.

It is difficult to regulate it. Yet naturally, when you have succeeded in taming it, you have something powerful in hand for realisation. It is that which can carry by storm the biggest obstacles. It is that which is capable of turning an idiot into an intelligent person — it alone can do so; for if one yearns passionately for progress, if the vital takes it into its head that one must progress, even the greatest idiot can become intelligent! I have seen this, I am not speaking from hearsay; I have seen it, I have seen people who were dull, stupid, incapable of understanding, who understood nothing — you could go on explaining something to them for months, it would not enter, as though one were speaking to a block of wood — and then all of a sudden their vital was caught in a passion; they wanted simply to please someone or get something, and for that one had to understand, one had to know, it was necessary. Well, they set everything moving, they shook up the sleeping mind, they poured energy into all the corners where there was none; and they understood, they became intelligent. I knew someone who knew nothing practically, understood nothing, and who, when the mind started moving and the passion for progress took possession of him, began to write wonderful things. I have them with me. And when the movement withdrew, when the vital went on strike (for sometimes it went on strike, and withdrew), the person became once again absolutely dull.

Naturally it is very difficult to establish a constant contact between the most external physical consciousness and the psychic consciousness, and oh! the physical consciousness has plenty of goodwill; it is very regular, it tries a great deal, but it is slow and heavy, it takes long, it is difficult to move it. It does not get tired, but it makes no effort; it goes its way, quietly. It can take centuries to put the external consciousness in contact with the psychic. But for some reason or other the vital takes a hand in it. A passion seizes it. It wants this contact (for some reason or other, which is not always a spiritual reason), but it wants this contact. It wants it with all its energy, all its strength, all its passion, all its fervour: in three months the thing is done.

So then, take great care of it. Treat it with great consideration but never submit to it. For it will drag you into all kinds of troublesome and untoward experiments; and if you succeed in convincing it in some way or other, then you will advance with giant strides on the path.

# 16 September 1953

*"The force that comes down into one who is doing Yoga and helps him in his transformation, acts along many different lines and its results vary according to the nature that receives it and the work to be done. First of all, it hastens the transformation of all in the being that is ready to be transformed. If he is open and receptive in his mind, the mind, touched by the power of Yoga, begins to change and progress swiftly. There may be the same rapidity of change in the vital consciousness if that is ready, or even in the body. But in the body the transforming power of Yoga is operative only to a certain degree; for the receptivity of the body is limited. The most material plane of the universe is still in a condition in which receptivity is mixed with a large amount of resistance. But rapid progress in one part of the being which is not followed by an equivalent progress in other parts produces a disharmony in the nature, a dislocation somewhere; and wherever or whenever this dislocation occurs, it can translate itself into an illness. The nature of the illness depends upon the nature of the dislocation."*
Questions and Answers 1929 (16 June)

*Why is the receptivity of the body limited?*

Because in the physical world, in order that things do not get mixed up, it was necessary that it should be somewhat fixed. If, for example, your body were so subtle and plastic that suddenly it began to melt just like that, in the presence of another person, it would be quite annoying! Or when you come nearer, if both were to get mixed up, it would be rather unpleasant! So, because of this, there was a greater concentration, a kind of fixity in the force to separate (it is indeed for the sake of separating) one individuality from another. And this fixity is just what prevents the body from progressing as rapidly as it could and should. And as one grows up and reaches one's normal height and constitution, one becomes still more rigid. For children have this plasticity of growth, they are changing all the time, they are visibly changing. Therefore so long as they are young and are growing and developing, they have a certain plasticity in them, but when you are over forty and as generally in life you then sit down and think that you have reached your goal and are about to gather the fruit of your labour, you become dry and hard like wood and even like stone in the end. And as the body is no longer able to adapt itself to the movement of inner transformation, it drags, it ages and cannot keep pace any more, it dries up.

*After death, does the inner being continue to progress?*

That depends altogether upon the person. For everyone it is different. There are people — for example, writers, musicians, artists — people who have lived on intellectual heights, who feel that they still have something further to do, that they have not finished what they had undertaken to do, have not reached the goal they had fixed for themselves, so they are ready to remain in the earth atmosphere as long as they can, with as much cohesiveness as possible and they try to manifest themselves and continue their progress in other human bodies. I have seen many such cases, I have seen the very interesting case of a musician who was a pianist (a pianist of great worth), who had hands which were a marvel of skill, exactness, precision, force, rapidity of movement, indeed, it was absolutely remarkable. This man died relatively young with the feeling that if he had continued to live he would have continued to progress in his expression of music. And such was the intensity of his aspiration that his subtle hands maintained their form without being dissolved, and each time he met anyone a little receptive and passive and a good

## 16 September 1953

musician, his hands would enter the hands of those who were playing — the person who was playing at the time could play well but in an ordinary way; but at that moment he became not merely a virtuoso but a wonderful artist during the time he played. It was the hands of the other that were making use of him. This is a phenomenon I know. I have seen the same thing in the case of a painter: it was also a matter of hands. The same thing with regard to some writers, and here it was the brain that kept quite a precise form and entered the brain of someone who was sufficiently receptive and suddenly made him write extraordinary things, infinitely more beautiful than anything he had written before. I saw that taking hold of someone. It was in the case of a composer of music — not one of those who execute, but who compose, like Beethoven, like Bach, like César Franck (but César Franck executed also). The composition of music is an extremely cerebral activity. Well, here also the brain of a great musician came in contact with one who was engaged in writing an opera and made him compose wonderful things and arranged on paper all the parts. He was busy writing an opera and it is extremely complex for the executors who have to bring out in the music the thought of the person who has composed; and that man (I knew him) when he received this formation had a blank paper before him and then he started writing; I saw him writing, putting lines, then some figures, on a big, very big page and when he reached the bottom, the orchestration of the Overture (for example, of a certain act) was completed (orchestration means the distribution of certain lines of music to each one of the instruments). And he was doing it simply on a paper, merely by this wonderful mental power. And it was not only his own: it was coming to him from a musical mind that incarnated in him.... Whilst I was there I saw him writing in front of me a page like that: it took him about half an hour or three-quarters of an hour. And he got such a reputation that even big well-known musicians brought him their works for orchestration. He did it better than anyone, and just in that way on his paper.

He had no need to hear or anything. Afterwards, it was tried out and it was always very good. There were so many violins, so many violoncellos, so many altos, all the instruments: some were playing this, others playing that, yet others playing other things, sometimes all together, at other times one after another (it is very complicated, not a simple thing), well, there, while playing, hearing or even reading (sometimes he took the score and read it) he knew which notes had to be distributed to which instrument, which notes had to be played by another, and so on. And he had very clearly the feeling of something entering into him and helping him.

*Do these beings who want to manifest themselves keep the same desire when they are born once again?*

No, it is not the same thing. It is not the whole being, it is the special faculty which remains in the earth atmosphere, does not leave it and go away, which remains in the earth atmosphere in order to continue manifesting itself. But the psychic being can very well return to the psychic world and it is the psychic being which takes a body again. I explained to you the other day that before leaving the physical body, the psychic being decides most often what its next rebirth will be, the environment in which it will take birth and what its occupation will be, because it needs a certain field for its experience. So it may happen that very big writers and very big musicians take birth another time in somebody quite imbecile. And you say: "What! it is not possible!" Naturally it does not always happen like that, but it may. There was a case in which the contrary happened: it was a violin player, the most wonderful of the century.... (*Mother tries to remember.*) Just wait, I knew his name and it is gone — it came back and is gone again. What was his name?... Ysayë! he was a Belgian and a violinist, truly the most wonderful violinist of the epoch. Well, that man had most certainly in him a reincarnation of Beethoven. Not perhaps a reincarnation of his entire psychic being, but in any case, that of his musical capacity. He had the appearance, the head of Beethoven, I saw him, I heard him (I did not know him, I knew nothing, I was at a concert in Paris and they were giving the concerto in D major), I saw him coming on the stage to play and I said: "Strange! How much this man looks like Beethoven, he is the very portrait of Beethoven!" Then it just started with a stroke of the bow, three, four notes.... Everything changed, the atmosphere was changed. All became absolutely wonderful. Three notes started off with such power, such grandeur, so wonderful it was, nothing stirred, all waited. And he played that from one end to the other in an absolutely unique manner with an understanding I have not met with in any other executant. And then I saw that the musical genius of Beethoven was in him.... But perhaps Beethoven's psychic being had taken body in a shoemaker or anybody else, one does not know! It wanted to have another kind of experience.

For what I saw in this man was a formation belonging to an earthly plane, it was mental-vital; and as Beethoven had disciplined his whole mental, vital and physical being around his musical capacity, that had remained in form, it was a living thing, and had incarnated in that man, just as it was, but not necessarily Beethoven's psychic being. In his first life it was the psychic being of Beethoven that had shaped all those other beings, the psychic being that had disciplined them around musical creation; but after his death, it cannot at all be said whether the psychic being remained there; it must have returned to the psychic world as is the usual rule. That however had been formed, had its own life, independent and existing in itself. It was formed for a certain manifestation and it remained to manifest itself. And as soon as it found a fit instrument, it entered there to manifest itself.

*Can a psychic being take birth in two bodies?*

It is not quite so simple as that.... The psychic being is the result of evolution, that is to say, evolution of the divine Consciousness which spread into Matter and slowly lifted up Matter, made it develop to return to the Divine. The psychic being was formed by this divine centre progressively through all the births. There comes a time when it reaches a kind of perfection, perfection in its growth and formation. Then, most often, as it has an aspiration for realisation, for a greater perfection to manifest yet better the Divine, it generally draws towards itself a being from the involution, that is to say, one of those entities belonging to what Sri Aurobindo calls Overmind, who comes then to incarnate in this psychic being. It can be one of those entities men generally call gods, some kind of deities. And when this fusion occurs the psychic being naturally is magnified and shares in the nature of the being incarnated in it. And then it has the power to produce emanations. These beings have the power to produce emanations, that is to say, they project out of themselves a part of themselves which becomes independent and goes into others to incarnate itself. So there can be not only two, but three, four or five emanations. That depends upon cases, it can happen thus. That is to say, one can have the same origin, psycho-divine, we might say. And generally when there are a number of emanations, the different persons feel themselves to be that being with reason, for they carry in themselves something of that godhead: it is as though a part of the godhead has flung itself out of itself and become independent in another being. It is not a redoubling but a kind of self-projection. (*To the child who put the question:*) Redoubling gives the idea that what has been redoubled has lost a part of its faculty: if you cut your body in two, only half of it will remain for you; but if you have the power to emanate something out of you, you remain quite whole, as you are, and at the same time, there is another Tara who is there in another person.... You understand? It is like that.

*When the hands of the pianist entered the hands of another, would the one who lent his hands be able to play?*

## 16 September 1953

I do not understand! The "hands" were what remained in the earth atmosphere of the dead pianist. So these hands which had been absolutely formed, had become like conscious, living and independent entities, entered the material hands, for they wanted to play actually on a piano. But when they played, they played through the hands of the other person, who might have been a good pianist but became a genius whilst those hands were there.

*I thought that the other one was alive!*

The other was alive? Which other? The first one... Ah! No! (*Laughter*)

*You have said: "The whole world is in a process of progressive transformation."[1] Then why do men fight among themselves?*

It is perhaps their way of progressing! (*Laughter*) You do not progress always in an apparently harmonious way. All who do Yoga know that it is not a thing that always goes on in peace and harmony, that sometimes there are inner battles, you have to give battle to enemies within you who want to prevent you from progressing. That means war. Well, when it is the whole earth that's progressing and there are things that resist and do not want to move, sometimes you have to give battle and that means war. You must not believe that progress consists in sitting down and meditating!... There are difficulties to be conquered. To conquer, what does it mean? — To fight

---

[1] "The action of the forces of Yoga hastens the movement of transformation of the being in those parts that are ready to receive and respond to the power that is at work upon it. Yoga, in this way, saves time. The whole world is in a process of progressive transformation; if you take up the discipline of Yoga, you speed up in yourself this process. The work that would require years in the ordinary course, can be done by Yoga in a few days and even in a few hours."

*Questions and Answers 1929 (16 June)*

against something. When you fight, it means war. There are small wars, there are big wars; but what is this war of men upon earth, if seen, for example, by Titans to whom men are no bigger than ants?... When you look at a war of ants, you find it quite natural! You can even look at it with interest and smile and say: "Look, the ants are having a fight." Well, to the titanic forces of the universe, men fighting on earth are like ants fighting, it is nothing at all. You must not judge things according to the measure of human consciousness.... For man Nature is a monstrous thing. It is so formidable, all the forces at her disposal, all the movements she creates. And what we know is only what is happening on earth! You know, directly or indirectly, by a kind of speculative knowledge, what is happening in the rest of the universe; but these are conflicts and plays of forces that are formidable in proportion to human consciousness. These are things that in comparison with human duration last almost eternally. So, in time it is immensity, in space it is immensity, and for the human consciousness it is something almost incomprehensible. But to these forces, human dimensions and movements have truly almost the same proportions as (perhaps are even less than) the consciousness of the swarming ant-world for us; it is the same thing. There are Nordic legends — Swedish and Norwegian — about these mighty universal Titans who are like that. And so stories are told naturally so that children may understand. It is said that there were two Titans sitting on some summit in the universe, not on earth, and then one Titan breathed a sigh. Then a thousand years pass, and the other asks, "Why do you sigh?" Another thousand years pass and the first one replies: "I am bored!" Yet another thousand years pass.... They try to give an idea. Probably the Titans took some hundreds of years to say, "I am bored." It is a question of proportions!

*Is it not possible, by yogic force, to prevent the body from being rigid?*

## 16 September 1953

It is possible. When you do gymnastics, is it not to make your body less rigid? And you go on progressing: what you cannot do the first year, you are able to do after a few years. There are people who obtain an almost total suppleness, those, for example, who do Asanas. Yes, one can obtain almost complete suppleness. But an ordinary man, if he tried to do these exercises, would break something in him. Well, it happens like that. With the mind, it is the same thing. It is through gymnastic exercises that you make yourself supple. It is a question of discipline, of development.

*Suppose a man endeavours in this life to become very intelligent, but if in the next life he is born an idiot, what is the use of all these efforts?*

No, I spoke a little briefly, but it is not that. His psychic being is not stupid! Granting, for example, that the psychic being has had the experience of a man who was a writer and could translate his experience through books and speeches; thus he covered a particular field of experience due to the associations and circumstances in which this being lived. But there is a field of experience he misses. For example, he says: "I have lived with my brain, with the reactions of an intellectual to life, now I want to live with my feeling." For usually this over-activity of the intellect in ordinary life diminishes very much the capacity of feeling. Therefore in order to have another field of experience, of development, he renounces his intellectual height; he is no longer a genius, a writer of genius, he becomes an ordinary man, but with a remarkable heart, very kind, very generous. I said "idiot", but it is a question of comparison. It is not rare, for example, that a psychic being which has reached its maximum growth, after having enjoyed the experiences of a ruling authority (of all that the life of an emperor or king may bring) may want to be able to work in an obscure life, without being fettered all the time by governmental pomps, and may very well choose to be born in quite an ordinary environment, an ordinary bourgeois family, in the most mediocre conditions, so as to have that kind of incognito which will allow it to work without being hampered by all the necessities of governmental display that are binding on one who is at the head of a country. So if you look at the thing from one point of view, you say: "How is it? what is this downfall?" It is not a downfall. It is meeting the problem from another angle, from another point of view. For the consciousness (I mean the true consciousness, the divine consciousness) success or failure are the same, glory or mediocrity are the same. What is important is the growth of the consciousness. And certain conditions that appear very favourable to human beings can be very unfavourable for the growth of the consciousness.... You may look at yourself. Naturally, if you are careful to be always at the height of your being, you do not fall into this error. But with ordinary thought, with ordinary reaction, you judge everything by success or failure, but that is the last way of judging, for it is the most artificial, the most external, that which is the very contrary of truth. In human life as it is at present organised, not once in a million can one find the true value in front, recognised. Usually a little *cabotinage* is always necessary. When a man gets success, great success, whatever it is, in whatever domain it may be, you may always think that somewhere there is some acting.

*What does* cabotinage *mean?*

This is said of actors who show off in a comedy, but the word is used also in speaking of someone who over-estimates his value, who shows more than he has, displays what he has not and who thinks above all of getting appreciated. That is the most important thing for him, to be appreciated.

*How can memory be enlarged?*

Widen your consciousness and your memory will grow.

## 16 September 1953

Consciousness is a much higher memory than the mechanical brain memory. I explained this to you one day, not so very long ago. I told you that the mechanical brain memory can forget — can confuse and deform — but if you are able to establish in you once again the state of consciousness in which you were at a given moment, you have exactly the same experience. And that is the only true memory. And this depends entirely on the development of your consciousness.

*You have said that on the material plane "receptivity is mixed with a large amount of resistance."[2] What is this resistance?*

Don't you have resistances in your body, don't you? When you want to do an exercise, can you do with your body whatever you want? And when you try to be in good health, does your body always obey? And when you want to learn your lesson, does your brain follow it without difficulty?... That is the resistance, it is all that refuses to progress. And I believe that unfortunately the amount of resistance is much greater than the amount of receptivity. One must work very hard to become receptive.

One does not know — it is perhaps something you will know one day, perhaps you will be told one day, perhaps one will be able to make you understand it — you cannot imagine the immense flood of force at your disposal! And generally you do not feel it even. When you feel it, something in you shrinks because it is too much and produces a kind of instinctive fear in your cells; and when you receive it, more than three-quarters of it you throw away like an overfilled vessel! It gushes out, spills over, because you are not able to hold it. I have met a very large number of people who complained that they were receiving nothing, that is to say, they said they did not have the forces they needed. It was because they were absolutely incapable of

[2] *Questions and Answers 1929 (16 June).*

receiving them, and there was a hundred thousand times more force than what they could receive. It is like that. You are all in a sea of tremendous vibrations, and you are not at all aware of it because you are not receptive. And there is such a resistance in you that if something succeeds in entering, three quarters of what enters is thrown out violently because you are not able to contain it.... I do not speak of this usually, but since we are talking about the subject, I am telling you. And perhaps one day I shall give you examples of it. It is something unbelievable. For example, just take the consciousness of the Forces, like the force of love, the force of understanding or the force of creation (for everything, it is the same: the force of protection, the force of growth, all that, and the power for progress, for everything); take Consciousness, simply this Consciousness which surrounds everything, enters into everything, which is everywhere, which is in everything.... Well, it is almost felt as a violence which seeks to impose itself upon the being that is unable to receive or bear it. And I am speaking of the very best; but in everyone there is a part more or less big, more or less important which does not yet have the goodwill, which is just on the border-line of bad will and does not want at any cost and rejects what is there. But if one were open and simply breathed in — nothing more, if one did that only — one would breathe in the Consciousness, the Light, the Understanding, the Force, the Love and all the rest. And all that is wasted upon Earth because the Earth is not ready to take it. *Voilà*.

# 23 September 1953

*"Each spot of the body is symbolical of an inner movement; there is there a world of subtle correspondences. But this is a long and complex subject and we cannot enter into its details just now. The particular place in the body affected by an illness is an index to the nature of the inner disharmony that has taken place. It points to the origin, it is a sign of the cause of the ailment. It reveals too the nature of the resistance that prevents the whole being from advancing at the same high speed. It indicates the treatment and the cure. If one could perfectly understand where the mistake is, find out what has been unreceptive, open that part and put the force and the light there, it would be possible to re-establish in a moment the harmony that has been disturbed and the illness would immediately go."*

Questions and Answers 1929 (16 June)

*Why is "each spot of the body symbolical of an inner movement"?*

Because the whole physical world is the symbol of universal movements. So our body is the symbol of our inner movements. The whole world, the whole physical world is like a crystallisation — it is a materialisation, a crystallisation — of the movements in other planes of the universe. It is like a finalisation, it is as though a projection on something that retains the image, fixes the image. Therefore, at every point it is the same thing as in the whole material universe.

*The material is a plane, isn't it?*

Yes, it is a final result. There is an increasing materiality and a decreasing materiality, and the physical plane is at the centre: it is like a screen on which all the intervening vibrations are projected and held, as upon a screen — it is an image, an image of all that is happening. We notice it because it is a thing done, something concrete. It is as though you viewed the whole universe as a movement of force and this movement of force were projected till it met a screen and on the screen it made an image, and this image on the screen is the physical world. And it is a mere image. The physical world which everyone takes as the only reality is simply an image. It is the image of all that happens in what we call the invisible. It becomes visible to us because there is a screen which intervenes and stops the vibrations and that produces an image. If there were no such screen the vibrations would move on and nothing would be seen. And yet all the movements would exist. But for us they would be invisible, if there were no screen to stop the vibrations.

For the ordinary consciousness it is the image alone that is true, and what happens behind it is more or less problematical, but in the true consciousness, all that happens behind or before is the true thing and what one sees externally is only an image, that is to say, a projection on a screen, of something which exists altogether independently. So, our body represents a small fragment in this set of images that is projected and it is a fragment which expresses exactly all the vibrations of the inner state corresponding to this little point that is the body.

*What is the cause of illnesses in animals?*

I think, as in men, so in animals, there are as many causes as there are illnesses. These are perhaps psychological movements, for animals have psychological movements. They are perhaps accidents, for there is a whole domain of accidents. In fact, scholars say that all diseases, even death, are always accidental. It is not a normal condition. So, for animals, it may be that, and it is perhaps also a psychological condition.

## 23 September 1953

For animals who live with man, it is a sure fact. What they have gained from this, these poor creatures, is to become as sensitive and unbalanced as men, without getting their intelligence! For example, animals possess a very sure instinct; you put a cow in a field where there are all kinds of grasses — good and bad, and some which are even poisonous; but never will a cow touch a bad and poisonous herb. Never. With the tip of its tongue it chooses quite surely what is good and leaves the rest aside. But if you cut the grass and mix up the good and bad together and you put that in the manger before the cow, it will eat up everything and poison itself, for it has a kind of trust — an ignorant trust — that what is placed there before it is for eating, and so it loses its instinct. Animals in their natural state do not ever overeat, they eat according to their hunger and if some food is left over and they do not want it to be eaten by others, they hide it, bury it; they hide it with great care so that they may find it again when they are hungry. But an animal living with man loses this instinct and eats not only all that is given but all that's left within its reach. I lived for some time in a small town in the south of France. There was a grocer there who kept goats and one of them had become quite greedy. He had just received a barrel of molasses — you know what molasses is?... How do you call it here? It is crude sugar, "jaggery". He had received a barrel of jaggery and he opened it — he opened the lid and forgot to put it back. And there it was and the goat was roaming around. The goat thought that it must be quite good since it was left there within its reach! It began to eat it and found it truly excellent. And it went on — as it had lost all its instinct — until literally it fell dead, having eaten too much. Well, a wild animal would never do that. These are the advantages of man's company!

No question?

Then we shall drop the subject. It seems this lady[1] was quite preoccupied with maladies.

---

[1] The one who put the questions in *Questions and Answers 1929*.

## Questions and Answers 1953

> *You said that this physical world was a projection of invisible worlds. Then why should the divine Emanations come into the physical world to transform it? They have only to do the work in the invisible planes; then the projections will be good.*

That indeed is a serious question!... You know the image sometimes given to the universe: a serpent biting its tail? And it is taken as the symbol of the infinite, of the universe. Well, it is a fact. In the creation there is a progressive, a greater and greater materialisation. But we could take another image (I am taking an approximate image): the universe is a circle or rather a sphere (but for the convenience of explanation, let us take a circle). There is a progressive descent from the most subtle to the most material. But the most material happens to touch the point of origin of the most subtle. Then, if you understand the image, instead of going all the way round to change matter, it is much more easy to do the thing directly, for the two extremities meet — the extremely subtle and the extremely material touch, since it is a sphere. Hence, instead of doing all that (*Mother draws a circle*), it is much better to do this (*Mother touches the extreme material end of the circle*). In fact, psychologically it is that. The rest will follow quite naturally. If that is done (*Mother touches the same extreme material end*), all the rest will get settled as a matter of course. And it is not even like this! It is precisely for the convenience of work that all has been concentrated or concretised at one point so that instead of having to spread oneself out in the infinite to change things, one can work just on the point that serves as the symbol of the whole universe. And from the occult standpoint, earth (which is nothing from the astronomical standpoint; in the immensity of the astronomical skies, earth is a thing absolutely without interest and without importance), but from the occult and spiritual point of view, earth is the concentrated symbol of the universe. For it is much more easy to work on one point than in a diluted vastness.

*23 September 1953*

This all people who work know. Well, for the convenience and necessity of work, the whole universe has been concentrated and condensed symbolically in a grain of sand which is called the earth. And therefore it is the symbol of all; all that is to be changed, all that is to be transformed, all that is to be converted is there. This means that if one concentrates on this work and does it there, all the rest will follow automatically, otherwise there will be no end — and no hope.

But that is also why this point appears as particularly bad! Because the whole thing is concentrated. And that can be particularly good also. For always there are the two, the two opposites are together. And always the best borders on the worst, or the worst borders on the best (it depends on the side you look from). But it is because of the worst that you can find the best and it is because of the best that you can transform the worst — the two act and react upon each other.... That was published in the *Bulletin*: the "Evil Persona".[2] It is always said that there is a dark double of all the stars and a luminous double of all the planets. In the occult way, it is said that there is a luminous earth. All that is the experience of the luminous earth. Sri Aurobindo has described the experience.

*What experience?*

---

[2] "What you say about the "Evil Persona" interests me greatly as it answers to my consistent experience that a person greatly endowed for the work has, always or almost always — perhaps one ought not to make a too rigid universal rule about these things — a being attached to him, sometimes appearing like a part of him, which is just the contradiction of the thing he centrally represents in the work to be done. Or, if it is not there at first, not bound to his personality, a force of this kind enters into his environment as soon as he begins his movement to realise. Its business seems to be to oppose, to create stumblings and wrong conditions, in a word, to set before him the whole problem of the work he has started to do. It would seem as if the problem could not, in the occult economy of things, be solved otherwise than by the predestined instrument making the difficulty his own. That would explain many things that seem very disconcerting on the surface."

Sri Aurobindo, *Letters on Yoga*, SABCL Vol. 24, p. 1660.

It is an experience that I had and I wrote about it to Sri Aurobindo. He answered me saying that it was an experience of Vedic times, an experience that happened in the luminous double of the earth.... That will come out somewhere one day.[3]

---

[3] The experience referred to is one which the Mother had on 26 November 1915. This has been described in her *Prayers and Meditations*. Sri Aurobindo's reply to the Mother, dated 31 December 1915, is published in *The Mother*, SABCL Vol. 25, p. 384.

# 30 September 1953

*"There is a plane in the mind where the memory of everything is stored and remains always in existence. All mental movements that belong to the life of the earth are memorised and registered in this plane. Those who are capable of going there and care to take the trouble, can read in it and learn anything they choose. But this region must not be mistaken for the supramental levels. And yet to reach even there you must be able to silence the movements of the material or physical mind; you must be able to leave aside all your sensations and put a stop to your ordinary mental movements, whatever they are; you must get out of the vital; you must become free from the slavery of the body. Then only can you enter into that region and see. But if you are sufficiently interested to make this effort, you can arrive there and read what is written in the earth's memory."*

Questions and Answers 1929 (23 June)

*You have said that in order to go to the place where all mental movements belonging to earthly life are recorded and preserved, one must silence the movements of the material and physical mind... and put a stop to ordinary mental movements. If the movements are stopped, what is going to happen? We have to do something or other the whole day long.*

No, just for that moment. Not permanently.

*Mother, but if one forgets? There is some work to do: at two o'clock one must do this, and at half past ten one must do that; if one forgets...*

277

No, you don't understand. To go to that place, at the time of going you must be able to completely silence the mind (and all the other things I have mentioned), but just for going there. For example, you decide: "Now, I am going to read such and such a chapter of earth's history", then you lounge comfortably in an easy-chair, you tell people not to disturb you, you go within yourself and completely stop your mind, and you send your mental messenger to that place.... It is preferable to have someone who can guide you there, because, otherwise you can lose your way and go elsewhere! And then you go. It is like a very big library with many many small compartments. So you find the compartment corresponding to the information you wish to have. You press a button and it opens. And inside it you find a scroll as it were, a mental formation which unrolls before you like a parchment, and you read. And then you make a note of what you have read and afterwards return quietly into your body with the new knowledge, and you may transcribe physically, if you can, what you have found, and then you get up and start your life as before.... This may take you ten minutes, it may take one hour, it may take half an hour, it depends upon your capacity, but it is important to know the way, as I said, in order not to make a mistake.

*Why then don't we do that instead of reading books!*

Because very few people would be able to do it, whereas many can read books (there are not many who understand them, but many can read them!). And this is still more difficult than understanding a book.

*And if it were taught to children when they are quite young?*

It is possible that this might replace the reading of books with advantage!

*30 September 1953*

All that has happened upon earth — from the beginning of the earth till now, all the movements of the mind have been exactly inscribed, all of them. So when you need any accurate information about something, you have only to go there, you find your way. It is a very strange place; it is made as though of small cells, they are like small pigeon-holes; and so, following the shelves and some kind of... how to put it? There are libraries of that kind. Why, I saw a picture shown to us at the cinema, the picture of a library at New York. Well, it is arranged somewhat like that. It is a similar arrangement. It interested me because of that. But instead of being books, these are like small squares. They are all closed. You put your finger, press a button and the thing opens. And then something like a scroll comes out and you unroll it and can read it — all that is written about a subject. There are millions and millions and millions of these. And happily, in the mind, one can go down, one can go up, one can go right on the top. You do not need a ladder!

*How does one read? As one reads a book?*

Yes, it is a kind of mental perception. It corresponds to that. You see quite, quite well all the description or the information (that depends on what it is). Sometimes they are pictures: it is as though a picture had been preserved. Sometimes it is a story. Sometimes it is simply an answer to a question. All possible and imaginable things recorded mentally are there. You can find many corrections too (exactly of those facts that have been put in books and are not correct). And you need not walk on or climb up: you send along quite simply something like a concentrated mental consciousness and that goes forward and touches the thing. Only, if you do this without completely detaching yourself from your own mental activity, I am afraid you will see only what is in your own head! Instead of seeing the thing as it is, perhaps you take a walk in your own brain and see only what is there — it is a danger. You must be able to silence your head absolutely and be completely detached, not to have (for example, when you are looking for the solution of a problem), not to have already in your head the solution that seems to you right or the best or most profitable. That must not be there. You must become absolutely like a blank paper, with nothing on it. And you proceed in that way, with a very sincere aspiration to know the truth, without assuming beforehand that it will be like this or like that; because otherwise you will see only your own formation. The very first condition is that the head must keep completely silent during the time one is observing.

And in order to be more sure (but here one must be fully trained, one must have a very good education), in order to be altogether sure of reporting clearly the knowledge received without deforming it in any way, it is better to say what one sees and what one reads (we say "reads", but rather it is what one perceives), to say it as one perceives it, and it should be someone else who notes it down.... I repeat: You lie quietly stretched in your easy-chair, without moving and altogether quiet, and you send a messenger from your head. Now, someone should be sitting by your side and when you reach the place and open the door and pull out the manuscript (or whatever you like to call it), you begin, instead of reading only with your eyes that are absent, to describe what you see. You acquire the habit of speaking aloud and as you go on observing up there, you speak here. You narrate precisely your journey through those vast halls and how you reached that place and how it had a small mark that was the sign of what you wanted to see. Then you open that little place and pull out the scroll and start reading. And you read it out aloud. And the person who is there, sitting by your side, goes on noting down what you are reading. In this way there is no danger of the thing getting changed when you return. For, the experience is very clear and precise to that part of your being which is there at the moment, but when you come back into the material world as it is, almost always something escapes and this does not escape when you speak directly at the

*30 September 1953*

time you are at work. So all that means very many conditions to fulfil: it is not so easy as taking a book in the library and reading it! This is within the reach of everybody. That is a little more difficult to accomplish.

*What is the theory of relativity?*[1]

(*Mother turns to a mathematician disciple*) Pavitra! Will you please explain that to these children?

Pavitra: *It means that the description of the universe varies with each observer — to put it in one sentence.*

Is that all! Why is there so much fuss over this discovery?

Pavitra: *It is a revolution, Mother!*

It is a revolution? That what one sees depends on who sees? Ah! Well...

Pavitra: *What one measures depends upon the physical*

---

[1] "Although it may be true in a general way and in a certain sense that a Yogi can know all things and can answer all questions from his own field of vision and consciousness, yet it does not follow that there are no questions whatever of any kind to which he would not or could not answer. A Yogi who has the direct knowledge, the knowledge of the true truth of things, would not care or perhaps would find it difficult to answer questions that belong entirely to the domain of human mental constructions. It may be, he could or would not wish to solve problems and difficulties you might put to him which touch only the illusions of things and their appearances. The working of his knowledge is not in the mind; if you put him some silly mental query of that character, he probably would not answer. The very common conception that you can put any ignorant question to him as to some superschoolmaster or demand from him any kind of information past, present or future and that he is bound to answer, is a foolish idea. It is as inept as the expectation from the spiritual man of feats and miracles that would satisfy the vulgar external mind and leave it gaping with wonder."

*Questions and Answers 1929 (23 June)*

*universe, from the point of view of the physical sciences.*

Physical sciences, yes. For measuring the universe, each one measures it in his own way.

*Pavitra: But then, complementary to that, it has been found that behind there is something independent of the observer.*

Ah! they have "discovered" that? (*laughter*) A still greater revolution!... (*loud laughter*) Good.

*Mother, you have said[2] there are many intermediary planes between the mental and the supramental, and that if an ordinary man came in contact with one of these intermediate planes, he would be dazzled. Why then, since man is in such an undeveloped condition, do we speak of the descent of the supramental plane, instead of the descent of the intermediate planes?*

For a very simple reason, because till now the whole physical, material world, the whole earth (let us take the earth) has been ruled by forces and the consciousness that come from what Sri Aurobindo calls the Overmind. Even what men call God is a force, a power coming from the Overmind and the whole universe was under the rule of the Overmind. To get there one has to pass through many intermediate planes and very few people can reach there without getting dazzled. But what Sri Aurobindo

---

[2] "Men are too easily inclined to believe that they have climbed into regions quite divine when they have only gone above the average level. There are many stages between the ordinary human mind and the Supermind, many grades and many intervening planes. If an ordinary man were to get into direct contact even with one of these intermediate planes, he would be dazzled and blinded, would be crushed under the weight of the sense of immensity or would lose his balance; and yet it is not the Supermind."

*Questions and Answers 1929 (23 June)*

## 30 September 1953

said is that now the time for the "rule" of the Overmind is coming to its end and is going to be replaced by the rule of the Supermind. All who have had spiritual experiences and have discovered the Divine and become united with Him, know what it is, the Overmind. But what Sri Aurobindo says is that beyond the Overmind there is something and that it is now the turn of this something to come and rule the earth, to manifest upon earth and rule the earth. Therefore, there is no need to speak of the Overmind, for many people have spoken about it already and have had the experience of it; whereas this is something new that is going to manifest itself in a new way and nobody has been aware of it before. That is why. The old accounts — there's no lack of people who have experienced these things or described them, or of books written on the subject. There is no need to repeat once more what others have said. Sri Aurobindo came to say something new. And it is precisely because people are unable to come out of the experiences they have known and heard being spoken of, that they try to identify this Force which Sri Aurobindo called supramental with their experience of the intermediary worlds including the Overmind. For they cannot conceive that there could be something else.... Sri Aurobindo always said that his Yoga began where the former Yogas ended, that to be able to realise his Yoga it was necessary first of all to have reached the extreme limit of what the older Yogas had realised, that is to say, the perception of the Divine, the union, the identification with the Divine. But that Divine, Sri Aurobindo says, is the Divine of the Overmind which is already something quite unthinkable, in comparison with the human consciousness, because even to reach there one must pass through several planes and in these planes one feels dazzled.

There are beings of the vital, if they appeared to men, or to say things more exactly, whenever they have appeared to men, men have taken them for the supreme God — these vital entities! If you like, we shall call that a disguise but it is a very successful disguise, because those who saw it were thoroughly convinced that they had seen the supreme Godhead. And yet, they were but beings of the vital. And these entities of the Overmind, these overmental gods are mighty entities in comparison with our humanity. When human beings come in relation with them, they become truly bewildered.

There is however a kind of Grace which makes it possible for us to profit by the experience of others. It is something similar to the way of teaching the sciences. If each scientist had to do all over again all the experiments of the past in order to arrive at a new discovery, go over all that the others had found, he would have to spend his whole life in that and there would be no time left to make his new discovery! Now one doesn't need to do all that: one opens a book and sees the results and starting from there can proceed further. Well, Sri Aurobindo wanted to do the same thing. He tells you where you can find the results of what others before him have found — the experiments they made and their results — and where you stand: historically where you stand in the spiritual history of the world. And then he takes you from there, and after the basis has been firmly laid for you, he makes you climb higher up the mountain.

*So, in the Ashram, there should be only those who have reached the overmental level? Instead of that...*

I don't want to speak of those who were there at the beginning, what they knew or did not know and their experience. But you all, my children, at what age did you come here? That was not an age to have realised the Overmind?!

*If you had around you people like Vivekananda, for example, your work would be more easy, wouldn't it? Instead of having unrefined stuff like us?* (laughter)

Probably they would have been more refractory!... For what is most difficult is to convince someone who has already had a

## 30 September 1953

realisation. He believes he is above all progress.

Not necessarily. It is not necessarily someone with experience who is most advanced. He lacks an element of simplicity, modesty, and the plasticity that comes from the fact that one is not yet totally developed. As one grows, something crystallises in the head; it gets more and more fixed and unless you try very hard you finish by becoming fossilised. This is what usually happens to people, particularly those who have tried for some realisation and succeeded in it or those who have come to believe they have reached the goal. In any case, it was their personal goal. They have reached it, they have attained. It is done, they remain there; they settle there, they say "that's it." And they do no more any more. So, after that they may live ten years more, or twenty or thirty, they will not budge. They are there, they will stay there. Such people lack all the suppleness of stuff that's necessary for going further and progressing. They are stuck. They are very good objects to be put in a museum, but not for doing work. They are like samples to show what can be done but they are not the stuff to do more. For me personally, I admit I prefer for my work someone who knows very little, has not laboured too much, but who has a great deal of aspiration, a great goodwill and who feels in himself this flame, this need for progressing. He may know very little, may have realised still less, but if he has that within him, it is good stuff with which one can go very far, much further. For one must know the way (it is the same thing here as with your library), one must know the way to go. Well, usually in life when you climb a mountain or go to an unknown land, you look for a man who has been there, who is a guide, and you ask him to direct you. It is the same thing. If you follow the guide, you can go much quicker than someone else who has made much effort, found his own way and is usually quite proud of himself and, in any case, has the feeling of having come to the end, reached the goal he aimed at, finally arrived — and he stops, settles down. And he does not move any more.

## Questions and Answers 1953

Naturally, at the beginning there were no children here and children were not accepted, children were all refused. It was only after the war that children were taken. But I do not regret that they have been accepted. For I believe there is much more stuff for the future among children who know nothing than among those grown-ups who believe they know everything.... I do not know if you have much knowledge of sculpture. But to do sculpture, you have to take some clay, soak it with water; it must be finely powdered clay, and you soak it with water and make a paste. You have to keep it wet all the time and you make a statue or whatever you want out of that. When it is finished, you bake it so that it does not move. And after that — indeed after that — it cannot move any more. If you want to change something, you must break it and make another. For otherwise, as it is, it is no longer pliable. It is hard and rigid like stone.... Something like that happens in life. You must not attain something and then remain crystallised, fossilised, immobilised. For otherwise you have to break it, take it to pieces, or else you can do nothing with it any longer.

So long as one remains thus clay-like, very soft, very malleable, not yet formed, not aware of being formed, something can be done. And as long as one remains a child... it is a blissful state. I was saying this yesterday, children have only one idea, to become grown-ups, and they do not know that when they are grown up, they will have lost three-fourths of their worth which consists in being something which can still be developed, formed, something malleable, progressive, which need not be broken into bits so that it may progress. There are people who are compelled to take a whole turn around the mountain, in that way, from the foot to the top, and they take an entire lifetime to reach the top. There are others who know the road, the shortest cut that can be taken by which one can go straight to the top. And then, once up there, they are still full of youthfulness and energy and they can see the horizon and the next mountain. On the contrary, the others are conscious of having done a considerable

## 30 September 1953

work by turning round and round and spending their whole life to reach the summit. But as for you, my children, it is being tried here to take you quite at the bottom and make you go up by the funicular railway right to the top, the shortest cut. And when you are on the top, you will have the vision of the spaces before you and you will be able to choose the mountain you wish to climb.

Above all, do not be in a hurry not to be a child any more! One must be a child all one's life, as much as one can, as long as one can. Be happy, joyful, content to be a child and remain a child, plastic stuff for shaping. *Voilà*.

*Can't you change someone who has already made progress? Can't one change men who are getting old?*

It can be done, it can be done. It is being done. It can be done but it is much more difficult and the more they are convinced of having attained something, the more difficult it is.

That can be done, it has been done, but it is much more difficult. And sometimes it takes more time.

*Why were children not accepted before the war?*

Ah, my children, it is very simple. Because where there are children, you have to be busy most of the time with them only! Children are very absorbing creatures. Everything must be organised for them, everything must be arranged in view of their welfare, and the whole aspect of life changes. Children are most important personages. When they are there, everything turns around them. And the entire organisation of the Ashram has completely changed. Formerly, it was quite different. First of all there was a kind of austerity that cannot be imposed upon children. There are simplicities and austerities of life that can be imposed upon grown-up people, because they are told: "Take it or leave it: if you cannot bear it, if you do not like it, well, you may go away. This is what it should be like; if you do not want it, you may leave the place, the door is always open." But with a child... What right have you to demand of a child things that have no normal relationship with its growth? Children must have reached a certain maturity before they are able to make a choice. You cannot compel them to do a thing before they have the capacity to choose. You have to give them quite normally all that they need. And this changes life completely. And I knew that very well. I already had the experience of what the life of solitary people or a group of solitary people is like or of a life in which children are admitted. It is absolutely, totally different. You have no right to demand of a person something when he has no free choice; and so long as a person is not formed, has not attained a certain maturity, you cannot make him choose. When one reaches this maturity, then one chooses. And the children here have not come of themselves. Most of you were not taller than a boot — when you came here, how old were you?... One cannot tell them: "You have chosen, therefore you have to take it or leave it, either you do this or you go away." They have been brought here, hence it is one's duty to give them what they need; and the needs of children are not at all the same as those of big people. It is much more complicated.

Now things are different, because now people are not told: "You are going to come here to do yoga"; they are told: "You are going to try to learn about the conditions under which earthly life can be bettered." So people come and study. When one thinks he knows what he wants to learn, he goes away. It is not the same thing. And it is not the same conditions as when one comes with a definite and single aim like realising the Divine in his physical life and nothing else in the world counts for him but that. In order to choose you must at least know a little the elements to choose from. And for that you must have a certain inner formation, a certain culture. And you certainly do not have that when you are five years old — except some; some among you (more than one would believe) knew very well why they

*30 September 1953*

had come, although they could not formulate it in words. They felt it very intensely. And when their parents tried to take them away, they refused stubbornly, saying: "No, no, I want to remain here." Even at the age of five, although they could not know in their head the reason why, because the brain was not formed. But the psychic consciousness was there, and they could feel. Well, these children are of an infinitely higher stuff than that of people who have already had three-fourths of their head blunted by the education they have been given in ordinary schools and who come here quite convinced that they know many things, that they are well acquainted with life. They have a formed character and have acquired many bad habits. There, then.

*Are remembrance and memory the same thing?*

Not necessarily. Memory is a mental phenomenon, purely mental. Remembrance can be a phenomenon of consciousness. One can remember in all the domains of one's being: one can remember vitally, one can remember physically, one can remember psychically, one can remember mentally also. But memory is a purely mental phenomenon. Memory can, first of all, be deformed and it can also be effaced, one can forget. The phenomenon of consciousness is very precise; if you can take the consciousness back to the state in which it was, things come back exactly as they were. It is as though you relived the same moment. You can relive it once, twice, ten times, a hundred times, but you relive a phenomenon of consciousness. It is very different from the memory of a fact which you inscribe somewhere in your brain. And if the cerebral associations are disturbed in the least (for there are many things in your brain and it is a very delicate instrument), if there is the slightest disturbance, your memory goes out of order. And then holes are formed and you forget. On the other hand, if you know how to bring back a particular state of consciousness in you, it comes back exactly the same as it was. Now, a remembrance can also be purely mental and it may be a continuation of cerebral activities, but that is mental remembrance. And you have remembrances in feeling, remembrances in sensation....

*The other day, you said: To enlarge your memory, you must widen your consciousness. Is it the same thing for remembrance?*

I meant to say that a phenomenon of memory should be replaced by a phenomenon of consciousness. I do not know in what sense I used the word memory the other day. It can be only in this sense.

*Memory in studying.*

Well, yes, it is that. That is what I meant: replace a purely mental memory by states of consciousness. That is exactly what I wanted to say. For, if you try to learn a thing by heart, after a time you are sure to forget it. Or else there are holes: you remember one thing and you do not remember another. But if you associate a particular knowledge with a phenomenon of consciousness, you can always bring it back and the knowledge will come back as it was.

*Voilà, au revoir* my children.

# 7 October 1953

> *"The method by which you will be most successful depends on the consciousness you have developed and the character of the forces you are able to bring into play. You can live in the consciousness of the completed cure or change and by the force of your inner formation slowly bring about the outward change. Or if you know and have the vision of the force that is able to effect these things and if you have the skill to handle it, you can call it down and apply it in the parts where its action is needed, and it will work out the change. Or, again, you can present your difficulty to the Divine and ask of It the cure, putting confidently your trust in the Divine Power."*
>
> Questions and Answers 1929 (23 June)

*What is this "consciousness of the completed cure"?*

This does not mean that there is a specific consciousness of the completed cure. It means: "To live in a state of consciousness that's conformable to a complete cure." How shall I explain it?... You have in your mind a picture or an image or formation which realises in itself all the necessary relations and elements for the cure to exist and be total. This is called "having the consciousness of a complete cure". It does not mean that there is a state of consciousness which is in itself a complete cure, and that if you get this consciousness, well, you get the cure. It is not like that. Have you understood the difference?

> *"In some the aspiration moves on the mental levels or in the vital field; some have a spiritual aspiration. On the quality of the aspiration depends the force that answers*

291

*and the work that it comes to do. To make yourself blank in meditation creates an inner silence; it does not mean that you have become nothing or have become a dead and inert mass. Making yourself an empty vessel, you invite that which shall fill it. It means that you release the stress of your inner consciousness towards realisation. The nature of the consciousness and the degree of its stress determine the forces that you bring into play and whether they shall help and fulfil or fail or even harm and hinder."*

*Questions and Answers 1929 (23 June)*

*What is the difference between mental aspiration, vital aspiration and spiritual aspiration?*

In what way do you aspire in the mind and in the vital or aspire spiritually?

A mental aspiration means that the thought-power aspires to have knowledge, for instance, or else to have the power to express itself well or have clear ideas, a logical reasoning. One may aspire for many things; that all the faculties and capacities of the mind may be developed and placed at the service of the Divine. This is a mental aspiration.

Or you may have an aspiration in the vital; if you have desires or troubles, storms, inner difficulties, you may aspire for peace, to be quite impartial, without desire or preference, to be a good docile instrument without any personal whims, always at the Divine's disposal. This is a vital aspiration.

You may have a physical aspiration also; that the body may feel the need to acquire a kind of equipoise in which all the parts of the being will be well balanced, and that you may have the power to hold off illness at a distance or overcome it fast when it enters trickily, and that the body may always function normally, harmoniously, in perfect health. That is a physical aspiration.

A spiritual aspiration means having an intense need to unite

7 October 1953

with the Divine, to give oneself totally to the Divine, not to live outside the divine Consciousness so that the Divine may be all in all for you in your integral being, and you feel the need of a constant communion with Him, of the sense of his presence, of his guidance in all that you do, and of his harmonising all the movements of the being. That is a spiritual aspiration.

*Mother, does aspiration come from the psychic?*

Not necessarily. Each part of the being can have its own aspiration.

*How can the physical manage to aspire, since it is the mind that thinks?*

As long as it is the mind that thinks, your physical is something that's three-fourths inert and without its own consciousness. There is a physical consciousness proper, a consciousness of the body; the body is conscious of itself, and it has its own aspiration. So long as one thinks of one's body, one is not in one's physical consciousness. The body has a consciousness that's quite personal to it and altogether independent of the mind. The body is completely aware of its own functioning or its own equilibrium or disequilibrium, and it becomes absolutely conscious, in quite a precise way, if there is a disorder somewhere or other, and (how shall I put it?) it is in contact with that and feels it very clearly, even if there are no external symptoms. The body is aware if the whole working is harmonious, well balanced, quite regular, functioning as it should; it has that kind of plenitude, a sense of plenitude, of joy and strength — something like the joy of living, acting, moving in an equilibrium full of life and energy. Or else the body can be aware that it is ill-treated by the vital and the mind and that this harms its own equilibrium, and it suffers from this. That may produce a complete disequilibrium in it. And so on.

One can develop one's physical consciousness so well that even if one is fully exteriorised, even if the vital goes completely out of the body, the body has a personal, independent consciousness which enables it to move, to do all kinds of very simple things without the vital's being there, quite independently. The body can learn how to speak: the mind and the vital may be outside it, very far away, busy elsewhere, but due to the link joining them with matter, they can still find expression through a body wherein there is no mind or vital, and which yet can learn to speak and repeat what the others say. The body can move; I don't mean that it can exert much, but it can move. It can do small, very simple things. It can write, for instance, learn how to write as it can learn to speak. It does speak: a little (how to put it?) slowly, with a little difficulty, but still it can speak clearly (sufficiently clearly) for one to understand. And yet the mind and vital may have gone out altogether, may be completely outside. There is a body-consciousness.

And so, when one has developed this body-consciousness, one can have a very clear perception of the opposition between the different kinds of consciousness. When the body needs something and is aware that this is what it needs, and the vital wants something else and the mind yet another, well, there may very well be a discussion among them, and contradictions and conflicts. And one can discern very clearly what the poise of the body is, the need of the body in itself, and in what way the vital interferes and destroys this equilibrium most often and harms the development so much, because it is ignorant. And when the mind comes in, it creates yet another disorder which is added to the one between the vital and the physical, by introducing its ideas and norms, its principles and rules, its laws and all that, and as it doesn't take into account exactly the needs of the other, it wants to do what everybody does. Human beings have a much more delicate and uncertain health than animals because their mind intervenes and disturbs the equilibrium. The body, left to itself, has a very sure instinct. For

**7 October 1953**

instance, never will the body if left to itself eat when it doesn't need to or take something which will be harmful to it. And it will sleep when it needs to sleep, it will act when it needs to act. The instinct of the body is very sure. It is the vital and the mind which disturb it: one by its desires and caprices, the other by its principles, dogmas, laws and ideas. And unfortunately, in civilisation as it is understood, with the kind of education given to children, this sure instinct of the body is completely destroyed: it is the rest that dominate. And naturally things happen as they do: one eats things that are harmful, one doesn't take rest when one needs to or sleeps too much when it is not necessary or does things one shouldn't do and spoils one's health completely.

> *Sometimes, Mother, when children are interested in something, they don't want to go to bed, then what should be done? Just a few minutes earlier they said they were sleepy, and then they start playing and say they don't want to go to bed.*

They shouldn't be allowed to play when they are sleepy. This is exactly the intrusion of vital movements. A child who doesn't live much with older people (it is bad for children to live much among older people), a child left to itself will sleep spontaneously whatever it may be doing, the moment it needs to sleep. Only, when children are used to living with older people, well, they catch all the habits of the grown-ups. Specially when they are told: "Oh! you can't do this because you are young! When you are older, you can do it. You can't eat this because you are small, when you are bigger you will be able to eat it. At this particular time you must go to bed because you are young...." So, naturally, they have that idea that they must grow up at any cost or at least look grown-up!

*"The very intensity of your faith may mean that the*

> *Divine has already chosen that the thing it points to shall be done. An unshakable faith is a sign of the presence of the Divine Will, an evidence of what shall be."*
> Questions and Answers 1929 (23 June)

> *A dynamic faith and a great trust, aren't they the same thing?*

Not necessarily. One should know of what stuff the faith and the trust are made. Because, for instance, if you live normally, under quite normal conditions — without having extravagant ideas and a depressing education — well, through all your youth and usually till you are about thirty, you have an absolute trust in life. If, for example, you are not surrounded by people who, as soon as you have a cold in the head, get into a flurry and rush to the doctor and give you medicines, if you are in normal surroundings and happen to have something — an accident or a slight illness — there is this certainty in the body, this absolute trust that it will be all right: "It is nothing, it will pass off. It is sure to go. I shall be quite well tomorrow or in a few days. It will surely be cured" — whatever you may have caught. That is indeed the normal condition of the body. An absolute trust that all life lies before it and that all will be well. And this helps enormously. One gets cured nine times out of ten, one gets cured very quickly with this confidence: "It is nothing; what is it after all? Just an accident, it will pass off, it is nothing." And there are people who keep it for a very long time, a very long time, a kind of confidence — nothing can happen to them. Their life is all before them, fully, and nothing can happen to them. And what will happen to them is of no importance at all: all will be well, perforce; they have the whole of life before them. Naturally, if you live in surroundings where there are morbid ideas and people pass their time recounting disastrous and catastrophic things, then you may think wrongly. And if you think wrongly, this reacts on your body. Otherwise, the body as it is can keep

## 7 October 1953

this confidence till the age of forty or fifty — it depends upon people — some know how to live a normal, balanced life. But the body is quite confident about its life. It is only if thought comes in and brings all kinds of morbid and unhealthy imaginations, as I said, that it changes everything. I have seen instances like that: children who had these little accidents one has when running and playing about: they did not even think about it. And it disappeared immediately. I have seen others whose family has drummed into them since the time they could understand, that everything is dangerous, that there are microbes everywhere, that one must be very careful, that the least wound may prove disastrous, that one must be altogether on one's guard and take great care that nothing serious happens.... So, they must have their wounds dressed, must be washed with disinfectants, and there they sit wondering: "What is going to happen to me? Oh! I may perhaps get tetanus, a septic fever...." Naturally, in such cases one loses confidence in life and the body feels the effects keenly. Three-fourths of its resistance disappears. But normally, naturally, it is the body which knows that it must remain healthy, and it knows it has the power to react. And if something happens, it tells this something: "It is nothing, it will go away, don't think about it, it is over"; and it does go.

That of course is absolute trust.

Now, you are speaking of "dynamic faith". Dynamic faith is something different. If one has within him faith in the divine grace, that the divine grace is watching over him, and that no matter what happens the divine grace is there, watching over him, this one may keep all one's life and always; and with this one can pass through all dangers, face all difficulties, and nothing stirs, for you have the faith and the divine grace is with you. It is an infinitely stronger, more conscious, more lasting force which does not depend upon the conditions of your physical build, does not depend upon anything except the divine grace alone, and hence it leans on the Truth and nothing can shake it. It is very different.

> *Sometimes children ask us why we are here. What should we tell them?*

That depends upon their age, my child, and upon what they are. It depends upon their sincerity. You can't give the same answer to everyone.

But do the tiny tots sometimes ask?... Do the youngest ask why they are here?

> *Not the youngest — Purnima, Tarulata.*

At that age, already it's the age when one questions and doubts.

The very tiny ones, if they ask this, it is wonderful. There is only one very simple answer to give them: "My children, it is because this is the divine will. It is due to the divine grace that you are here. Be happy, be calm, be at peace, do not question, all will be well." And when they grow older they already begin to reason, then it is no longer so well, no longer so easy. But that depends, as I said, that depends upon how intelligent they are, how great is their opening. There are those who are predestined, who are here because they should be here. With these it is easy. You have only to tell them: "My children, it is because you belong to a future which is being built up, and it is here that it is being built." For them it is very simple, it is true. There are those who are here because their parents are here, for no other reason. So it is difficult to tell them that unless you tell them quite simply: "Because your father and mother are here."

> *But how can we understand?*

Ah! that indeed depends upon you.

The first thing is to learn how to know by identity. That is indispensable when one has the responsibility for others. To learn how to guide other people, the first indispensable step is to know how to enter into their minds so as to know them

## 7 October 1953

— not to project one's thought, imagine what they are, but go out of oneself and enter into them, to know what is happening there. Then, in this way, one knows them because one is they. When one knows only oneself in others, that means one knows nothing. One may be completely mistaken. One imagines it is like this or that — one judges by appearances or else through mental preferences, preconceived ideas; that is to say, one knows nothing. But there is one condition in which one doesn't even need to know, to try to know what somebody is like: one can't do otherwise but feel what he is, for he is a projection of oneself. And unless one knows how to do that, one can never do what is necessary for people — unless one feels as they feel, thinks as they think, unless one is able to enter into them as though one were they themselves. That is the only way. If you try to know with a small active mind, you will never know anything — nor by looking at people and telling yourself: "Why, he does this in this way and that way, so he must be like that." That is impossible.

So, the first task of those who have a responsibility — for instance, those who are in charge of educating other children, taking care of others, from rulers to teachers and monitors — their first task is to learn how to identify themselves with the others, to feel as they do. Then one knows what one should do. One keeps one's inner light, keeps one's consciousness where it ought to be, very high above, in the light, and at the same time gets identified, and so one feels what they are, what their reactions are, what their thoughts, and one holds that before the light one has: one succeeds in thinking out perfectly well what should be done for them. You will tell each one what he needs to hear, you will act with each one as is necessary to make him understand. And that is why it is a wonderful grace to have the responsibility for a certain number of people, for that obliges you to make the most essential progress. And I hasten to tell you that ninety-nine times out of a hundred, people don't make it. But that is exactly why things are in such a bad way. Particularly those who have the responsibility of governing a country — this is the last thing they think about! They are very eager rather to keep their way of seeing and their way of feeling, and fiercely refrain from realising the needs of those over whom they rule. But indeed one can see that the result is not up to much; so far it is evident that it can't be said that governments have been remarkable institutions. It is the same thing on all the levels: there are small governments, there are big governments. But the laws are the same, for all. And unless, when giving a lesson, you are able, there and then, to take in the entire atmosphere, to gather the vibrations around people, put them all together, keep all that before you, and become aware of what you can do with this stuff (with the vibrations you can spread, the forces you can give out, those which will be received, those which will be assimilated), unless you do that, mostly you are wasting your time, you too. In order to do the least work, one must make a lot of progress.

> *"The supramental does not take interest in mental things in the same way as the mind. It takes its own interest in all the movements of the universe, but it is from a different point of view and with a different vision. The world presents to it an entirely different appearance; there is a reversal of outlook and everything is seen from there as other than what it seems to the mind and often even the opposite. Things have another meaning; their aspect, their motion and process, everything about them, are watched with other eyes. Everything here is followed by the supermind; the mind movements and not less the vital, the material movements, all the play of the universe has for it a very deep interest, but of another kind."*
> Questions and Answers 1929 (23 June)

*In what does the supermind take interest?*

It takes interest in the transformation of the world — in the descent of forces in the material world and its transformation, in

## 7 October 1953

its preparation so that it may be able to receive the supramental forces. And it is conscious of the difference between the world as it is and the world as it ought to be. Every moment it sees the gulf between what is and what should be, between the truth and the falsehood that is expressed. And constantly it keeps this vision of the Truth which broods over the world, so that as soon as there is a little opening, it may descend and manifest itself. And what to the ordinary awareness seems quite natural is for it usually a play of obscure, ignorant, altogether unconscious forces. And it does not find that at all natural. It finds that a detestable accident and tries with all its strength to remedy it. It seeks, looks, and if there is any receptivity anywhere, it intensifies its action. It does not see men in their outward appearance but as vibrations more or less receptive and more or less dark or luminous, and wherever it sees a light it projects its force so that it may have its full effect. And instead of treating each being like a pawn on a chess-board, a small, well-defined person, it sees how forces enter, go out, stir, move and make all things move, how vibrations act. And it sees those vibrations which ascend and lead to progress and it sees those vibrations which fling you further and further into the darkness, which make you go down. And at times someone comes to you with ready-made words which he has learnt generally from books, though words of aspiration and goodwill, and he is answered by a strong rebuff and told that he should try to be sincere — he does not understand. This is because the Force sees that there is no sincerity — the Force does not see the words, does not hear the words, doesn't even see the ideas in the head but only the state of consciousness, whether the state of consciousness is sincere or not. There are other instances of people who seem to be quite frivolous and stupid and busy with useless things, and suddenly one helps them, encourages them, treats them like friends and comrades, for one sees shining in the depth of all that a sincerity, an aspiration which may have a childish form outwardly but which is there and very pure at times. And so one does many things for them which people don't understand, for they cannot see the reality behind the appearance. That is why I say that it is in an entirely different way that the supermind is interested, an entirely different way that it sees, an entirely different way that it knows.

*Isn't it more important to know oneself than to try to know others?*

Very important, of capital importance! Besides, that's the field of work given to each one. It is this one must understand, that each one — this totality of substance constituting your inner and outer body, the totality of substance with which your being is built from the outermost to the inmost — is a field of work; it is as though one had gathered together carefully, accumulated a certain number of vibrations and put them at your disposal for you to work upon them fully. It is like a field of action constantly at your disposal: night and day, waking or asleep, all the time — nobody can take it away from you, it is wonderful! You may refuse to use it (as most men do), but it is a mass to be transformed that is there in your hands, fully at your disposal, given to you for you to learn to work upon it. So, the most important thing is to begin by doing that. You can do nothing with others unless you are able to do it with yourself. You can never give a good advice to anyone unless you are able to give it to yourself first, and to follow it. And if you see a difficulty somewhere, the best way of changing this difficulty is to change it in yourself first. If you see a defect in anyone, you may be sure it is in you, and you begin to change it in yourself. And when you will have changed it in yourself, you will be strong enough to change it in others. And this is a wonderful thing, people don't realise what an infinite grace it is that this universe is arranged in such a way that there is a collection of substance, from the most material to the highest spiritual, all that gathered together into what is called a small individual, but at the disposal of a central

7 October 1953

Will. And that is yours, your field of work, nobody can take it away from you, it is your own property. And to the extent you can work upon it, you will be able to have an action upon the world. But only to that extent. One must do more for oneself, besides, than one does for others.

*Is it possible to know others before knowing oneself?*

Nothing is impossible. One can't say it is not possible. But if one is unaware of certain movements in oneself, it is certainly an anomaly to be conscious first of these in others. It is an anomaly. It may exist. There may be people so decentralised that they are more sensitive about others than in themselves. But still, usually they are considered a little morbid. This does not give them a very great inner equilibrium, they become unbalanced. There are people who are all at sea, they are like a cork upon the waves: it goes here and there, jumps this way and that. They have no line of consciousness.... It is not an enviable state. I don't think, truly, sincerely I don't think that it is possible to help anyone unless one has already helped oneself first. If you are unconscious, how do you expect to bring consciousness into others! This seems to me an insoluble problem. That is what people usually do, but that's no reason for approving it. This is exactly why, I believe, things go so wrong. It is like those who seeing others quarrelling rush forward and begin shouting louder than they to tell them, "Keep quiet!"

*You said that to each individual is given a problem to solve. So each man upon earth has to live individually, for, in living collectively one has the difficulty of the collectivity also: it is not only one's own difficulty.*

Yes, but man happens to be a social animal, and so, instinctively, he forms groups. But that also is why those who wished to go fast and did not feel themselves sufficiently strong retired into solitude. That is the reason, the justification of the ascetic who goes away into solitude, for he tries to cut himself off from the world. Only... there is an "only". One can do that physically to a certain extent, up to a point, cut oneself off from physical nature — not totally. It has been noticed, for instance, that ascetics who went away to sit under a tree in the forest, in a very short while became extraordinarily interested in all the animals living in the forest: it is the need of physical relationship with other living beings. It is possible that some do not need this, but it is a fairly general rule.

But solidarity does not stop there. There is a vital solidarity and a mental solidarity which you cannot prevent. There is, despite everything (though men are much more individualised than animals), there is a spirit of the species. There are collective suggestions which don't need to be expressed in words. There are atmospheres one cannot escape. It is certain (for this I know by experience), it is certain that there is a degree of individual perfection and transformation which cannot be realised without the whole of humanity having made a particular progress. And this happens by successive steps. There are things in Matter which cannot be transformed unless the whole of Matter has undergone transformation to a certain degree. One cannot isolate oneself completely. It is not possible. One can do the work, one can choose: there are people who have chosen to go into solitude and try to realise in themselves the ideal they saw — usually they reached a certain point, then stopped there, they could not go further. It has been thus historically. I was saying the other day: "There are perhaps people upon earth whom I don't know who have realised extraordinary things" but exactly because they have isolated themselves from the earth, the earth does not know them. This is just to say that nothing is impossible. It seems doubtful, is all that I can say. But it is impossible, even if one isolates oneself physically, to do so vitally and mentally. There is the vast terrestrial atmosphere in which one is born, and there is a sort of spirit or genius of the human race; well, this genius

*7 October 1953*

must have reached a certain degree of perfection for anyone to be able to go farther. It is not that one has to wait till all have done it, no; but it is as though all had to reach a certain level for one to be able to take one's spring and go farther.... Surely the individual will always be ahead of the mass, there's no doubt about that, but there will always be a proportion and a relation.

*On what plane are men most united?*

You mean "most interdependent"?

*No, I mean a common will.*

A common will? You must not mix up things. If you are telling me about the goodwill among human beings, this is in the psychic, there's no shadow of a doubt about it. But there is a kind of vital interdependence, quite considerable, more than the physical, I believe. For instance, the First World War was the result of a tremendous descent of the forces of the vital world (hostile forces of the vital world) into the material world. Even those who were conscious of this descent and consequently armed to defend themselves against it, suffered from its consequences. The world, the whole earth suffered from its consequences. There was a general deterioration from the vital point of view, I could say, which was inevitable even for those who consciously knew whence the force came, whence the deterioration came, and who could therefore fight against it consciously — they could not prevent certain effects being produced in the earth atmosphere. Naturally, men do not know what happened to them; all that they have said is that everything had become worse since the war. That was all that they could affirm. For example, the moral level went down very much. It was simply the result of a formidable descent of the vital world: forces of disorder, forces of corruption, forces of deterioration, forces of destruction, forces of violence, forces of cruelty.

## Questions and Answers 1953

*Why this descent?*

Perhaps it was a reaction, for there was another Force coming down which wanted to do its work, and perhaps those forces did not want it — it disturbed their habits. It is like a government which fears that it will be thrown out and so intervenes violently in order to keep in power.

# 14 October 1953

> Q. "If the Divine that is all love is the source of the creation, whence have come all the evils abounding upon earth?"
>
> "All is from the Divine; but the One Consciousness, the Supreme has not created the world directly out of itself; a Power has gone out of it and has descended through many gradations of its workings and passed through many agents. There are many creators or rather 'formateurs', form-makers, who have presided over the creation of the world. They are intermediary agents and I prefer to call them 'Formateurs' and not 'Creators'; for what they have done is to give the form and turn and nature to matter. There have been many, and some have formed things harmonious and benignant and some have shaped things mischievous and evil. And some too have been distorters rather than builders, for they have interfered and spoiled what was begun well by others."
>
> Questions and Answers 1929 (30 June)

*You say, "Many creators or rather 'formateurs', form-makers, have presided over the creation of the world." Who are these 'formateurs'?*

That depends. They have been given many names. All has been done by gradations and through individual beings of all kinds. Each state of being is inhabited by entities, individualities and personalities and each one has created a world around him or has contributed to the formation of certain beings upon earth. The last creators are those of the vital world, but there are beings of the Overmind (Sri Aurobindo calls this plane the Overmind), who have created, given forms, sent out emanations, and these emanations again had their emanations and so on. What I meant is that it is not the Divine Will that acted directly on Matter to give to the world the required form, it is by passing through layers, so to say, planes of the world, as for example, the mental plane — there are so many beings on the mental plane who are form-makers, who have taken part in the formation of some beings who have incarnated upon earth. On the vital plane also the same thing happens.

For example, there is a tradition which says that the whole world of insects is the outcome of the form-makers of the vital world, and that this is why they take such absolutely diabolical shapes when they are magnified under the microscope. You saw the other day, when you were shown the microbes in water? Naturally the pictures were made to amuse, to strike the imagination, but they are based on real forms, so magnified, however, that they look like monsters. Almost the whole world of insects is a world of microscopic monsters which, had they been larger in size, would have been quite terrifying. So it is said these are entities of the vital world, beings of the vital who created that for fun and amused themselves forming all these impossible beasts which make human life altogether unpleasant.

*Did these intermediaries also come out of the Divine Power?*

Through intermediaries, yes, not directly. These beings are not in direct contact with the Divine (there are exceptions, I mean as a general rule), they are beings who are in relation with other beings, who are again in relation with others, and these with still others, and so on, in a hierarchy, up to the Supreme.

*If they came out of the Divine, why are they evil?*

Evil? That I think I have explained to you once: it is enough just not to remain under the direct influence of the Divine and

## 14 October 1953

not to follow the movement of creation or expansion as willed by the Divine; this rupture of contact is enough to produce the greatest of disorders, that of division. Well, even the most luminous, the most powerful beings may choose to follow their own movement instead of obeying the divine movement. And though in themselves they may be quite wonderful and if human beings saw them they would take them for the very Godhead, they can, because they follow their own will instead of working in harmony with the universe, be the source of very great evils, very great disorders, very great massive obstructions. But don't you see, the question is badly put, I laughed just now when I read the question.[1] It is a childish way of speaking. This person says: "If God is everything in the world, why are there evil things in the world?" Now, if she had told me that, I would have simply answered: there is nothing which is not God, only it is in a disorder. One must try to remedy it — God is not love alone, He is all things, and if that appears to us — to us — altogether wrong, it is because it is not arranged properly. There have been movements exactly of the kind I spoke to you about.

You may ask why it happened. Well, certainly it is not the mind, you know, which can say why it happened. It happened, that is all. In reality the only thing that concerns us is that it has happened. It is perhaps an accident to begin with.... If you look at the thing from a philosophical point of view, it is evident that the universe in which we live is a movement among many others and this movement follows a law which is its own (and which is perhaps not the same in the others), and if the Will was for the world to be built on the principle of choice, of the freedom of choice, then one cannot prevent disorderly movements from taking place until knowledge comes and the choice is enlightened. If one is free to choose, one can also choose bad things, not necessarily the good, for if it were a

---

[1] "If the Divine who is all love be the source of the creation, whence have come all the evils abounding upon earth?"

thing decided beforehand, it would no longer be a free choice. You see, when such questions are put, the mind only answers and it reduces the problem, it reduces it to a more or less elementary mental formula; but that corresponds only very vaguely and superficially and incompletely with the reality of things.

To be able to understand, one must become. If you want to understand the why and how of the universe, you must identify yourself with the universe. It is not impossible but it is not very easy either, particularly for children.

This was one of the most childish questions that she put — altogether childish: "If He is just, why is there injustice? If He is good, why is there wickedness? If He is love, why is there hatred?" — But He is all! So He is not merely this or that, or only, exclusively this — He is all. That is, to be more correct, it should be said that all is He. There are notions about creation, very widespread upon earth, which have been accepted more or less for a long time in human thought, that are quite simplistic! There is "something" (truly speaking, one does not know what), and then there is a God who puts this something into form and creates the world out of it. So if you have such notions, you have a justifiable right to say to this God: "Well, you have indeed created a world, it's a pretty one, that world of yours!" Although, according to the story, after seven days of labour, he declared that it was very good — but it was good for him. Perhaps it may have amused him immensely, but as for us who are in the world, we do not find it good at all! Don't you see, the conception and the way of putting it are altogether childish. It is just like the story of the potter who puts his pot in shape — this God is a human being, formidable in proportions and power, but looking strangely like a man. It is man who makes God in his image, not God who makes man in his image! So each time a question is put in an incomplete or childish way, it is impossible to give an answer to it truly, for the question is badly put. You say something, you affirm it. But what right have you to assert it? Because you affirm that, you conclude: "Since that

## 14 October 1953

is this, how does it happen that it is so?" But "that is this" is your statement. It does not mean that it is so!

There is only one single solution to the problem — not to make any distinction between God and the universe at the origin. The universe *is* the Divine projected in space, and God *is* the universe at its origin. It is the same thing under one aspect or another. And you cannot divide them. It is the opposite conception to that of the "creator" and his "work". Only, it is very convenient to speak of the creator and his work, it makes explanations very easy and the teaching quite elementary. But it is not the truth. And then you say: "How is it that God who is all-powerful has allowed the world to be like this?" But it is your own conception! It is because you yourself happen to be in the midst of a set of circumstances that seems to you unpleasant, so you project that upon the Divine and you tell him: "Why have you made such a world?" — "I did not make it. It is you yourself. And if you become Myself once again, you will no longer feel as you do. What makes you feel as you do is that you are no longer Myself." This is what He could tell you in answer. And the fact is that when you succeed in uniting your consciousness with the divine consciousness, there is no problem left. Everything appears quite natural and simple and all right and exactly what it had to be. But when you cut yourself off from the origin and stand over against Him, then truly everything goes wrong, nothing can go right!

But if you ask for a logic that pushes things to the extreme end, you question how it is that the Divine has tolerated parts of his own self to be separated from him and all this disorder to be created. You may say that. And I then will reply: "If you want to know, it is better to unite yourself with the Divine, for that is the only way of knowing why He has done these things." It is not by questioning Him mentally, for your mind cannot understand. And I repeat it, when you reach such an identification, all problems are solved. And this feeling that things are not all right and that they should be otherwise, comes just because there is a divine will for a constant unfolding in perpetual progress and things that were must give place to things that shall be and shall be better than what the others were. And the world that was good yesterday is no longer good tomorrow. The whole world that could appear absolutely harmonious and perfect at one time, well, today it is discordant, no longer harmonious, because now we conceive and see the possibility of a better world. And if we were to find it all right we would not do what we ought to do, that is, make the effort needed for it to become better.

There comes a time when all these notions appear so childish! And this happens solely because one is shut up within oneself. With this consciousness which is your own, which is like a grain of sand in the infinite vastness, you want to know and judge the infinite? It is impossible. You must first of all come out of yourself, and then unite with the infinite and only afterwards can you begin to understand what it is, not before. You project your consciousness — what you are, the thoughts you have, the capacity of understanding you have — you project this upon the Divine and then say: "That is all wrong." I quite understand! But there is no possibility of knowing unless you identify yourself. I do not see how, for example, a drop of water could tell you what the ocean is like. That's how it is.

> *"When one takes up the human body, one accepts along with it a mass of these general suggestions, race ideas, race feelings of mankind, associations, attractions, repulsions, fears."*
>
> Questions and Answers 1929 (30 June)

*When one takes up a human body, is it necessary to accept suggestions of fear?*

It seems more inevitable than necessary!... One doesn't even perceive that one is accepting them. We said the other day that

## 14 October 1953

when a psychic being enters a body, it is as though it fell on its head — it is a little stunned for a time. So during this period it is under the influence of these suggestions without even knowing it. But as soon as it wakes up, it can come out of that; it is not at all necessary to accept them. Only, one must know that they are suggestions. One must be able to separate oneself from the purely human consciousness, the body consciousness. And once you can look at it from above, you can free yourself from these suggestions quite well. You can free yourself from all suggestions, but for that you must rise above them. If that were not possible, it would be impossible to do yoga.

But you do not become aware of it, it is a constant thing. For example, there is that formidable collective suggestion of death. But how can you get rid of that idea unless you are able to create in you an immortal consciousness? Once you have created in you the immortal consciousness, you can be freed of the suggestion. Otherwise it is not possible. And you are not aware of it because you live in it quite normally — you are full of the movements and ideas belonging to the human race, which are not personal to you at all. You are not aware of them because they are very intimately bound up with your consciousness. But the moment you can free yourself from this human consciousness and enter a domain where, for example, life in the body becomes almost an accident — it can be here, it can be there, it can be over there — you are no longer tied to the body. You look at it and say: it is almost like an accident (it may be a choice also, but most often it is an accident). Then, from that moment you are no longer tied down, for you are conscious in a being which is no longer merely, exclusively human. But till that moment you are not even aware. You have no means of becoming aware. And if you come to the purely mental domain, there are such strong ideas; for example, that the infinite cannot be within the finite, that what begins will surely have an end — ideas of this kind which seem wonderfully luminous, and yet are idiocies. But all that belongs to the collective human mentality and there is nothing more difficult than to drive this out of the head of people who think themselves very clever.... Perhaps you have not yet put these problems to yourselves because you have not yet begun studying philosophy, but when you begin, you will see. And this will be given to you as deathless verities which cannot be touched! Yet this is nonsense. One day I would like... (*turning to Nolini*) You don't have the *Advent* here? It is in the *Advent*, that text of Sri Aurobindo's. One day we shall translate it together from English into French. He has made a wonderful observation upon logic and reason[2]... And all that never even crossed your mind: that these are collective suggestions and one must come out of them. Not only does it not appear to you as slavery, but it appears to you as an illumination. Well, it's not that at all!

*Mother, sometimes we are terribly afraid. What should we do in such a case?*

Ah! that depends on the nature of the fear. Is it a fear without a cause or is it based on a cause? Because the remedy differs.

*It is based on a cause.*

Ah! For example, when someone is ill, one is afraid of catching the illness....

*No, someone is dead.*

And one is afraid to die.

There are two remedies. There are many, but two at least are there. In any case, the use of a deeper consciousness is essential.

---

[2] Perhaps the reference is to the following Aphorism of Sri Aurobindo quoted in the *Advent* of August 1953:
"Logic is the worst enemy of Truth, as self-righteousness is the worst enemy of virtue; for the one cannot see its own errors nor the other its own imperfections."
(*Thoughts and Aphorisms: CWSA Vol. 12, p. 428*).

## 14 October 1953

One remedy consists in saying that it is something that happens to everyone (let us take it on that level), yes, it is a thing that happens to everybody, and therefore, sooner or later, it will come and there is no reason why one should be afraid, it is quite a normal thing. You may add one more idea to this, that according to experience (not yours but just the collective human experience), circumstances being the same, absolutely identical, in one case people die, in another they do not — why? And if you push the thing a little further still, you say to yourself that after all it must depend on something which is altogether outside your consciousness — and in the end one dies when one has to die. That is all. When one has to die one dies, and when one has not to die, one does not die. Even when you are in mortal danger, if it is not your hour to die, you will not die, and even if you are out of all danger, just a scratch on your foot will be enough to make you die, for there are people who have died of a pin-scratch on the foot — because the time had come. Therefore, fear has no sense. What you can do is to rise to a state of consciousness where you can say, "It is like that, we accept the fact because it seems to be recognised as an inevitable fact. But I do not need to worry, for it will come only when it must come. So I don't need to feel afraid: when it is not to come, it will not come to me, but when it must come to me, it will come. And as it will come to me inevitably, it is better I do not fear the thing; on the contrary, one must accept what is perfectly natural." This is a well-known remedy, that is to say, very much in use.

There is another, a little more difficult, but better, I believe. It lies in telling oneself: "This body is not I", and in trying to find in oneself the part which is truly one's self, until one has found one's psychic being. And when one has found one's psychic being — immediately, you understand — one has the sense of immortality. And one knows that what goes out or what comes in is just a matter of convenience: "I am not going to weep over a pair of shoes I put aside when it is full of holes! When my pair of shoes is worn out I cast it aside, and I do not weep." Well, the psychic being has taken this body because it needed to use it for its work, but when the time comes to leave the body, that is to say, when one must leave it because it is no longer of any use for some reason or other, one leaves the body and has no fear. It is quite a natural gesture — and it is done without the least regret, that's all.

And the moment you are in your psychic being, you have that feeling, spontaneously, effortlessly. You soar above the physical life and have the sense of immortality. As for me, I consider this the best remedy. The other is an intellectual, common-sense, rational remedy. This is a deep experience and you can always get it back as soon as you recover the contact with your psychic being. This is a truly interesting phenomenon, for it is automatic. The moment you are in contact with your psychic being, you have the feeling of immortality, of having always been and being always, eternally. And then what comes and goes — these are life's accidents, they have no importance. Yes, this is the best remedy. The other is like the prisoner finding good reasons for accepting his prison. This one is like a man for whom there's no longer any prison.

Now, a third thing also one must know, but for this one has to be a mighty yogi. For this means knowing that death is not an inevitable thing, it is an accident which has been occurring till now (which seems in any case to have always occurred till now), and that we have put it into our head and our will to conquer this accident and overcome it. But it is so terrible, so formidable a battle against all the laws of Nature, against all collective suggestions, all earthly habits, that unless, as I have said, you are a first-rate warrior whom nothing frightens, it is better not to begin the battle. You must be an absolutely intrepid hero, for at every step, at every second you have to fight a battle against all established things. So it is not a very easy thing. And even as an individual it is a battle against oneself, because (I think I have already told you this once), if you want your physical consciousness to be in a state which admits of physical

## 14 October 1953

immortality, you must be free to such an extent from everything which at present represents the physical consciousness that it becomes every second a battle. All feelings, all sensations, all thoughts, all reflexes, all attractions, all repulsions, all existing things, all that forms the fabric of our physical life must be overcome, transformed and freed from all their habits. This is a battle of every second against thousands and millions of enemies. Unless you feel you are a hero, it is better not to try. Because this solution, well... I do not know, but I believe I was asked this question once before: "Has anyone succeeded so far?" To tell you the truth I don't know, for I have not met such a person.... I do not have the feeling that anyone has succeeded till now. But it is possible. Only, he or she who has done it has not declared it, at least, not till now.

The other two solutions are safe and sure and within your reach. Now, there is a small remedy which is very very easy. For it is based on a simple personal question of one's common sense.... You must observe yourself a little and say that when you are afraid it is as though the fear was attracting the thing you are afraid of. If you are afraid of illness, it is as though you were attracting the illness. If you are afraid of an accident, it is as though you were attracting the accident. And if you look into yourself and around yourself a little, you will find it out, it is a persistent fact. So if you have just a little common sense, you say: "It is stupid to be afraid of anything, for it is precisely as though I were making a sign to that thing to come to me. If I had an enemy who wanted to kill me, I would not go and tell him: 'You know, it's me you want to kill!' " It is something like that. So since fear is bad, we won't have it. And if you say you are unable to prevent it by your reason, well, that shows you have no control over yourselves and must make a little effort to control yourselves. That is all.

Oh! There are many ways of curing oneself of fear. But in reality everyone finds his own way, the one good for him. There are people to whom you have simply to say: "Your fear is a weakness", and they would immediately find the means to look at it with contempt, for they have a horror of weakness. There are others, you tell them: "Fear is a suggestion from hostile forces, you must push it away, as you drive off hostile forces", and this is very effective. For each one it is different. But first of all you must know that fear is a very bad thing, very bad, it is a dissolvent; it is like an acid. If you put a drop of it on something, it eats into the substance. The first step is not to admit the possibility of fear. Yes, that's the first step. I knew people who used to boast about their fear. These are incurable. That is, quite naturally they would say, "Ah, just imagine, I was so frightened!" And then what! It is nothing to be proud of. With such people you can do nothing.

However, when once you recognise that fear is neither good nor favourable nor noble nor worthy of a consciousness a little enlightened, you begin to fight against it. And I say, one man's way is not another's; one must find one's own way; it depends on each one. Fear is also a terribly contagious collective thing — contagious, it is much more catching than the most contagious of illnesses. You breathe an atmosphere of fear and instantly you feel frightened, without even knowing why or how, nothing, simply because there was an atmosphere of fear. A panic at an accident is nothing but an atmosphere of fear spreading round over everybody. And it is quite curable. There have been numerous cases of a panic being stopped outright simply because some people refused the suggestion and could counteract it with an opposite suggestion. For mystics the best cure as soon as one begins to feel afraid of something is to think of the Divine and then snuggle in his arms or at his feet and leave him entirely responsible for everything that happens, within, outside, everywhere — and immediately the fear disappears. That is the cure for the mystic. It is the easiest of all. But everybody does not enjoy the grace of being a mystic.

*Sometimes there are latent powers in us of which we are*

## 14 October 1953

*unaware. To do a work, how is one to know whether one is capable of doing it or not?*

How can one know whether one is capable of doing it or not! By *trying*. That's the best thing. And if you do not succeed immediately, persevere. And you must know that if a strong urge, a very strong urge to do something comes to you, that means this work has something to do with you and you are capable of doing it. But one can have powers which are so well hidden that one has to dig long before finding them. So you must not get discouraged at the first setback, you must persist.

# 21 October 1953

*When a true artist concentrates and sees the Divine in himself, can he use art to express the Divine?*

And why not? Whom do you call an artist, first of all? A painter, a sculptor — Is that all? What else? What meaning do you give to the word "artist"? Of whom do you think when you speak of an artist? Of a painter or a sculptor?

*Someone who can draw.*

Yes, a painter, a draughtsman, it is the same thing. Of a painter, a sculptor, that's all? Painter and sculptor? Not of a musician or a writer or... I am asking you because the answer would be different according to the instances....

*I had thought of a draughtsman.*

For instance, there were in the Middle Ages — there still are today, but they were already there in the Middle Ages — men who made stained-glass windows, designs with pieces of coloured glass and in various forms. In the churches, in cathedrals, there were always stained-glass windows. Instead of ordinary windows, there were these coloured panes which made designs. It is a wonderful material, for there is the sun behind (in any case the full light), and these glasses were transparent; so they gave out a colour which was as though self-luminous, and these men made designs, made pictures with these coloured glasses cut out, you know, in special forms and painted in different colours. And that indeed was art. In all the cathedrals, the big churches, there were stained-glass windows; some of them were quite marvellous. And they expressed, for instance, the life of a

## 21 October 1953

saint or scenes from the life of Christ or... all kinds of things like that.

So, what is your question? Put it clearly.

*Whether one can express the Divine himself...*

Whether one can express the Divine himself in art? But in what can one express Him? I mean, what exactly do you call "expressing the Divine"? In words? In teachings? In books, finally? Or how else? Who has expressed the Divine completely in the material world?... It is only when the material world is transformed that it will be possible to express the Divine in his purity. And I don't see what difference there can be between art and any other activity. It is something which has the capacity to become fused, but not entirely, and it remains (how to put it?) an instrument for giving a form. And I don't see what difference this makes, whatever may be the form. If one can express the Divine with words, one can express Him with colours, express Him with sounds, express Him with forms. But in none of these instances is the expression perfect, for the union is not perfect. But when the world is transformed and the Divine is able to manifest Himself without being deformed, the expression will be perfect. But for the moment all expressions are on the same plane. None of them is better than any other. One mode of expression (I mean in itself) is not better than another. There is always *something* of the human personality, the being in form, which is there to give a limitation or deformation to what has to be expressed.

Art is just one activity like all others. Truly speaking, I was too polite to tell that lady[1] this, but I thought: "Why do you make distinctions like that, all this is the same thing." Do you catch what I mean?

---

[1] The one who asked the question in the conversation of 28 July: see *Questions and Answers 1929*.

*When one is identified with the Divine, does one see Him in the form one thinks He has?*

Usually. It is very rare — unless one is able to get rid of one's mental formation completely — it is very rare to see Him quite objectively. Besides, Sri Aurobindo always used to say that the relation with the Divine depended on what one wanted it to be. Everyone aspires for a particular form of relation, and for him the relation takes that form.

*Then, what is it in truth?*

Probably something that escapes form totally — or that can take all forms. There is no limitation to the expression of the Divine. He can express Himself without form and He can express Himself in all forms. And He expresses Himself in everyone according to each one's need. For even if somebody succeeds in becoming sufficiently impersonal so as to identify himself completely with the Divine, at that moment he will not be able to express it. And as soon as he is in a condition to express it, there will be something of the limited personality intervening and through this the experience has to pass. The moment of the experience is one thing and the expression of this experience is another. It may be simultaneous: there are people who while having the experience express what they feel in some form or other. Then it is simultaneous. But that does not prevent that which has the experience in its purity and that which expresses it from being two fairly different modes of being. And this difference is enough for one to be able to say in truth that it is impossible to know the Divine unless one becomes the Divine.

As for expressing Him, there is always a shifting; it always causes something like this (*gesture of changing levels*), whatever the mode of expression.

There remains only one field in which the experience has not been totally achieved, that is the purely material field. And there, it may be asked if truly, when the divine Consciousness descends into the body, the transformations will not be sufficient for there to be a possibility of integral expression.... But that is yet to come; it has not yet been done. And so long as it is not done, one cannot know. For even in the highest mental expression there is something which intervenes, due to the physical body. For the inspiration to come right down to the paper, for instance, well, despite everything, it must pass through very material vibrations which may change it. But if these very vibrations are transformed, then in that case it is possible that the outer expression is absolutely identical with the inner; that is, the corporal manifestation truly becomes a manifestation of the divine essence.

Is that all?

*Aren't the incidents of the Mahabharata and the Ramayana true?*

True, in what sense? Whether it all really happened on earth like that? Hanuman and the monkeys and the?... (*laughter*) I can't tell. I have the feeling that it is symbolical; that, for instance, when one speaks of Hanuman, this represents the evolutionary man, and Rama is the involutionary being, the one who comes from above. But...

*What do you mean by the involutionary and evolutionary being?*

The evolutionary being is the one that's the continuation of the animals, and the other is a being from higher worlds who, when the earth was formed, materialised itself upon earth — it does not come from below, it has come from above. But in the evolutionary being there is that central light which is the origin of the psychic being, which will develop into the psychic being, and when the psychic being is fully formed, there is a moment when it can unite with a being from above which can incarnate in it. So this being from above which descends into a psychic being is an involuntary being — a being of the Overmind plane or from elsewhere.

That is all?

*Was Anatole France's "jongleur" an artist?*

I don't know. That depends (that's just what I was asking Parul), it depends on the definition you give to the word "artist".

If you ask me, I believe that all those who produce something artistic are artists! A word depends upon the way it is used, upon what one puts into it. One may put into it all that one wants. For instance, in Japan there are gardeners who spend their time correcting the forms of trees so that in the landscape they make a beautiful picture. By all kinds of trimmings, props, etc. they adjust the forms of trees. They give them special forms so that each form may be just what is needed in the landscape. A tree is planted in a garden at the spot where it is needed and besides, it is given the form that's required for it to go well with the whole set-up. And they succeed in doing wonderful things. You have but to take a photograph of the garden, it is a real picture, it is so good. Well, I certainly call the man an artist. One may call him a gardener but he is an artist.... All those who have a sure and developed sense of harmony in all its forms, and the harmony of all the forms among themselves, are necessarily artists, whatever may be the type of their production.

*You did not finish telling us about Rama and Hanuman.*
(Laughter)

I did not finish? But yes, I said... Oh! because he asked what difference there was between an involuntary and an evolutionary being. But that's enough as it is. Once you know that you have the key to the whole story. Besides, I don't know whether there

## 21 October 1953

is a single authentic text or many texts of the Ramayana. For I have heard different versions. There are different versions, aren't there? Above all, for two very important facts (*Mother turns to Nolini*) concerning the end: the defeat and death of Ravana, and then the death of Sita. I have heard it narrated very differently, with different significances, by different pandits. According to their turn of mind, if I may say so, some who were very very very orthodox told me certain things and others who were not orthodox told me something very different. So I don't know if there are several texts or whether it was their own interpretation.

(Nolini) *There are several texts. There is one text in the North and another in the South.*

Ah! as for Buddhism. The people of the South and the North have different kinds of imagination. The southern people are generally more rigid, aren't they?... I don't know, but for Buddhism, the Buddhism of the South is quite rigid and doesn't allow any suppleness in the understanding of the text. And it is a terribly strict Buddhism in which all notion of the Godhead in any form whatsoever, is completely done away with. On the other hand, the Buddhism of the North is an orgy of gods! It is true that these are former Buddhas, but still they are turned into gods. And it is this latter that has spread into China and from China gone to Japan. So, one enters a Buddhist temple in Japan and sees... There is a temple where there were more than a thousand Buddhas, all sculptured — a thousand figures seated around the central Buddha — they were there all around, the entire back wall of the temple was covered with images: small ones, big ones, fat ones, thin ones, women, men — there was everything, a whole pantheon there, formidable, and they were like gods. And then too, there were little beings down below with all kinds of forms including those of animals, and these were the worshippers. It was... it was an orgy of images. But the Buddhism of the South has the austerity of

Protestantism: there must be no images. And there is no divine Consciousness, besides. One comes into the world through desire, into a world of desire, and abandoning desire one goes out of the world and creation and returns to Nirvana — even the nought is something too concrete. There is no Creator in Buddhism. So, I don't know. The Buddhism of the South is written in Pali and that of the North in Sanskrit. And naturally, there is Tibetan Buddhism written in Tibetan, and Chinese Buddhism written in Chinese and Japanese Buddhism in Japanese. And each one, I believe, is very very different from the others. Well, probably there must be several versions of the Ramayana. And still more versions of the Mahabharata — that indeed is formidable!

(Nolini) *Of the Ramayana also.*

Then texts have been added later.

*Did it exist, Mother, the Mahabharata?*

I suppose something did exist. In all these things, there is "something" that's true and then what has been made of it. These are two very different things. But in all religions, everywhere, it is the same thing: there is something which is there, something exists, and then one makes quite a different thing of it. That's the difference between history and legend — but history itself is a legend.

The same story, even taken quite objectively, when it is repeated several times, changes; and so after thousands of years it is altogether deformed. Which are the original texts — I mean the first recognised original texts — of the Mahabharata? It was related orally for a very long time, wasn't it? So you can imagine how it could have changed. These were oral traditions for a very long time. But who wrote the first version?

21 October 1953

(Nolini) *Vyasa.*

Ah!

(Nolini) *At first there were 36,000 verses. Now it is more than a lakh or two.*

Oh! Oh! it has grown: from 36,000 it has become quite inflated! But the Gita — are there several versions?

(Nolini) *No.*

But the Gita is a part of the Mahabharata.

(Nolini) *Yes.*

Is the Ramayana more recent?

(Nolini) *No.*

Is it of the same period? And is the author known?

(Nolini) *Valmiki.*

Yes, and this has not changed so much.

(Nolini) *Not as much as the other. Not so much as the Mahabharata.*

But there are differences. There is one tradition which says that Ravana died deliberately, that it was deliberately he chose the role of the Asura and that he died willingly in order to shorten his "stay" outside the Divine. He dissolved into Rama when he died, saying that thus he had succeeded sooner in uniting with him definitively. Which version is this? Is it orthodox or not?

327

(Nolini) *Everything is orthodox!*

It is orthodox. The idea (it is an idea, isn't it?) is that the Asuras have chosen to be Asuras because they will be dissolved by the Divine and thus return more quickly, unite more swiftly with the divine essence than the gods or sages who take a big round of labour before being able to return to the Divine. The Asuras, on the other hand, having chosen to be very wicked, will be destroyed much more quickly, they will return much faster. It is an idea! (*Laughter*)

In the same way, I have heard two versions (but as I said, one was broad-minded and the other extremely orthodox) about the end of Sita; one said that Sita chose to be swallowed up in the earth to prove her innocence, whilst the very orthodox version said that it was just because she was not innocent that she was swallowed up! (*Laughter*)

*Flowers fell from the skies, didn't they?*[2]

Ah! that again is another story.... I heard the Ramayana from a man called Pandit, and he was the son of a pandit and had come to Paris to study Law. But he had remained orthodox, as orthodox as one could be, it was tremendous! And he had with him a Ramayana translated into English, with pictures, and he showed it to me. And he told me the story. And then, when he came to the end he told me that. So I said: "What do you mean?" He told me: "You understand, for an Indian, if a woman has lived even for a few hours in another man's house, she is impure...." Oh! it is terrible... So, it was because she was impure that she was swallowed up.... I remember, he was quite short. He was from a Bombay family — not Bombay proper but from that side. He was a Gujarati. I believe he spoke Gujarati.

---

[2] According to the texts, it seems, flowers fell from the skies after Sita's disappearance, proving her innocence.

**21 October 1953**

And then the other version, I heard that from... that man was called Shastri. He was another pandit. He was in Japan. There we are, then.

Is that all? No questions? You... Be quick, it is late.

*In one of your writings you have said that beauty is universal and that one must be universal in order to see and recognise it.*

Yes. I mean one must have a universal *consciousness* in order to see and recognise it. For instance, if your consciousness is limited to one place, that is, it is a national consciousness (the consciousness of any one country), what is beautiful for one country is not beautiful for another. The sense of beauty is different. For example (I could make you laugh with a story), I knew in Paris the son of the king of Dahomey (he was a negro — the king of Dahomey was a negro) and this boy had come to Paris to study Law. He used to speak French like a Frenchman. But he had remained a negro, you understand. And he was asked (he used to tell us all kinds of stories about his life as a student), someone asked him in front of me: "Well, when you marry, whom will you marry?" — "Ah! a girl from my country, naturally, they alone are beautiful...." (*Laughter*) Now, for those who are not negroes, negro beauty is a little difficult to see! And yet, this was quite spontaneous. He was fully convinced it was impossible for anyone to think otherwise.... "Only the women of my country are beautiful!"

It is the same thing everywhere. Only those who have developed a little artistic taste, have travelled much and seen many things have widened their consciousness and they are no longer so sectarian. But it is very difficult to pull a person out of the specialised tastes of his race — I am not even speaking now of the country, I am speaking of the race. It is very difficult. It is there, you know, hidden right at the bottom, in the subconscious, and it comes back without your even noticing it, quite spontaneously, quite naturally. Even on this very point: the woman of your race is always much more beautiful than the woman of other races — spontaneously, it is the spontaneous taste. That's what I mean. So, you must rise above that. I am not even speaking of those who find everything that's outside their own family or caste very ugly and bad. I am not speaking at all of these people. I am not even speaking of those for whom one country is much more beautiful than another. And yet, these people have already risen above the altogether ordinary way of thinking. I am not even speaking of a question of race.... It is very difficult, one must go right down, right down within oneself into the subconscious — and even farther — to discover the root of these things. Therefore, if you want to have the sense of beauty in itself — which is quite independent of all these tastes, the taste of the race — you must have a universal consciousness. Otherwise how can you have it? You will always have preferences. Even if these are not active and conscious preferences, they are subconscious preferences, instincts. So, to know true beauty independent of all form, one must rise above all form. And once you have known it beyond every form, you can recognise it in any form whatsoever, indifferently. And that becomes very interesting.

So that's all. *Au revoir*, my children.

# 28 October 1953

> *"True art is a whole and an ensemble; it is one and of one piece with life. You see something of this intimate wholeness in ancient Greece and ancient Egypt; for there pictures and statues and all objects of art were made and arranged as part of the architectural plan of a building, each detail a portion of the whole. It is like that in Japan, or at least it was so till the other day before the invasion of a utilitarian and practical modernism. A Japanese house is a wonderful artistic whole; always the right thing is there in the right place, nothing wrongly set, nothing too much, nothing too little. Everything is just as it needed to be, and the house itself blends marvellously with the surrounding nature. In India, too, painting and sculpture and architecture were one integral beauty, one single movement of adoration of the Divine."*
> 
> Questions and Answers 1929 (28 July)

*Mother, I did not understand what you have said: "True art is a whole and an ensemble; it is one and of one piece with life."*

What I have said? Nothing else but that true art is the expression of beauty in the material world; and in a world entirely changed spiritually, that is to say, one expressing completely the divine reality, art must function as a revealer and teacher of this divine beauty in life; that is to say, an artist should be capable of entering into communion with the Divine and of receiving inspiration about what form or forms ought to be used to express the divine beauty in matter. And thus, if it does that, art can be a means of realisation of beauty, and at the same time a teacher of what beauty ought to be, that is, art should be an element in the education of men's taste, of young and old, and it is the teaching of true beauty, that is, the essential beauty which expresses the divine truth. This is the *raison d'être* of art. Now, between this and what is done there is a great difference, but this is the true *raison d'être* of art.

Have you understood? A little!

*Why are today's painters not so good as those of the days of Leonardo da Vinci?*

Because human evolution goes in spirals. I have explained this.[1] I said that art had become an altogether mercenary affair, obscure and ignorant, from the beginning of the last century till its middle. It had become something very commercial and quite remote from the true sense of art. And so, naturally, the artistic spirit does not come! It followed bad forms, yet it tried to manifest to counteract the degradation of taste which prevailed. But naturally, as with every movement of Nature in man, some having gone to one extreme, others went to the other extreme; and as these made a sort of servile copy of life — not even that, in those days it was called "a photographic view" of things, but now one can no longer say that, for photography has progressed so much that it would be doing it an injustice to say this, wouldn't it? Photography has become artistic; so a picture cannot be criticised by calling it photographic; nor can one call it "realistic" any longer, for there is a realistic painting which is not at all like that — but it was conventional, artificial and without any true life, so the reaction was to the very opposite, and naturally to another absurdity: "art" was no longer to express physical life but mental life or vital life. And so came all the schools, like the Cubists and others, who created from their head. But in art it is not the head that dominates, it is the feeling for beauty. And they produced absurd and ridiculous and

---

[1] See *Questions and Answers 1929 (28 July)*.

# 28 October 1953

frightful things. Now they have gone farther still, but that, that is due to the wars — with every war there descends upon earth a world in decomposition which produces a sort of chaos. And some, of course, find all this very beautiful and admire it very much.

I understand what they want to do, I understand it very well, but I cannot say that I find they do it well. All I can say is that they are trying.

But it is perhaps (with all its horror, from a certain point of view), it is perhaps better than what was produced in that age of extreme and practical philistinism: the Victorian age or in France the Second Empire. So, one starts from a point where there was a harmony and describes a curve, and with this curve one goes completely out of this harmony and may enter into a total darkness; and then one climbs up, and when one finds oneself in line with the old realisation of art, one becomes aware of the truth there was in this realisation, but with the necessity of expressing something more complete and more conscious. But in describing the circle one forgets that art is the expression of forms and one tries to express ideas and feelings with a minimum of forms. That gives what we have, what you may see (I believe we have reproductions of the most modern painters in the University Library). But if one goes a little farther still, this idea and these feelings they wish to express and express very clumsily — if one returns to the same point of the spiral (only a little higher), one will discover that it is the embryo of a new art which will be an art of beauty and will express not only material life but will also try to express its soul.

Anyway, we have not yet come to that, but let us hope we shall reach there soon. So that's all.

*Why does evolution go in spirals instead of being a constant progress?*

It is a constant progress. But if you made it in a straight line, you would cover only a single part — the world is a globe, it is not a line.

*If it were a cylinder!*

Even for a cylinder, if you drew only one line, one part of the cylinder would escape you altogether. This movement in a spiral is precisely to try and make everything enter this phenomenon of evolution — so that not only one thing may advance whilst the others remain behind. And so, according to the centre where the progress is concentrated, one seems to move away from one thing and enter into another. But in the long run, when one evolves consciously, one does not forget one thing in order to do another. What is bad at present is forgetfulness; it is that when following a certain activity for a realisation, one forgets all the others or they go into the background, they have no longer any intensity. But this is a human shortcoming which can be corrected — it ought to be corrected.

*Do all progress in a spiral, and all together or separately?*

I fear it is not very harmonious, for the world seems to me rather chaotic! If indeed the march were totally organised, it would be a harmonious development, and if one could see where one is going — having the line of what has been done, one could prolong these lines and see what would come. But for the moment this is open only to an élite. And the mass follows the movement, and all the movements are not homogeneous and simultaneous — certain things are slower to put into line and movement than others. So, even a little difference like this suffices for it to create an immense difference in the movement.

There is even a considerable number of spirals intersecting and giving the impression of contradiction. If one could follow in its totality the movement of universal progress, one would see that there is such a great number of spirals which intersect, that

## 28 October 1953

finally one does not know at all whether one is advancing or going back. For, at the same moment some things are going up and others falling back into the darkness, and all these are not absolutely independent of one another. There is a kind of coordination, so that instead of imagining a spiral like that, we should have to think of spherical spirals. If this could be described, the ensemble of all these spirals would make an immense globe. And it is at the intersection of these spirals that there are moments of progress. But before the progress is coherent, total, there must be an inner organisation of life, different from that of Nature, arranged in accordance with a plan. For Nature — her plan is only made with an aspiration, a decision and a goal. And the road seems quite fantastic, following the impulses of every minute — trials, set-backs, contradictions, progress and demolition of what has already been done; and it is such a chaos that one can understand nothing there. She has the air of somebody doing things impulsively — giving out certain impulses and destroying them, beginning others again, and going on and on like that. She makes and unmakes, she remakes and again demolishes, she mixes, destroys, constructs and all this at the same time. It is incomprehensible. And yet, she evidently has a plan, and herself goes towards a certain goal which is very clear to her but quite veiled to human consciousness.... It is very interesting. If one could construct something like that, it would give an idea: a globe made of intersecting spirals of different colours, and each representing one aspect of Nature's creation. And these aspects are made to complete one another — but so far they are rather in competition than collaboration, and it seems she is always obliged to destroy something in order to make another, which makes for a terrible wastage, and a still greater disorder. But if all this were seen in its ensemble, it would be extremely interesting. For it is an extremely complex criss-crossing, in all possible directions, of a spiralling ascent.

Now, for your question, there could be another answer. What I have said just now is also exactly the same for art, it also follows an evolution and at a certain moment seems to drift away from its goal and at others it draws close to a greater height. But there is something else, that is a social point of view: there is a period, like the Age of Louis XIV for example, in which what predominated was the sense of artistic creation, and this sense seems to have given a certain perception of beauty at that moment; but afterwards social evolution brought in other needs and other ideas, and now, for more than a century it is commercialism which is uppermost in the world, and there is nothing more in contradiction with art than commerce. For it is precisely the vulgarisation of something which ought to be exceptional. It is putting within everybody's range something which could be understood only by an élite. And as we are in an age of mechanisation and commercialism, it is a time altogether uncongenial for a blossoming of art. And probably this is why art, not finding the conditions necessary for its full flowering, tries to seek another outlet and enters the mental and vital field for its expression. That is the reason. When the time comes to shake off, so to say, to reject this mercantilism and to wake up to a more beautiful reality, then art too will be reborn in a greater consciousness of harmony.

*Is self-complacency an obstacle to art?*

Yes, it is even an obstacle to intelligence. Fatuity is one of the greatest of human follies. There is a very great difference between having faith in what can be done, the will to realise it, the certitude of the possibilities open in creation (and also the certitude that these possibilities will be realised), and self-complacency; these are two things which turn their backs completely on each other. To be convinced that nothing is impossible if one puts in the time, energy, will, trust, sincerity and all else, is very essential, but to be self-satisfied in any way whatever is always, without exception, a folly. And this is one of the things that takes you farthest away from the divine realisation, for it

*28 October 1953*

makes you foolish. And it is at the same time one of the things most contrary to the goodwill of Nature, for Nature laughs at you immediately. You become an object of ridicule at once. For, in truth, there is no human being who is something by himself. He is only a possibility created by the Divine and one which can be developed only by the Divine, which exists only by the Divine, and which should live only for the Divine. And so, in this I do not see any place for self-complacency; for, as we are nothing in ourselves but what the Divine makes of us, and as we can do nothing by ourselves except what the Divine wants to do through us, I don't see what satisfaction one can have in that. One can only have the feeling of one's perfect powerlessness. Only, what is very bad is to have this the wrong side out — for there is always a wrong side and a right to every state of consciousness — and, fundamentally, it is the same vanity which makes you say: "I can do nothing, I am good for nothing, I am incapable of doing anything whatsoever"; that, that is the wrong side of "I can, I am great, I have all sorts of powers in me." It is the same thing. One is the shadow and the other the light, but they are exactly alike: one is no better than the other. And if really one were aware of being nothing at all, one would not bother to know what one is like. That would already be something. But truly, sincerely, I tell you, and I have a sufficiently long experience of life, I know nothing so grotesque as people who are satisfied with themselves. It is truly ridiculous. They make themselves utterly ridiculous. There are people like that; some of them came to see Sri Aurobindo telling him all that they were capable of, all that they had done and all they could do, all that they had realised — and so Sri Aurobindo looked at them very seriously and replied: "Oh! you are too perfect to be here. It would be better for you to go away."

> *"Music too is an essentially spiritual art and has always been associated with religious feeling and an inner life. But, here too, we have turned it into something*

*independent and self-sufficient, a mushroom art, such as is operatic music. Most of the artistic productions we come across are of this kind and at best interesting from the point of view of technique. I do not say that even operatic music cannot be used as a medium of a higher art expression; for whatever the form, it can be made to serve a deeper purpose. All depends on the thing itself, on how it is used, on what is behind it. There is nothing that cannot be used for the Divine purpose — just as anything can pretend to be the Divine and yet be of the mushroom species."*

*Questions and Answers 1929 (28 July)*

*What do you mean by "mushroom species"?*

Don't you know what a mushroom is? how mushrooms grow? Mushrooms spring up anywhere and seem not to belong to any cultivation. The idea is of a kind of spontaneous growth which has no roots in the totality of creation. These are things which do not belong to a whole, which are as though extraneous. Instead of mushrooms I could have said parasites on trees. You know there are parasites on trees, like the mistletoe on the oak; here too I have seen them on certain trees; I have seen plants grow clinging to the tree, plants which lived on the life of the tree, which did not have their own separate life, their own roots, which did not take their food directly from the soil; they clung to another plant, as though they made use of others' work. The others work to obtain the food and these cling upon them and live by it. Really, how parasites live on animals!

I don't know, I thought I went into great detail. But I have said enough about it for those who know.... In the old days, I mean in the artistic ages, as for instance in Greece or even during the Italian renaissance (but much more in Greece and Egypt), buildings were made for public utility. Mostly too, in Greece and Egypt, a kind of sanctuary was built to house their

## 28 October 1953

gods. Well, what they tried to do was something total, beautiful in itself, complete. And in that they used architecture, that is to say, the sense of harmony of lines, and sculpture to add to architecture the detail of expression, and painting to complete this expression, but all this was held in a coordinated unity which was the created monument. The sculpture formed a part of the building, the painting was a part of the building. These were not things apart, just put there one knew not why — they belonged to the general plan. And so, when these people made a temple, for example, it was a whole wherein were found almost all the manifestations of art, united in a single will to express the beauty they wished to express, that is, a garment for the god they wished to adore. All the beautiful periods of art were of this kind. But precisely, these days, though not quite recently — at the end of the last century, art became commercial, mercenary, and pictures were made to be sold; they were painted on canvas, a frame was put and then, without any definite reason, a picture was put here or another there, or else some sculpture was made representing one thing or another, and it was put no matter where. It had nothing to do with the house in which it was placed. It did not fit in. Things could be beautiful in themselves but they had no meaning. It was not a whole having cohesion and attempting to express something: it was an exhibition of talent, cleverness, the ability to make a picture or a statue. So too the architecture of those days, it had no precise meaning. One did not build with the idea of expressing the force one wanted to incarnate in that building; the architecture was not the expression of an aspiration or of something that uplifts your spirit or the expression of the magnificence of the godhead one wanted to house. It was simply just mushrooms. They put up a house here, a house there, made this and that, pictures, statues, objects of all kinds. So, on entering a house one saw, as I have just told you, a bit of sculpture here, a bit of painting there, showcases with a heap of bizarre objects having no connection with one another. And all this, why? To make a sort of exhibition, a show of art-objects which had nothing to do with art and beauty! But that — one must understand the deep meaning of art to feel to what an extent this was shocking. Otherwise, when one is accustomed to it, when one has lived in that period and that milieu, it seems quite natural — but it is not natural. It is a commercial deformation.

There is only one justification, that is to make it a means of education. Then it becomes a museum. If you make a museum, it is a historical sampling of all that has been done. It serves to give you a historical knowledge of things. But a museum is not something beautiful in itself, far from it! For an artist it is something quite shocking. From the point of view of education it is very good, for specimens of all kinds of things have been collected there in a single place; and in this way you may learn, acquire erudition. But from the point of view of beauty, it is frightful.

And so there was an attempt, later, to return (for instance, at the beginning of this century — I am speaking of the first years of this century) an attempt to create what was called "decorative art", that is, to try to get back to a vision of the ensemble and to make, when arranging a house, a coordinated whole in which things were in a certain place because they were meant to be there, and where every object had not only its *raison d'être* but its exact place and could not be displaced. An ensemble was created, a whole. So that was already a little better. They were trying.

Here (in India), it is altogether different, for there is a tradition of art which has remained, the whole country is full of things which were made at a fine moment of the artistic history of the country. One lives in its midst. One has hardly undergone the after-effects of what happened in the rest of the world, above all in Europe. Only those parts of India which are a little too anglicised have lost the sense of beauty. There are certain schools in Bombay, schools of artists, which are frightful. And then, there was that attempt of the Calcutta School to revive Indian art, but that was only on a very small scale. From the point of view of

28 October 1953

art what you have most within your reach are the old creations, the old temples, old pictures. All that was very good. And that had been made to express a faith. And it was done precisely with a sense of the whole, not in disorder.

You have followed very little of this movement of art I am speaking about, which is related to European civilisation, it has not been felt much here — just a little but not deeply. Here, the majority of creations (this is a very good example), the majority of works, I believe even almost all the beautiful works, are not signed. All those paintings in the caves, those statues in the temples — these are not signed. One does not know at all who created them. And all this was not done with the idea of making a name for oneself as at present. One happened to be a great sculptor, a great painter, a great architect, and then that was all, there was no question of putting one's name on everything and proclaiming it aloud in the newspapers so that no one might forget it! In those days the artist did what he had to do without caring whether his name would go down to posterity or not. All was done in a movement of aspiration to express a higher beauty, and above all with the idea of giving an appropriate abode to the godhead who was evoked. In the cathedrals of the Middle Ages, it was the same thing, and I don't think that there too the names of the artists who made them have remained. If any are there, it is quite exceptional and it is only by chance that the name has been preserved. Whilst today, there is not a tiny little piece of canvas, painted or daubed, but on it is a signature to tell you: it is Mr. So-and-so who made this!

*It is said that a synthesis of western and eastern art could be made?*

Yes. One can make a synthesis of everything if one rises sufficiently high.

*What will come out of it?*

341

If it is necessary, it will be done. But fundamentally, these are things in the course of making. For, the advantage of modern times and specially of this hideous commercialism is that everything is now mixed up; that things from the East go to the West, and things from the West to the East, and they influence each other. For the moment this creates a confusion, a sort of pot-pourri. But a new expression will come out of it — it is not so far from its realisation. People cannot intermix, as men today are intermixing, without its producing a reciprocal effect. For instance, with their mania of conquest, the nations of the West which conquered all sorts of countries in the world, have undergone a very strong influence of the conquered countries. In the old days, when Rome conquered Greece it came under the influence of Greece much more than if it had not conquered it. And the Americans — all that they make now is full of Japanese things, and perhaps they are not even aware of it. But since they occupied Japan, I see that the magazines received from America are full of Japanese things. And even in certain details of objects received from America, one now feels the influence of Japan. That happens automatically. It is quite strange, there always comes about a sort of equilibrium, and he who made the material conquest is conquered by the spirit of the vanquished. It is reciprocal. He made the material conquest, he possesses materially, but it is the spirit of the conquered one who possesses the conqueror.

So, through mixing... The ways of Nature are slow, obscure and complicated. She takes a very long time to do a thing which could probably be done much more rapidly, easily and without wastage by means of the spirit. At present there is a terrible wastage in the world. But the thing is done. She has her own way of mixing people.

*Is it intentional?*

Not the way men understand "intentional". But it is certainly

## 28 October 1953

the expression of an intention and a goal towards which one is going. Only, all depends on the amount of consciousness. For a man this seems a confusion, for he can see only details, and it appears to be a terrible loss of time, because for him the idea of time is limited to the duration of his person. But Nature has eternity before her. And it is all the same to her to waste, for she is like someone who had a huge cauldron; she throws things in and makes a mixture, and if that does not succeed she throws all this out, for she knows that by taking back the same things she will make another mixture. And that is how it is. Nothing is lost, for it comes into use again all the time. Forms are broken and the substance is taken back, and it goes on constantly like that. It is made, it is unmade, it is turned inside out — what harm can it do her to try a hundred thousand times if it so pleases her! For there is nothing that is wasted, except her work. But her work is her pleasure. Without work she would not exist.

*It is a pleasure for her, not for men!*

No, certainly, I quite agree. I find it a little too cruel an amusement. *Voilà.*

# 4 November 1953

Before beginning the class Mother spoke for a few minutes about the "sphere with spirals" which the children had constructed to give an idea of what She had explained the preceding week:

... The sphere is touched only by a part of the curve, the rest is evolved inside. It cannot be made. This one is opaque. But it was... there was at the centre of the sphere an intersection of all the spirals.

What you have done there makes it flat, the way it is done. It is flat. As I saw it, the edge was touched by a section of the curve. Each curve has one part of the edge as section. And the colours were seen distinctly and one could see right through.... I think you could do this geometrically. The whole surface is taken up by one section of the curve of the spiral.

Pavitra: *Are these spirals on the surface of the sphere or inside?*

No, the spirals are inside.

*Hence towards the centre.*

They are intersecting. Their direction is such that the whole sphere is formed by sections of each spiral.

*Is the whole of the inside of the sphere filled with spirals?*

The whole inside was naturally full of spirals. But as there was no substance (there were only spirals), one could see through. They were not so joined up as to make an opaque mass. And

*4 November 1953*

one could follow: the colours were brilliant, they were luminous. One could follow the line inside. And so it should be inferred that they were countless.

*Were they drawing closer inwards forming smaller and smaller curves?*

Not regularly as to have all the first rounds at the centre. It was not a series of spirals beginning with the first circle and working towards the centre.

*And beginning again from the centre outwards?*

No, not at all. The finishing-point was not the same as the starting-point. Still, in this way, seen from far, it gave that impression a little. It was much more complex than that. And then there were none of those dull things.

*Mother, what do the colours represent?*

Here you have three greens and only one blue. That one is blue, but greenish blue. Then there are two browns, one black and one grey, two reds... These colours are dead colours, aren't they? They can be given a particular meaning.
There there was no black.

After reading the part of the conversation of 4 August 1929 on sacrifice and self-giving, the Mother continues:

*"The spiritual life reveals the one essence in all, but reveals too its infinite diversity; it works for diversity in oneness and for perfection in that diversity. Morality lifts up one artificial standard contrary to the variety of life and the freedom of the spirit. Creating something mental, fixed and limited, it asks all to conform to it. All*

*must labour to acquire the same qualities and the same ideal nature. Morality is not divine or of the Divine; it is of man and human. Morality takes for its basic element a fixed division into the good and the bad; but this is an arbitrary notion. It takes things that are relative and tries to impose them as absolutes; for this good and this bad differ in differing climates and times, epochs and countries."*

Questions and Answers 1929 (4 August)

*In the past, why did men offer human sacrifices in temples?*

I don't quite understand the question. Why should they not do it! There is not much difference between killing a goat and killing a man. I don't know. In any case, what has come down to posterity and what really happened may be two very different things. When they spoke of sacrifice, it was perhaps only symbolic. Certain religions, we are told, have massacred men by thousands. It is possible, it is the same instinct which makes men destroy things. And these were certainly religions which tended towards destruction. Now, there are many different cases, and if someone asks why people offered material sacrifices, one should first be sure about it. As for me, I am not sure of it. It is possible. It depends on the way one looks at life. And in any case, if one arrogates to oneself the right to make use of another man's existence to offer a sacrifice to the Divine, or if one looks at it in a certain way, it is a pretty bad attitude. I was saying at the beginning I don't see why one should make a difference between any other animal and a human animal. It is a very curious thing.

In the majority of religions, I believe it used to be as it still is here where there is a temple of the headless Kali[1] — it is an

---

[1] In whose honour, every year, men wring the necks of a huge number of chickens.

4 November 1953

extremely dark and ignorant affair. It comes from a sort of unhealthy fear of a monstrous god who needs either blood or force or no matter what in order to be satisfied and not to do harm. And all this comes from a dread and a conception of the Divine which is a monstrosity. But even were it admitted, there would be only one tolerable sacrifice, the sacrifice of oneself. If one wants to sacrifice something to the Divine, I don't see by what right one can seek the life of another, be it human being or animal, to offer it in one's own stead. If one wants to sacrifice, it is one's own self one must sacrifice, not others. And as the movement itself is sufficiently ugly and obscure and unconscious, I don't see why there should be such a difference between sacrificing a goat and sacrificing a human being. From the goat's point of view it is an intolerable idea — if a goat were to be asked why....

Men have strange ideas about their own importance in the world and the respective worth of their person. It does not make much difference. If they are told, "You have no right to take the life of another", it is defensible; but then do not offer sacrifices, or if you want to sacrifice, sacrifice your own self; if you believe there is a terrible God who needs to be given blood or whatever else it may be, vital forces to satisfy him, do it. But by what right are you going to take the life of others to give it? That is an intolerable tyranny. Even were it only all those chickens one kills! But I believe there is another reason for that — it is that men have a fine feast! It is simply an opportunity to swallow a considerable amount of food.

I don't know, for me it does not make a great difference.

*Is it possible to feel the divine Presence even when one is surrounded by a bad atmosphere, a mental and vital disturbance?*

Provided the atmosphere is not within oneself! For if so, it is difficult. And yet! We have had frequent instances of people who used to lead a more than doubtful life and who had revelations.

There is the instance of a drunkard who, in his drunkenness, suddenly had a contact with the Divine — which, moreover, changed his life and, I must tell you, prevented him from drinking in future. But still, at the time he had the revelation of the divine Presence, he was in an intoxicated state. I don't think — here again we fall back into the same things — I don't think the Divine is a moralist. It is man who is a moralist, not the Divine. If it happens that, just then, at that moment, there is a concurrence of events and perhaps an opening in the being, the Divine, who is always present, manifests himself. On the other hand, for the sage or the saint who is quite infatuated with his own importance and his own worth, and full of pride and vanity, there is not much chance that the Divine will manifest in him, for there is no place for the expression of the Divine! There is no place except for the important personality of the wise man and his moral worth.

Naturally, there is a state in which one may be perfectly pure, perfectly wise, and be in contact with the Divine! But then, that means that one has reached a certain degree of perfection and lost the sense of one's personal importance and personal worth. I believe that's most important. The greatest obstacle to the contact with the Divine is pride and the sense of one's personal worth, one's personal capacities, personal power — the person becomes very big, so big that there is no place for the Divine.

No, the one truly important thing is the intensity of the aspiration. And this intensity of aspiration comes in all kinds of circumstances.

There are two things we must not confuse: certain necessities (which are purely necessities if one wants to succeed in completely controlling physical matter), and then moral notions. These are two very different things. One may, for instance, refrain from poisoning one's body or besotting one's brains or annulling one's will because one wants to become master of one's physical consciousness and capable of transforming one's body. But if one does these things solely because one thinks one will gain moral merit by doing so, that will lead you nowhere,

## 4 November 1953

to nothing at all. Because it is not meant for that. One does it for purely practical reasons: for the same reason, for instance, that you are not in the habit of taking poison, for you know it will poison you. And then, there are some very slow poisons taken by people (they think, with impunity, because the effect is so slow that they cannot discern it easily), but if one wants to succeed in becoming entirely master of one's physical activities and capable of putting the light into the reflexes of one's body, then one must abstain from these things — but not for moral reasons: for altogether practical reasons, from the point of view of the realisation of the yoga. One must not do this with the idea of gaining merit, or the idea that because you will gain merit God will be very pleased and come and manifest within you! It is not at all that, not at all! Perhaps even, He feels closer to him who has made mistakes, who is conscious of his faults and has the sense of his weakness, and aspires sincerely to come out of it all — He feels perhaps closer to him than to one who has never made a mistake and is satisfied with his external superiority over other human beings. In any case, that does not make a great difference. What does make a lot of difference is the sincerity, the spontaneity, the intensity of the aspiration — the need, that need which seizes you and which is so powerful that nothing else in the world counts.

As I have said elsewhere about surrender and sacrifice, if one regrets something, that means that one is not in a spiritual state of consciousness. If one regrets that one can no longer satisfy one's desires, that means the desires are at least as important as, if not more than, the thing one aspires for. You may say, "Desires are something of which I am quite conscious, whilst if I give up my desires with the idea of getting the Divine, I am yet not sure that I shall have Him; hence I call this a sacrifice." But I, I call that bargaining! It is bargaining with the Divine. One tells Him, "Give and take; I, I give You the joy I have in satisfying my desires, You must give me in exchange the joy of feeling You within myself, else it is not just." — This is not self-giving, this is bargaining.

This is something I have heard so often, so often: "I have sacrificed so many things, I have made so much effort, have taken so much trouble, and now see, I have nothing in exchange." All that I can answer is, "No wonder!"

*Can a very proud person have a great aspiration?*

Why not? The very proud person may receive blows and become sensible; besides, when he receives a blow, that may awaken him a little! Then he has an aspiration. And if it is someone who has intensity in his nature and some strength, well, then his aspiration is powerful.

*And without receiving blows?*

That may happen. Only in that case it will be very mixed up. In all instances it will be very mixed — but always everything is mixed. A long time is necessary for things to become clear. One may begin anywhere at all, at any state whatever and in any condition. One can always begin. Only, in some cases it takes a very long time. For the mixture is such that with every step forward one takes half a step back. But there is no reason for this. Fundamentally, as it is the true *raison d'être* of life and of individual existence to become aware of the Divine, that may emerge anywhere at all, at any moment whatsoever. If there is the least possibility, it springs up. Naturally, if one is perfectly satisfied, then that is an obstacle, because one sleeps in self-satisfaction. But that cannot last. In life, in the world as it is at present, an egoistic satisfaction, a personal satisfaction cannot last, and — as long as it lasts, yes, one may grow hard, not aspire at all. But it does not last.

Anything else?
Nobody has anything to say?
Then, *au revoir* my children, good-night!

# 11 November 1953

*Mother is about to begin reading the first pages of* Quelques Paroles, Quelques Prières.

The first texts were written in 1912. Many of you were not yet born. It was a small group of about twelve people who met once a week. A subject was given; an answer was to be prepared for the following week. Each one brought along his little work. Generally, I too used to prepare a short paper and, at the end, I read it out. That is what is given here — not all, only these two. These two first ones. Later, it was something else. The others appeared in *Words of Long Ago*.

There were four meetings. The subject for the first meeting was: What is the aim to be achieved, the work to be done, the means of achievement? And here is my answer:

*Mother reads the text of 7 May 1912:*[1] *"The general aim to be achieved is the advent of a progressive universal harmony."*

This is the Supermind.

I did not know Sri Aurobindo at that time and he had not written anything yet.

*"... To become the perfect representatives on earth of the first manifestation of the Unthinkable in his three modes, his seven attributes and twelve qualities... "*
What do you call the "three modes, seven attributes and twelve qualities"?

---

[1] For a similar English translation of the complete text, see *Words of Long Ago*, MCW Vol. 2, pp. 47–48.

### Questions and Answers 1953

I no longer remember. The three formed modes — love, light and life — which correspond to Sachchidananda. The seven attributes... I have a list somewhere. There is an old tradition which says that the world was created seven times, that is, the first six times it returned into the Creator. This is the idea of *pralaya*.[2] It is said that this happened six times and that we are now the seventh creation, and that this is the last one. It is the one which will persist, and it is the "creation of Equilibrium". All these creations I have also noted down somewhere, it is written down. I no longer know their order. There are six creations, one after another, created in accordance with this special mode, found imperfect and withdrawn into the Origin, recreated and withdrawn into the Origin — six times thus. And it is a progressive order. When one knows that order, one understands the principle of each creation. Well, this tradition said that the principle of our latest creation, at present, is the principle of Equilibrium, and that this is the last. That means the world will not go back again into *pralaya*, and there will be a perpetual progress. And this is the creation of Equilibrium.

Consequently, now, there is no longer anything good or bad: there is what is in equilibrium and what is not in equilibrium. There is imbalance and balance. That's all. And what I have said there was based upon that.

The twelve qualities — that is something else still. That too is noted somewhere. In order that the world may continue, it must realise a perfect equilibrium of all its elements by means of these twelve qualities, all present there. And then it will be a world which, whilst progressing indefinitely, will constantly be in harmony, and hence will not be open to destruction.

*"... To give to the world once again, under a new form adapted to the present state of its mentality, the eternal*

---

[2] The end of a world preceding a new creation.

> *word. This will be the synthesis of all human knowledge... "*
>
> *You speak here of "the eternal word"?*

I am using "word" in the sense of truth. There is an eternal Truth which is eternally true, but which finds expression in definite forms, and these definite forms are changing, fluctuating; they may become distorted; and to have the truth one must always go back to the source, which is... it may be called the eternal word, that is, the creative Word. It is a truth which is eternal, which manifests itself through all possible words and ideas. I use "word" in a literary sense — it is what is called elsewhere the creative Word. It is the origin of all speech and all thought.

*I did not understand "the aim to be achieved".*

The aim to be achieved? What have I said? It is the harmonisation of the earth, I think, isn't it?

> *"In regard to the earth, the means of achieving this aim is the realisation of human unity by the awakening in all and the manifestation by all of the inner Divinity who is one.*
>
> *In other words: to create unity by establishing the kingdom of God which is in all.*
>
> *Hence, the most useful work to be done is:*
>
> *1) For everyone individually the becoming aware in oneself of the divine Presence and one's identification with it."*

Yes, you do not understand? I have said it fifty thousand times already, haven't I? ... Ah, you understand now? (*laughter*)

> *"2) The individualisation of states of being which have so far never been conscious in man and, consequently, the*

> *putting the earth into touch with one or several sources of universal force which are yet sealed to it."*

"The individualisation of states of being which have so far never been conscious in man", that is to say, there are superposed states of consciousness, and there are new regions which have never yet been manifested on earth, and which Sri Aurobindo called supramental. It is that, this was the same idea. That is, one must go into the depths or the heights of creation which have never been manifested upon earth, and become conscious of that, and manifest it on earth. Sri Aurobindo called it the Supermind. I simply say these are states of being which were never yet conscious in man (that is, that man has so far never been aware of them). One must get identified with them, then bring them into the outer consciousness, and manifest them in action. And then, I add (exactly what I foresaw — I did not know that Sri Aurobindo would do it, but still I foresaw that this had to be done):

> *"3) To speak to the world, under a new form adapted to the present state of its mentality, the eternal word."*

That is, the supreme Truth, Harmony. It was the whole programme of what Sri Aurobindo has done, and the method of doing the work on earth, and I had foreseen this in 1912. I met Sri Aurobindo for the first time in 1914, that is, two years later, and I had already made the whole programme.

> *"4) Collectively, to found the ideal society in a place suited to the flowering of the new race, that of 'the Sons of God'."*

*Where did you decide to found the Ashram?*

Where did I decide to do it?... I never decided anything at all! I had simply said that it had to be done. I did not have the

## 11 November 1953

least idea, except that I had a great desire to come to India. But still, I did not even know if it corresponded to something. I had decided nothing at all. Simply, I had seen that state, what had to be done.

Then the children come back to the conversation of 4 August 1929:

*"The ordinary social notions distinguish between two classes of men,—the generous, the avaricious. The avaricious man is despised and blamed, while the generous man is considered unselfish and useful to society and praised for his virtue. But to the spiritual vision, they both stand on the same level; the generosity of the one, the avarice of the other are deformations of a higher truth, a greater divine power. There is a power, a divine movement that spreads, diffuses, throws out freely forces and things and whatever else it possesses on all the levels of nature from the most material to the most spiritual plane. Behind the generous man and his generosity is a soul-type that expresses this movement; he is a power for diffusion, for wide distribution. There is another power, another divine movement that collects and amasses; it gathers and accumulates forces and things and all possible possessions, whether of the lower or of the higher planes. The man you tax with avarice was meant to be an instrument of this movement. Both are important, both needed in the entire plan; the movement that stores up and concentrates is no less needed than the movement that spreads and diffuses."*

*Questions and Answers 1929 (4 August)*

*What do you mean by "soul-type"?*

What is the sentence?... (*Mother looks at the text*) Ah! it is the spirit of the type; just as we said that behind each animal type there was a spirit of the type, so behind each type of man there is a spirit of the type. This is what I call soul-type. It is a soul-type which may be progressive, but which is indestructible.

The soul-type corresponds, individually or in groups, to the *dharma* of things. Sometimes it is also called the truth of things, of each thing.

*Is generosity a deformation of the truth?*

Yes, all human qualities are deformations of a truth which is behind them. All that you call either qualities or defects are always a deformation of something which is behind, and which is neither this nor that but something else. But I say, moreover, what truth is found behind generosity: it is the movement of the spreading forces. But in order that these forces may spread, they must first become concentrated. So there is a sort of movement of pulsation: the forces are concentrated, then they spread, and then they are again concentrated and again spread.... But if you always want to spread out without ever concentrating, after a certain time you have nothing left to spread. For the forces — all forces — it is the same thing. I have written, besides, (or rather I shall write some time) that money is a force, it is nothing but that. And that is why nobody has the right to own it personally, for it is only a force, just like all other forces of Nature and the universe. If you take light as a force, it would never occur to anyone to say: "I possess the light", and to want to shut it up in his room and not give it to others! Well, with money people are so stupefied as to imagine that it is something they can possess and keep, as though it belonged to them, and make something personal of it. It is exactly the same thing. I am not speaking of money as paper, naturally, because that would be just like the light you put in a lamp, you may own the lamp, and so you say: "It is my light." Money, your notes, your pieces of silver, that is *your* money. But that is not money. This is a force

## 11 November 1953

which is behind all that, the power of exchange which is money. That does not belong to anybody. It belongs to everyone. It is something which is alive only if it circulates. If you want to heap it up, it decays. It is as though you wanted to enclose water in a vase and keep it always; after some time your water would be absolutely putrefied. With money it is the same thing. And people have not yet understood that. Later on I shall write about it.

That won't last always.

*When there is avarice for material things...*

Avarice for *all* things — there is an avarice for spiritual things also. There are misers who want to keep all the forces for themselves and never give them. But I have just told you the truth about it: one must have the power to accumulate in order to have the power of spreading. If you have only one of the two, that causes an imbalance. And it is then that it becomes avarice or wastage. One must have both in a balanced, rhythmic movement — the equilibrium we just spoke about. For it would be quite easy to prove that in fact at present equilibrium is the true thing: one must be neither here nor there, that is what Buddha called "the middle path". The middle path is the path of equilibrium. And so one must know how to manage as when rope-walking with a stick to keep one's balance.

But the most generous man in the world could give nothing if he had nothing to begin with. Hence, if it is not he who has accumulated, it is someone else who has accumulated for him. But if he has nothing in his pocket, he cannot distribute anything! That is evident. And the power of accumulation is as important as the power of distribution. It is only when these two things become egoistic that they are deformed, altogether deformed, and lose all their value.

*Voilà*, my children.

## 18 November 1953

*"In rebirth it is not the external being, that which is formed by parents, environment and circumstances, — the mental, the vital and the physical, — that is born again: it is only the psychic being that passes from body to body. Logically, then, neither the mental nor the vital being can remember past lives or recognise itself in the character or mode of life of this or that person. The psychic being alone can remember; and it is by becoming conscious of our psychic being that we can have at the same time exact impressions about our past lives.*

*Besides, it is much more important for us to fix our attention upon what we want to become than upon what we have been."*

2 April 1935; Words of the Mother, MCW Vol. 15, p. 135

*If it is not the mind, vital or physical which take birth again but only the psychic being, then the vital or mental progress made before is of no value in another life?*

It happens only to the extent the progress of these parts has brought them close to the psychic, that is, to the extent the progress lies in putting all the parts of the being successively under the psychic influence. For all that is under the psychic influence and identified with the psychic continues, and it is that alone which continues. But if the psychic is made the centre of one's life and consciousness, and if the whole being is organised around it, the whole being passes under the psychic influence, becomes united with it, and can continue — if it is necessary for it to continue. Indeed, if the physical body could be given the same movement — the same movements of progress and the same capacity to ascend that the psychic being has — well, it wouldn't

## 18 November 1953

be necessary for it to decompose. But that indeed is the difficulty.

And only that which is in contact with the psychic lasts, and only what can last can remember, for the rest disappears, is again dissolved into small pieces and utilised elsewhere — as the body is dissolved again to dust and used elsewhere. It goes back to the earth, plants use the soil, men eat the plants. It is in this way that it goes on. And then it returns to the earth and begins again. That's the way Nature progresses. In order to progress she makes a heap of forms, then, when that seems no longer important or necessary to her, she demolishes them, takes up all the elements again, chemical or other, and reconstitutes something else, and so it goes on changing all the time, coming and going. And she finds that very good, for she sees very far, her work extends over centuries, and a small human life is nothing, just a breath in eternity. So she takes up, shapes; she takes a certain time, it's fun for her, she finds it very good; and then, when it is no longer so good, she demolishes it — she takes up, mixes everything, begins another form, makes something else. And so perhaps with this process which is evidently very slow, finally the whole of matter progresses. It is possible — always in this way, intermingling, breaking up, remixing, breaking up again. Essentially, it is as though one made a heap of small objects and then destroyed them, remade something from the dust, remade other toys, and again broke them, and remade others out of that. Each time one adds something so that it mixes well. And then, one day, perhaps all that will produce something. In any case, she is in no hurry. And when we are in a hurry, she says: "Why are you in such a haste? It is sure to happen one day. You don't need to worry, it will surely come. Wait quietly." Then we tell her: "But it is not I who am waiting!" — "Ah! that's because you call 'I' that thing which comes and goes away. If you were to call consciousness — the one, eternal and divine consciousness — if you were to call that 'I', then you would see everything, you would be present at everything. Nobody prevents you from doing it! It is only because you identify yourself with this (*indicating the body*).

You have only to stop identifying yourself with that."

"*Justice is the strict logical determinism of the movements of Universal Nature.*

"*Illnesses are this determinism applied to the material body. The medical mind, basing itself upon this ineluctable Justice, strives to bring about the conditions which should lead logically to good health.*

"*The moral consciousness acts in the same way in the social body and* tapasya *in the spiritual domain.*

"*The Divine Grace alone has the power to intervene and change the course of Universal Justice.*

"*The great work of the Avatar is to manifest the Divine Grace upon earth. To be a disciple of the Avatar is to become an instrument of the Divine Grace. The Mother is the great dispensatrix — through identity — of the Divine Grace with a perfect knowledge — through identity — of the absolute mechanism of Universal Justice.*

"*And through her mediation each movement of sincere and confident aspiration towards the Divine calls down in response the intervention of the Grace.*

"*Who can stand before You, O Lord, and say in all sincerity: 'I have never made a mistake'? How many times in a day we commit faults against Your work, and always Your Grace comes to efface them!*

"*Without the ceaseless intervention of Your Grace, who would not oftentimes have come under the merciless blade of the Law of Universal Justice?*

"*Each one here represents an impossibility to be resolved, but as for Your Divine Grace all things are possible. Your work will be, in the detail as in the ensemble, the accomplishment of all the impossibilities transformed into divine realisations.*"

15 January 1933; Words of the Mother, MCW Vol. 14, p. 86

18 November 1953

*What is the meaning of "Justice is the strict logical determinism of the movements of Universal Nature"?*

You know the law of determinism, don't you? You have not studied philosophy at all? (*Turning to a professor*) Pavitra, explain what determinism is to them. Try to be brief and clear.

Pavitra: *I think determinism is this: when something happens, it always has the same effect.*

If it is the same thing — on condition it is identically the same thing. Are there two identical things in the universe? No.

Nolini: *The same cause produces the same effect.*

Yes. The same cause produces the same effect. That is the principle on which science is founded. But I have used the word here in a little more general and precise a way at once. I mean that each thing (whether the same or not) always produces an effect and that this effect produces still another and that other produces yet another and so on — always a cause produces an effect and each effect becomes the cause of another effect, and so on, indefinitely. And so justice means that each thing, as Nolini said, the same cause always produces the same effect automatically. And hence one cannot say a word, make a movement without its being the cause of something else. And this something else is the cause of yet another thing. And all this follows automatically and strictly, and that is universal justice.

An act carried out has always a consequence and this consequence brings along another and so on. And this is absolutely ineluctable. That is universal justice. You have a bad thought, it has a result. And that result has yet another. And you cannot escape it except through the intervention of Grace. Grace is exactly something which has the power of changing all that. But only the Grace can change it. It is so strict a law and so terrible that once one has entered within it, one cannot get out. And the moment one is upon earth, one enters therein. The whole earthly existence is like that, constructed in this way. And each thing one does, each thing one says, each thing one thinks, each thing one feels has a consequence. And this consequence brings another, and so on. Now, if one wants to have a more practical point of view, one may take examples and say: "If you do this, it will automatically produce that." For instance, in societies organised by men, if you commit a crime, you will be punished for your crime. In your own conscience, if you make a mistake, you suffer for the mistake you have made. And in the law as man has made it, it is always said that to be ignorant of the law is no excuse. If you are ignorant of the law, you are punished. If you make a mistake without knowing that it is a mistake, that does not protect you, you are punished. Well, in Nature it is the same thing. If you take poison without knowing that it is poison, it will poison you all the same. Do you understand?... Unless the Grace intervenes. And as the Grace is omnipotent, it can change everything. That is what I have explained. But without the Grace there is no hope. For precisely it is ignorance that's the constant factor of mankind.

I was thinking today how many deplorable and frightful experiences man has had to go through before knowing how to make use of Nature's things. It is possible that there was just this Grace which made him find things instinctively; but if he had to learn his lesson... I thought about that because... there are a certain number of fruits on the trees: there are fruits which are good, and then others which are poisoned — this is not written upon the tree. Now, there is always someone to tell you: "No, do not eat this, this will poison you." But if there were nobody to tell you that, how would you know? — By eating it and poisoning yourself. And then it would be somebody else who would have the benefit of your experience.

I thought of that because some fruits, when ripe, are excellent; they have a great nourishing power, they are very useful.

## 18 November 1953

But if they are not ripe they poison you. And it is the same fruit. Take, for instance, the avocado, (butterfruit, I think), take the butterfruit; if you eat an unripe butterfruit (you won't eat it because it tastes very bad), but if you eat an unripe butterfruit, it poisons you radically, whilst as soon as it is ripe, it is excellent. Now, in some countries as in South America or certain parts of Africa, these trees grow as high as the tallest mango trees. And all the fruits hang down in the same way. Somebody who comes along not knowing the tree, not knowing anything and without anyone to warn him, takes the fruit, cuts it, eats it and dies. Then someone else comes by a month later, all the fruits are ripe; he takes them, eats them, finds himself well nourished — it is excellent, it is wonderful. Now, somebody tells him: "Ah! how is it you have eaten that fruit, and the other man is dead.... " So how many experiences are necessary to learn that it is because one ate the unripe fruit and the other the ripe. And when it is not ripe, it is bad and when ripe, good.

And we benefit by all the experiences of those who were upon earth before us. But if we had to come to a country about which we knew nothing, and had to learn everything by ourselves, we would have very unpleasant experiences. There are other fruits like that, this is not the only one, there are many such. For example, the fig — the unripe fig — if you touch the white juice that oozes from the fig — but it's awful — you have boils all over the mouth and become quite ill, and you get ulcers in the stomach also. But when the fig is ripe and you take care not to touch the white juice, it is a perfect food. I could give you a great many examples of this kind. But now we know this because we have been told. Those who told us learnt it from others. But who first made the experiment, who learnt all that, all the things in Nature?... There are many, there are countless things in Nature. Well, take plant life in Nature, we don't yet know everything today. For instance, some people tell you: "The remedy is always there along with the illness, in Nature; Nature has made it thus." I don't know if this is strictly so, but in any case, in a way it works, it is true. It is said, for instance, that if a snake has its hole somewhere, you may be sure you will find beside it a plant which will cure you if bitten. But which plant? There are so many there and who will teach you? There are people who go up to the mountains in the moonlight and collect herbs which cure diseases generally considered incurable. How have they learnt that? Who has made the experiment?

*And mushrooms?...*

Ah! yes, it is the same thing. You have side by side, just next to one another, a mushroom that's an excellent food and another which will send you to the other world immediately. We benefit by an accumulated knowledge. And I dare say much of this knowledge must have been lost, for many men have discovered things like these and never noted them down; and we too, we may make discoveries but don't always take care to note them down and make them accessible to others. And Nature is an almost infinite field of study and discovery.

Pavitra: *Those who discovered explosives — how many died and how many had accidents....*

That's man, it is his own fault. If he had not meddled with that, it would not have happened.

*Often he may have touched it accidentally, without knowing it, without doing it on purpose.*

But it is still an explosive. It is always the fault of another man, isn't it?

*Those who studied chemistry and alighted upon explosives.*

If they didn't know what it was, yes. For instance, you take some

18 November 1953

potassium chlorate, quite harmless, white, pretty, crystallised, charming. But then you take a hammer and start hitting it with all your might, and suddenly it explodes. Yes, it is like that.

But the number of plants — nobody has ever known and nobody will probably ever know the number of different plants there are upon earth. Yet when a list is made of the number of plants men know and use, it is ridiculously small. I believe, when I was in Japan, the Japanese used to tell me that Europeans eat only three hundred and fifty types of different plants, whilst they use more than six hundred. That makes a considerable difference. They used to say: "Oh, how you waste your food! Nature produces infinitely more than you know; you waste all that." Have you ever eaten (not here, but in Europe) bamboo sprouts?... You have eaten bamboo sprouts? You have eaten palm-tree buds? Coconut buds? — That, indeed, makes a marvellous salad, coconut flowers. Only, this kills the tree. For a salad, one kills a tree. But when there is a cyclone, for instance, which knocks down hundreds of coconut trees, the only way of utilising the catastrophe is to eat all the buds and make yourself a magnificent dish. Haven't you ever eaten coconut buds? As for me, I was not surprised, for I had eaten bamboo sprouts before they sprang up from the ground — somewhat like the asparagus. It is quite a classical dish in Japan. And their bamboos are much more tender than the bamboos here. Their bamboos are very tender and their sprouts are wonderful.

Still, that's how it is. It seems in Europe one knows how to use only three hundred and fifty varieties of vegetables from the vegetable kingdom, whilst in Japan they use six hundred of them and more. But perhaps if people knew, they would not die of hunger, at least those who live in the countryside. *Voilá*.

In any case, things are like that. We don't know how it would be if it were only justice reigning over the world. But I believe it wouldn't be fun! For, as I have said, there is not a single person who can stand before the Lord and tell him: "I have never made a mistake." And when I speak of making a mistake, ignorance is not an excuse; for whether you touch the fire through ignorance or knowing it, the difference is rather in favour of the stupidity of touching it when one knows, for one can take precautions. But when one touches the fire through ignorance, without knowing, one burns oneself completely. And then one can't tell Nature: "Oh! I should not have been burnt, for I did not know that it burnt." It burns, nobody will listen to you!

*Does the intervention of the Grace come through a call?*

When one calls? I think so. Anyway, not exclusively and solely. But certainly, yes, if one has faith in the Grace and an aspiration and if one does what a little child would when it runs to its mother and says: "Mamma, give me this", if one calls with that simplicity, if one turns to the Grace and says "Give me this", I believe it listens. Unless one asks for something that is not good for one, then it does not listen. If one asks from it something that does harm or is not favourable, it does not listen.

*What is the cause of this effect? of the call?*

Perhaps one was destined to call. That is: Did the hen produce the egg or the egg the hen? I don't know whether it is the Grace which makes you call the Grace or whether because the Grace is called the Grace comes. It is difficult to say.

Essentially, it is quite possible that what is most lacking is faith. There is always a tiny corner in the thought which doubts and debates. So that spoils everything. It is only just when one is in an absolutely critical situation, when the mind realises that it can do nothing, absolutely nothing, when it stands there quite stupid and incapable, then, at that moment, if one aspires for a higher help, the aspiration has exactly that kind of intensity which comes from despair, and that takes effect. But if your thought continues to argue, if it says: "Yes, yes, I have aspired, I

## 18 November 1953

have prayed, but God knows if this is the moment, and whether it will come and whether it is possible", well, then it is finished, it doesn't work. This is one of the commonest of things. People are told: "If you want to advance in the yoga, you must have no desires". One goes even a little further and says: "You must not have any needs." One goes a little further still and says: "Never ask anything from the Divine." Well, I don't know, more than ninety-nine times out of a hundred, people's reaction is: "Ah! if I don't ask, I won't have what I need." They don't see that they cut the whole movement at the very root! They don't have faith. "I need this...."

I am not even discussing the idea of need, for it is quite arbitrary. I knew a Dutch painter who had come here, and done Sri Aurobindo's portrait (it seems this portrait is still existent). This Dutch painter was practising a yoga. And so, one day, he told me this: "Oh! as for me, I think I can do without anything. Truly I believe one can reduce one's needs to a minimum. But all the same, I must have a tooth-brush." I had not yet lived in India at that time, otherwise I would have told him: "There are millions of people who have never had a toothbrush and whose teeth are quite clean. This is not the only way of keeping one's teeth clean." But at that time he was quite convinced that one could do without everything except keeping one's mouth clean. And for him, to keep one's mouth clean meant having a tooth-brush. That gives a very exact picture of what goes on in people's minds. They cling to something and think they need it. And surely it is a complete ignorance, for perhaps there is a real necessity like that of having a clean mouth (that seems to be in any case quite necessary), but that association of the tooth-brush with the necessity of having a clean mouth is quite arbitrary. For it is not so very long ago that tooth-brushes were invented.

There was someone else also who told me: "Oh! I can absolutely do without anything at all" — we were speaking of a walking-tour with a minimum of baggage on the back (when you are compelled to carry it for miles on end, four or five kilometres a day, you try to reduce the weight of your bag as much as possible); so we discussed about what was indispensable and had to be put in the bag. He said his tooth-brush. Another told me he needed a piece of soap (usually this spins round very simple tiny things of this kind). But here how many people there are who have never used soap, and that doesn't prevent them from being clean! There are other ways of being clean. That's how it is, one is fixed in all kinds of small ideas and believes these are indispensable needs. And then, if you travel a little around the world, you notice that what is a need for you is for others something they don't even know of, something they have never seen in their life, which doesn't exist and hasn't the slightest importance of any kind. Hence it is not indispensable. It is just the result of an education and life in a particular environment. And these things are quite relative, and not only relative but transitory.

*Voilà.*

# 25 November 1953

*You have said: "It is in proportion to our trust in the Divine that the Divine Grace can act for us and help."[1] If someone has no trust in the Divine, but calls very sincerely when he is in difficulty, in danger, what will happen to him?*

How can he call? The two things are contradictory. If he has no trust, he won't even think of the Divine! He won't think of calling. It is contradictory. He thinks of calling exactly in proportion to his trust.... So?

*You have said here: "To smile at an enemy is to disarm him."[2] "Smile" means what? One ought not to smile at an enemy!*

One ought not to!... What I have stated here is an experience. It is the record of an experience which I expressed in general terms. But if, at a particular moment, somebody comes along with the blackest intentions, if one smiles at him, he is completely disarmed, he can do nothing any longer. But one must smile sincerely. One must not just grin or simper and think one... *(laughter)* I take "smile" in a rather complete meaning. That is to say, if one can be sufficiently master of oneself and above things, in a much higher consciousness which can see from above — even that which appears the most terrible and most dramatic to the ordinary human consciousness makes you smile as at a childishness. And so, if one is in that consciousness in which one can smile at everything (for one understands the causes of everything, and one also sees the forces working in

---

[1] *Words of the Mother*, MCW Vol. 14, p. 96.
[2] Ibid., p. 191.

all things), if one can be in that consciousness and then smile at what happens, immediately things change. Only, this is not a little external and social smile: it must be the psychic being which smiles.

*Doesn't the Divine help if he is not called?*

It is not altogether like that.... The divine Consciousness works always, everywhere and in the same way. The divine Grace is active everywhere, and in all circumstances in the same way. And so on. But according to your personal attitude, you create within yourself the conditions for receiving what is done or not receiving it. And trust — indeed, trust in the Truth, trust in the Grace, trust in the divine Knowledge — this puts you in that state of receptivity in which you can receive these things. Whilst, if you have no trust... you may still try to receive something — there are people, for instance, who fling a sort of challenge, they throw a challenge at the Divine and tell him: "Here's the situation such as it is, I am in these conditions which seem to me at least inextricable, it is impossible to get out of them. But if the Divine pulls me out of the difficulty, I shall put my trust in him." There are many people — they do not formulate it like this but many feel and think in this way. Well, this is the worst of all possible conditions. Generally it puts you into a complete hole. And it is exactly the state most opposed to trustfulness. And besides, it is quite a vulgar bargaining: "If you do this for me, I shall have faith that you exist. I am going to try and see if you really exist and whether you are what they say. Do this, and we are going to see clearly if you succeed. Then I shall trust in you." And many people do that, even without being aware of it. Any number of men say: "How can I have trust in the Divine? I have such a lamentable and unhappy life!" That is to say, they limit the divine Consciousness to their little personal needs.

*If one has the trust, does the help come automatically?*

25 November 1953

Even an atom of sincerity suffices, and it comes. And if, truly, one calls very sincerely (not just calling and at the same time saying, "We are going to see now if it is going to succeed" — that naturally is not a very good condition), but if one calls very sincerely and sincerely needs the answer, one waits and it *always* comes. And if one can silence one's mind and be a little quiet, one even perceives the coming of the help and what form it takes.

*From where do the gods come?*

That means?... "From where" means what? What is their origin? Who has formed them?... But everything, everything comes from the one Origin, from the Supreme, the gods also.

There is a very old tradition which narrates this. I am going to tell you the story as one does to children, for in this way you will understand:

One day "God" decided to exteriorise himself, objectivise himself, in order to have the joy of knowing himself in detail. So, first of all, he emanated his consciousness (that is to say, he manifested his consciousness) by ordering this consciousness to realise a universe. This consciousness began by emanating four beings, four individualities which were indeed altogether very high beings, of the highest Reality. They were the being of consciousness, the being of love (of Ananda rather), the being of life and the being of light and knowledge — but consciousness and light are the same thing. There we are then: consciousness, love and Ananda, life and truth — truth, that's the exact word. And naturally, they were supremely powerful beings, you understand. They were what are called in that tradition the first emanations, that is, the first formations. And each one became very conscious of its qualities, its power, its capacities, its possibilities, and, suddenly forgot each in its own way that it was only an emanation and an incarnation of the Supreme. And so this is what happened: when light or Consciousness separated

371

from the divine Consciousness, that is, when it began to think it was the divine Consciousness and that there was nothing other than itself, it suddenly became obscurity and inconscience. And when Life thought that all life was in itself and that there was nothing else but its life and that it did not depend at all upon the Supreme, then its life became death. And when Truth thought that it contained all truth, and that there was no other truth than itself, this Truth became falsehood. And when love or Ananda was convinced that it was the supreme Ananda and that there was no other than itself and its felicity, it became suffering. And that is how the world, which was to have been so beautiful, became so ugly. Now, that consciousness (if you like to call it the Divine Mother, the Supreme Consciousness), when she saw this she was very disturbed, you may be sure, she said to herself: "This has really not succeeded." So she turned back to the Divine, to God, the Supreme, and she asked him to come to her aid. She said to him: "This is what has happened. Now what is to be done?" He said: "Begin again, but try to manage in such a way that the beings do not become so independent! ... They must remain in contact with you, and through you with me." And it was thus that she created the gods, who were quite docile and not so proud, and who began the creation of the world. But as the others had come before them, at every step the gods met the others. And it was in this way that the world changed into a battlefield, a place of war, strife, suffering, darkness and all the rest, and for each new creation the gods had to fight with the others who had gone ahead: they had preceded them, they had plunged headlong into matter; and they had created all this disorder and the gods had to put straight all this confusion. That is where the gods came from. They are the second emanations.

*Mother, the first four who changed, was it by chance or was it deliberately?*

No. What is chance?

*25 November 1953*

It is said also — that is the continuation of the story or rather its beginning — that the Divine wanted his creation to be a free creation. He wanted all that went forth from him to be absolutely independent and free in order to be able to unite with him in freedom, not through compulsion. He did not want that they should be compelled to be faithful, compelled to be conscious, compelled to be obedient. They had to do it spontaneously, through the knowledge and conviction that that was much better. So this world was created as a world of total freedom, freedom of choice. And it is in this way that at every moment everyone has the freedom of choice — but with all the consequences. If one chooses well, it is good, but if one chooses ill, ah well, what's to happen happens — that is what has happened!

The story may be understood in a much more occult and spiritual sense. But it is like all the stories of the universe: if you want to narrate them so that people may understand, they become stories for children. But if one knows how to see the truth behind the symbols, one understands everything. Even with what I have told you, which seems like a little story for children, even like that, if you understand what I have told you and the meaning of what I have told you, you can have the secret of things.

There are traditions which say that it is an "accident", in the sense that it could have been otherwise. But it happened like that. It is true, it came about like that. Only, it was quite understandable that, every one of these elements having its origin in the Supreme, being quite close to the Emanation at that moment, quite close to the Origin, carried in itself the consciousness of its divinity and superiority, necessarily, since this is not a creation made with something foreign to the Divine: it is simply the Divine who has emanated himself, as though he were looking at himself — he objectivises himself in order to become aware of all that he is; instead of being in an inner static state of concentration in which all is unmanifested, he projects that outside himself "in order to see", as though he wanted to see all that is within him, that is, all the infinity of possibilities. So, all was possible. It happened like that — it could have happened otherwise. Besides, nothing tells you that alongside our universe such as it is, there do not exist others which are so different that there cannot be any relation between one universe and another. It can very well be that our universe is not the only exteriorisation of the Divine. Ours is such as we know it; there may be others which are in much less sorry a state than this one! Besides, it is lamentable only in its appearance. If you go behind the appearance, you become aware that it is not lamentable at all. It is only one way of seeing.

> *"When we have made a decisive spiritual progress the invisible enemies of the Divine always try to have their revenge and when they cannot injure the soul they strike the body, but all their efforts are in vain and will finally be defeated as the Divine Grace is with us."*
> Words of the Mother, MCW Vol. 15, p. 22

*What are these "invisible enemies of the Divine"?*

They are precisely those four persons who have naturally put forth innumerable emanations, which have again put forth others, which have made formations. And so there are millions and millions and millions of them, and it is these who have formed between themselves a certain habit and have the logic to preserve it and continue not to want any other rule than theirs to govern. These are what are called in India the Asuras, the beings of darkness. It is through a sort of logic that they are like that. They began by going wrong, they continue. Now, I must say, there are some among them who change their mind. But this is mentioned in the Gita also; I believe they speak of those who will be converted, and then of those who absolutely refuse any conversion, who prefer to disappear, to be destroyed rather than

## 25 November 1953

be converted. And that's how it is. Some are of one kind, others of another.

*Which are "the others" who have been converted?*

Ah, you know that? You have a good memory. There is one of them who has been converted, and who even collaborates, he is the one of Consciousness and Light.

*If he is converted, the difficulty must go of itself.*

Naturally, but his power remains. This becomes a formidable being.

*You said that consciousness had changed into inconscience. But when consciousness is converted, inconscience must go?*

It becomes once again consciousness and light — it becomes once more what it was.

*Hasn't it become that again?*

But I have just said a minute ago that when it became inconscience or darkness, it produced innumerable formations — emanations, formations, creations. And its conversion does not mean that all the rest follow. They obey that same law of freedom, freedom of choice. They may be converted or not. There are those who are converted, there are those who refuse. And I believe that in fact there are many more who refuse.

But the one who does the greatest harm is the "Lord of Falsehood". He it is indeed who is the biggest obstacle in the universe, this constant negation of the truth. And he has a very strong hold on the terrestrial world, on the material world. Besides, here (on the earth), those who see him, see him as an absolutely marvellous, splendid being. He entitles himself the "Lord of the Nations", and he appears formidable, luminous, powerful, very impressive.... Historically, he was the inspirer of certain heads of State, and he proclaims himself the Lord of the Nations because it is he who governs the peoples. He is evidently, at the source, the supreme organiser of these last two wars. It was on that occasion that he manifested himself as the Lord of the Nations. And he declared, besides, that he would never be converted. And he knows that his end will come — naturally, he will try to make it as late as possible. And he declared that he would destroy all he could before being destroyed.... We may expect all possible catastrophes.

*In February you gave a message saying "a new light shall break upon the earth",* [3] *and just after that [on 5 March 1953], Stalin died. Does this signify anything?*

That would truly be a small result. The death of Stalin (unfortunately not any more than the death of Hitler) has not changed the present state of the world. Something more than that would be necessary. For this is like the assassin who is guillotined: when his head is cut off, his spirit remains behind and is projected outside him. It is a vital formation and it goes and takes shelter in one of the benevolent spectators, who suddenly feels a criminal instinct in himself. There are many men like that, specially very young criminals who when questioned have acknowledged this. They have been asked: "When did this desire to kill come to you?" and the frequent reply is: "It got hold of me when I saw so-and-so executed."

So, this is of no use, the death of this one or that other. That does not help very much — the thing goes elsewhere. It is only

---

[3] The reference is to a message given to the Bengali journal *Srinvantu*: "Let the Light of the Truth be born upon earth from today and for ever."

*(21 February 1953)*

## 25 November 1953

one form. It is as though you did something very wicked with a particular shirt on and then threw away your shirt and said: "Now, I shall no longer do harm." You continue with another shirt on!

*If life has been converted into death, why doesn't it itself die?*

Because it protects itself well. What you say is quite true, but it takes good care not to incarnate on earth. And in the vital world there is no death, it does not exist there. It is in the material world that this exists, and it takes very good care not to incarnate.

*Was Stalin predestined to be what he was?*

Stalin? I am not quite sure that he was a human being... in the sense that I don't think he had a psychic being. Or perhaps he did have one — in all matter, in every atom there is a divine centre — but I mean a conscious psychic being, formed, individualised. I don't think so. I believe it was a direct incarnation of a being of the vital world. And that was the great difference between him and Hitler. Hitler was simply a man, and as a man he was very weak-minded, very sentimental — he had the conscience of a petty workman (some said of a petty shoemaker), in any case of a little workman or a little school-master, something like that, a very small conscience, and extremely sentimental, what is called in French "fleur bleue", very weak.

But he was possessed. He was rather mediocre by nature, very mediocre. He was a medium, a very good medium — the thing took hold of him, besides, during spiritism séances. It was at that moment that he was seized by those fits which were described as epileptic. They were not epileptic: they were attacks of possession. It was thus that he had a kind of power, which however was not very great. But when he wanted to know something from that power, he went away to his castle, and there, in "meditation", there truly he invoked very intensely what he called his "god", his supreme god, who was the Lord of the Nations. And everything seemed to him magnificent. It was a being... it was small — it appeared to him all in silver armour, with a silver helmet and golden plume! It was magnificent! And a light so dazzling that hardly could the eyes see and bear that blaze. Naturally it did not appear physically — Hitler was a medium, he saw. He had a sort of clairvoyance. And it was at such times that he had his fits: he rolled on the ground, he drivelled, bit the carpet, it was frightful, the state he was in. The people around him knew it. Well, that being is the "Lord of the Nations". And it is not even the Lord of the Nations in its origin, it is an emanation of the Lord of the Nations, and a very powerful emanation.

*If it chooses to disappear, would that be a loss of power for the Divine?*

What? What are you saying! Disappear where? What do you call disappearing? — Disappear where? You know the story of the Ramayana. What did Ravana choose? You know that? Very well, this is what is called choosing to disappear: that is to say, he has no longer any individuality.

*What happened to Ravana after his death we are not told.*

We are not told? To me it has been told. It is said that Ravana chose to disappear into the Supreme, and that he was completely dissolved in Him, that is, he lost his individuality, he was no longer a separate being, he returned to the Origin, he was dissolved in the Supreme. And even before doing it, he had chosen to play that part, his part as a hostile being, because the road is much shorter than for those who are devotees and obey. One goes much more rapidly, for, one day, the Divine decides

## 25 November 1953

that it is enough, and he just destroys them. He cannot go out of the Divine, for all is divine! He may lose his individuality, that is, may be fused, dissolved into the Supreme.

Besides, nothing disappears, it is the form which disappears but the constituent elements continue. Everything is eternal, for everything is the Divine, and nothing can go out of the Divine, for everything is divine. But the forms disappear. And it is through this identification with the form that the impression of death comes; but the constituent elements are eternal, for all is eternal. It is the form which disappears.

So, some of those beings prefer to be just completely dissolved and to disappear totally like that, into the infinite, the oneness (that is, they lose their personal consciousness, they have no longer any personal consciousness, they exist no longer as a personal consciousness), they prefer that, rather than having a personal consciousness which gives itself to the Divine and becomes by this very fact consciously and personally immortal. They like dissolution and personal disappearance better than conversion, that is, self-giving.

*Why?*

Through pride, I suppose. It is always pride. Fundamentally, from the very beginning it is pride — but almost all the religions have said it. It is pride, that is, a sort of consciousness of one's power and one's importance.

*You said that these four emanations were parts of the Supreme. Then how can they have another consciousness than His?*

Another consciousness? But there is no other consciousness! The very principle of emanation is an objectivisation of a part of himself, which potentially keeps the qualities of the emanator. But if this emanation is made (as they were made) with a will

379

to give freedom of choice, as I said, these emanations can either follow that freedom and independence or continue to keep the connection with the emanator, for there is a freedom of choice. That strength and force which they hold in themselves is quite sufficient to give them the impression of their importance and power. If they choose not to remain in a voluntary contact, in a relation of surrender to the Supreme, if they choose to use the amount of power and consciousness and force they contain in themselves to do what they must do independently, by that very fact they cut themselves off from their source — but in spite of that the constituent elements of their being are those which belonged to the Source. And it is because of this that, even if they cut themselves off voluntarily, there is in the very depth of the consciousness a link which is indestructible. It is the link of identity. But in the outer manifestation, as they were emanated with this essential quality of freedom of choice, well, they are free to choose to do this or that. That is why, even in the worst criminal, there is somewhere in the depths, somewhere, the divine light. I believe you have read that passage of Vivekananda where he says (I don't know the exact words), that the criminal must be told: "Awake, awake, being of light, and shine forth!"

Just a while ago, when I told you I shall narrate the story to you as one does to children, that is precisely because I narrated it as if it were a material story. And so, told thus, it becomes a child's story. But these things must be seen in their own domain, which is a spiritual domain and not a material one. Things do not happen as they would here.

But still, yes! What happens here is symbolically the same thing, in the sense that the child who is born is nothing else but a little piece of his mother, even materially, altogether materially, for during almost — completely during a few hours, about two days, and to a lesser extent though still very perceptibly during at least two months — this link of substance is so great that it feels really like a physical material prolongation of herself, but outside herself. That is just the element of emanation. Well, this

## 25 November 1953

does not prevent children, when they grow up, from becoming quite independent of their parents and at times completely different, but at the source, at the beginning, it is the same thing. It is simply the same matter, absolutely the same, simply exteriorised, that's all.

And for the emanations, it is the same phenomenon, but instead of being on a material plane it is on the highest spiritual plane. And what happens here is a symbol of what happens up above.

Well, doesn't it ever occur to you to say: "How is it that this child whose father and mother are so good, so honest, so generous, so truthful, how is it that he is such a rascal?" You may wonder at it, but it does not seem anything impossible. So, this is the same thing. Fundamentally, all depends on the inner constitution of the being. There are no two beings who are exactly alike; there are no two constitutions which are the same. And all depends on the inner organisation, the integral organisation of the being, on the order in which the elements are organised and what their inner relation is — even as the external form differs because the cells are not organised in the same way. But as this is a phenomenon you constantly see, in the midst of which you are born, which you see every day, it seems quite natural to you. But it is the same thing. It seems quite natural to you that a child is different from its mother and father — and yet this is the same thing. And in an emanation of the Supreme, to begin with, one part is necessarily different from the whole, though it may potentially contain the whole, but the whole is not expressed. And as the whole is not expressed, it is perforce different from the whole, for the inner organisation is different. There then, I think that is enough.

We have almost touched philosophy.

*Au revoir*, my children.

# 9 December 1953

*"We are always surrounded by the things of which we think."*

Words of the Mother, MCW Vol. 14, p. 366

This is very important.

If you think of nasty things, you will be surrounded by nasty things.

*"To get over our ego is not an easy task.*

*"Even after overcoming it in the material consciousness, we meet it once more — magnified — in the spiritual."*

Ibid., p. 278

*How can one meet one's ego in the spiritual consciousness?*

There is a spiritual ego even as there is a physical, vital and mental ego. There is a spiritual ego. There are people who have made a great effort to overcome all their egoism and all their limitations, and attained a spiritual consciousness; and there, they have all the vanity and the sense of their importance and contempt for those who are not in the same condition as they. Indeed, all that is ridiculous and bad in the ego, they find there once again. There are many, many like that. They have overcome what was there in the physical or vital consciousness but the very effort they have made to master themselves and this victory they have gained give them the sense of their extreme importance. So they become puffed up and assert their authority.

This happens so frequently that it is not even noticed.

9 December 1953

*I didn't understand this: "The so-called forces of Nature are but the exterior activities of beings out of proportion with man by their size and the powers at their disposal."*

Words of the Mother, MCW Vol. 15, p. 12

Didn't understand?... For instance, take the wind which blows; now scientists will tell you: "These are manifestations of forces of Nature, and it is the result of such and such a phenomenon", they will speak about heat and cold, high and low, etc., and they will tell you: "That's the cause of the wind's blowing, these are currents of air produced in the atmosphere." But it is not this. There are entities behind, only they are so huge that their form eludes us. It would be like your asking an ant to describe the form of a man — it couldn't, could it? It sees at the most the tiny end of the little finger and it takes a walk on the foot — it is a great journey, and it would not know what a man's form would be like. Well, it is almost the same thing. These forces which bring about wind, rain, earthquakes, etc. are manifestations of — call them gestures, if you like — of movements of certain beings so formidably huge that we hardly see the end of their foot and don't realise their size.

*Still, the spiritual ego is better than the ordinary ego, isn't it?*

It is much more dangerous than the ordinary one! For one is not aware that it is the ego. Outwardly, when one is egoistic, not only does one know it oneself but others make you realise it still more, and circumstances prove it to you every moment. But there, as unfortunately you meet people who respect you highly, you are not even aware that you are terribly egoistic.

Very dangerous. Spiritual vanity is much more serious than physical vanity.

383

*Then, Sweet Mother, with the ego can one realise the Divine?*

Not at the moment one unites with Him. It is evident that at that moment the ego disappears. But that state does not last. Or in any case we can put it in another way: those who have brought along their ego with them cannot keep the consciousness for long. They become aware of themselves again whilst having the experience. It is that which is most terrible. They look at themselves having the experience and admire themselves. And they feel they are exceptional beings, much higher than others, and then that becomes deplorable.

*Here, you have said: "Whether Thou choosest for me life or death, happiness or sorrow, pleasure or suffering, all that comes to me from Thee will be welcome."*
*Does the Divine give suffering or sorrow?*

Well, my child, that text, you know what it is: it is Radha's prayer to Krishna. And so, it is such a personification of divine forces that one is obliged to extend human feelings to the Divine in order to be able to express oneself. To understand it in its true form a whole long explanation would be required, and then it is no longer artistic — it becomes dogmatic or in any case pedagogic. It is to give the idea that all is in the Divine and all is divine. And necessarily, if one changes the state of consciousness and is identified with the Divine, that changes the very nature of things. For example, what seemed pain or sorrow or misery — one becomes aware quite on the contrary that it is an opportunity for the Divine's growing closer to you, and that from this event perhaps one may draw a still greater joy than that experienced from something satisfying. Only, you must understand it like that, in that spirit and with that consciousness, for otherwise, if taken in the ordinary sense, it is the very contradiction of the principle that all is divine.

## 9 December 1953

The same thing, exactly the same vibration, according to the way in which it is received and responded to, brings either an intense joy or considerable despair, exactly the same, according to the state of consciousness one is in. So there is nothing of which it could be said: it is a misfortune. There is nothing that could be called suffering. All that is necessary is to change one's state of consciousness. That is all. Only (I have written this somewhere, I don't know where now), if you yourself succeed in changing your state of consciousness and enter this condition of bliss, you can see others still quarrelling, fighting, being unhappy, suffering and feeling miserable, and you yourself feel that everything is so harmonious, so wonderful, so sweet, so pleasant, and you say: "Well, why don't they do what I do?" But the trouble is that everybody is not ready to do that! And for those who remain in the ordinary consciousness, for them suffering is something very real.

Now, there are people who don't care to be happy all alone and agree to renounce this perfect bliss in order to help others to walk a little farther on the path.

Attitudes in the world — attitudes towards virtue — are very subjective. And what may succeed with one may not do so with another. And every one must follow his own path. That is why it is always difficult to say to people: "Do what I do." This is what all gurus usually say: "Do as I do and you will reach the goal." All that one may say is: "Do as I do and you will be like me."

*(Silence)*

Ah! I wanted to ask you a question. We said at the beginning: one is surrounded by what one thinks about. You understand quite well what this means? *(Turning to a child)* Every time you think of something, it is as though you had a magnet in your hand and were attracting that thing towards yourself — you understand. Now, there are people who have a very, very bad habit of always thinking about all possible catastrophes, and are in a sort of constant apprehension about some calamity befalling them the next moment. I know many like that, there are some here. And so, those people have as though a magnet in their hands to attract calamities, not only upon themselves but upon others also. That lays a big responsibility upon them. And if one can't stop all the time from thinking about something — some have a head that runs on and they haven't found a way of stopping it — well, why not make it run on the right lines instead of letting it run on the others! Once your head begins to run, let it run on all the good things that can happen. If it is obliged to turn round and round, well, turn then to the good side! That is, if somebody is ill, instead of saying: "What is going to happen, perhaps this is going to be very serious, and if it is that disease... and a calamity comes so quickly", instead of all that, if one thinks: "Oh! that is nothing, illnesses are outer illusions translating some deeper vibrations which are not seen, that is why one doesn't speak about them, but that's how it is. And these deeper vibrations may come and set in order what has been disturbed. And this imbalance, this illness or bad thing that has come, well, it will be absorbed by the Grace and will disappear, no trace of it will remain, except that of things agreeable and pleasant." One may continue to think in this way uninterruptedly.... People always need to make their mind run, run, run, but then make it run on the right lines, you will see that it has an effect. For instance, let it go like this: that I shall learn better and better, shall know better and better, become healthier and healthier, and all difficulties will vanish, and wicked people will become sweet and good, and ill people will be cured, and houses which should be built will be built, and those things which should disappear will disappear, but giving place to better things, and the world will move in a constant progress, and at the end of that progress there will be a total harmony, and so on, and continue thus.... You can go on endlessly. But then you will have around you and around

9 December 1953

your head all kinds of pretty things. Those who perceive the atmosphere see certain inky stains, like an octopus there, yes, like that, with its tentacles to try and upset your mind — instead of that, one will see happy formations, formations of light or rays of sunlight or perhaps beautiful pictures, all that. One will see beautiful things — there are painters who do that and they always catch thoughts.

> *Sweet Mother, you have said: "Each meditation ought to be a new revelation, for in each meditation something new happens."[1] After the meditation, is one conscious of what has happened?*

But that's exactly the thing; I say: pay attention and become conscious. If one is very attentive, one becomes conscious. One must be very concentrated and very attentive, then one becomes conscious.

> *Mother, suffering comes from ignorance and pain, but what is the nature of the suffering and pain the Divine Mother feels for her children — the Divine Mother in Savitri?*

It is because she participates in their nature. She has descended upon earth to participate in their nature. Because if she did not participate in their nature, she could not lead them farther. If she remained in her supreme consciousness where there is no suffering, in her supreme knowledge and consciousness, she could not have any contact with human beings. And it is for this that she is obliged to take on the human consciousness and form, it is to be able to enter into contact with them. Only, she does not forget: she has adopted their consciousness but she remains in relation with her own real, supreme consciousness. And thus, by joining

---

[1] *Words of the Mother*, MCW Vol. 14, p. 53.

the two, she can make those who are in that other consciousness progress. But if she did not adopt their consciousness, if she did not suffer with their sorrow, she could not help them. Hers is not a suffering of ignorance: it is a suffering through identity. It is because she has accepted to have the same vibrations as they, in order to be able to enter into contact with them and pull them out of the state they are in. If she did not enter into contact with them, she would not be felt at all or no one could bear her radiance.... This has been said in all kinds of forms, in all kinds of religions, and they have spoken very often of the divine Sacrifice, but from a certain point of view it is true. It is a voluntary sacrifice, but it is true: giving up a state of perfect consciousness, perfect bliss, perfect power in order to accept the state of ignorance of the outer world so as to pull it out of that ignorance. If this state were not accepted, there would be no contact with it. No relation would be possible. And this is the reason of the incarnations. Otherwise, there would be no necessity. If the divine consciousness and divine force could work directly from the place or state of their perfection, if they could work directly on matter and transform it, there would be no need to take a body like man's. It would have been enough to act from the world of Truth with the perfect consciousness and upon consciousness. In fact that acts perhaps but so slowly that when there is this effort to make the world progress, make it go forward more rapidly, well, it is necessary to take on human nature. By taking the human body, one is obliged to take on human nature, partially. Only, instead of losing one's consciousness and losing contact with the Truth, one keeps this consciousness and this Truth, and it is by joining the two that one can create exactly this kind of alchemy of transformation. But if one did not touch matter, one could do nothing for it.

*Did Savitri foresee what she was going to do?*

She said so. You have not read it? She had even been told that

# 9 December 1953

she would be alone. And she said: I am ready to be alone. You have not read it? It is in the canto they recited last year.[2]

*Did she know she would meet the "Mother of Sorrows", the "Mother of Might"?*

Indeed she did. It is said all along that she knew all that was going to happen. It is written clearly. Indeed, to each of them she says clearly: I shall bring to you what you need. Consequently, she knows it. Else she would not say so. If she did not know it, how could she say so?

*In* Savitri *the "Mother of Sorrows" says:*
*"Perhaps when the world sinks into a last sleep,*
*I too may sleep in dumb eternal peace."*
Savitri, CWSA Vol. 34, p. 505

Ah! that, that is the human consciousness. It is the human consciousness. It is the idea of the human consciousness that when all suffering will be over, well, "I shall sleep". It is indeed of this that Sri Aurobindo speaks. When there is this aspiration for a supreme peace, one feels that if there were a *pralaya* and the world disappeared, well, at least there would be peace. But the phrase itself is self-contradictory, for if there were a *pralaya*, there would be no more peace to be felt — there would be nothing at all any longer!

But this is just one of the contradictions of the human consciousness: "As long as the world is there and suffering there, I shall suffer with the world. But if ever the world enters into peace, disappears in the peace of Non-Being, then I too shall rest." It is a poetic way of saying that as long as misery is there in the world, I shall suffer with the world. Only when it ceases to be there, it shall cease for me also.

---

[2] Sri Aurobindo, *Savitri*, CWSA Vol. 34 pp. 503–21, recited at the School Annual function of 1 December 1953.

### Questions and Answers 1953

*Then what will the "Mother of Sorrows" do? What else can she do?*

She will be the "Mother of Delight".

*Savitri represents the Mother's Consciousness, doesn't she?*

Yes.

*What does Satyavan represent?*

He is the Avatar, isn't he? He is the incarnation of the Supreme.

# 16 December 1953

*Sweet Mother, you have said: "... Many methods have been framed to attain this perception [of the psychic being in us] and finally to achieve this identification [with the psychic being]. Some methods are psychological, some religious, some even mechanical."*

"The Science of Living", On Education

*Will you give some examples of this?*

Mechanical, these are the Asanas, Hathayoga. It is done with this intention. Religious, these are for those who believe in a particular religion and pray and perform religious ceremonies. When one believes in a religion — no matter which — one abides by the discipline of the religion and prays and asks, one undergoes the discipline according to the teaching and observing the beliefs of the religion. The psychological method is Yoga. To seek within oneself through introspection what is permanent, what is constant. That's all.

*"Your aim should be high and wide, generous and disinterested."*

Ibid.

*What does this mean?*

You are asking what that means! High?... For instance, there are those whose aim is to make a fortune, and there are those whose aim is to find a cure for a disease. That of making one's fortune is obviously more self-seeking and lower than the one of finding a remedy for an illness. There are those who have for their aim in life a comfortable and quiet living, with a family and children, wanting the best in the best of possible worlds. That is a pretty low aim, in any case quite an ordinary one. There are those who seek the betterment of the whole of society or those who study to make new discoveries, like Mr. and Mrs. Curie, for example, who discovered radium. That is a higher aim. "Disinterested", that means what is not for one's own small personal profit, for one's personal pleasure, but solely for helping others. Naturally, the highest aim is to unite with the Divine and fulfil His work, but that, that's right at the top of the ladder. In this first chapter I took good care not to say anything of this kind, for I wrote it intentionally for everybody, even for those who have no mystical conception. But still, it goes without saying that the discovery of the Divine in oneself and uniting with Him and accomplishing His work is the highest and most disinterested aim, and the least selfish.

What adjectives have I used?

*High and wide, generous and disinterested.*

Yes. Wide, it is something that's not limited to a small purely personal consciousness and its small purely selfish advantages, something embracing a whole — which may be a group, a nation, a continent or the entire earth. For man an action working on the entire earth is surely a wide action.

*After that you have said: "This will make your life precious to yourself and to all."*

Yes. If you are useless, it is not precious, if you are useful, it becomes precious! There is nothing more disgusting than to be busy with all the little details of a narrow personal existence. One feels empty, hollow, useless. One has no interest in life. There are people all shut up in their little family, and if the baby coughs, they spend hours in fretting, if the dinner is not well-cooked, they quarrel, or if the gentleman has lost his job and is

## 16 December 1953

looking for another, he laments: "How shall I feed my family?" — That's existing like an earth-worm in a hole.

*In everybody, is the psychic always pure or has it to be made pure?*

It is always pure. But it is either more or less individualised and independent in its action. What is psychic in the being is always pure, by its very definition, for it is that part of the being which is in contact with the Divine and expresses the truth of the being. But this may be like a spark in the darkness of the being or it may be a being of light, conscious, fully formed and independent. There are all the gradations between the two.

*Usually is it veiled?*

It is the outer consciousness that is not in contact with it, for it is turned outwards instead of being turned inwards — for it lives amidst all the external noises and movements, in what it sees, what it does, what it says, instead of looking within, into the depths of the being and listening to the inner inspirations.

*Has the psychic any power?*

Power? It is usually the psychic which guides the being. One knows nothing about it because one is not conscious of it but usually it is that which guides the being. If one is very attentive, one becomes aware of it. But the majority of men haven't the least idea of it. For instance, when they have decided, in their outer ignorance, to do something, and instead of their being able to do it, all the circumstances are so organised that they do something else, they start shouting, storming, flying into a rage against fate, saying (that depends on what they believe, their beliefs) that Nature is wicked or their destiny baleful or God unjust, or... no matter what (it depends on what they believe).

Whilst most of the time it is just the very circumstance which was most favourable for their inner development. And naturally, if you ask the psychic to help you to fashion a pleasant life for yourself, to earn money, have children who will be the pride of the family, etc., well, the psychic will not help you. But it will create for you all the circumstances necessary to awaken something in you so that the need of union with the Divine may be born in your consciousness. At times you have made fine plans, and if they had succeeded, you would have been more and more encrusted in your outer ignorance, your stupid little ambition and your aimless activity. Whilst if you receive a good shock, and the post you coveted is denied to you, the plan you made is shattered, and you find yourself completely thwarted, then, sometimes this opposition opens to you a door on something truer and deeper. And when you are a little awake and look back, if you are in the least sincere, you say: "Ah! it wasn't I who was right — it was Nature or the divine Grace or my psychic being who did it." It is the psychic being which organised that.

*Is it the psychic will which wants the being to be identified with the Divine?*

Yes, surely. It is the will of the psychic. It is also the very reason of its existence. It is for that it is there. For example, in the mind certain activities (and even at times in the physical and vital) certain activities awaken to the influence of the psychic without even knowing it. That is why those parts adhere to it and begin to aspire also for the divine knowledge, the divine union, the relation with the Divine.

*How does the psychic manifest the truth?*

I have said that it manifests the truth?

*16 December 1953*

> *"We give the name 'psychic' to the psychological centre of our being, the seat within of the highest truth of our existence, that which can know and manifest this truth."*
>
> *"The Science of Living", On Education*

Oh! the truth of our existence — not just the Truth. The truth of the being, that is, the central *raison d'être* of an existence. It is that, indeed, which organises circumstances so that the truth of the being may be expressed or the superficial outer being be led to turn round within — not find any support outside, for instance, and turn within to have a support; it finds the psychic support.

> *"The body has a wonderful capacity of adaptation and endurance. It is fit to do so many more things than one can usually imagine. If instead of the ignorant and despotic masters that govern it, it is ruled by the central truth of the being, one will be surprised at what it is capable of doing. Calm and quiet, strong and poised, it will at every minute put forth the effort that is demanded of it, for it will have learnt to find rest in action, to recuperate through contact with the universal forces the energies it spends consciously and usefully."*
>
> Ibid.

*How can one have "rest in action"?*

That comes from a kind of certitude of inner choice. When one aspires for something, if at the same time one knows that the aspiration will be heard and answered in the best way possible, that establishes a quietude in the being, a quietude in its vibrations; whilst if there is a doubt, an uncertainty, if one does not know what will lead one to the goal or if ever one will reach it or whether there is a way of doing so, and so on, then one gets disturbed and that usually creates a sort of little whirlwind around the being, which prevents it from receiving the real thing. Instead, if one has a quiet faith, if whilst aspiring one knows that there is no aspiration (naturally, sincere aspiration) which remains unanswered, then one is quiet. One aspires with as much fervour as possible, but does not stand in nervous agitation asking oneself why one does not get immediately what one has asked for. One knows how to wait. I have said somewhere: "To know how to wait is to put time on one's side." That is quite true. For if one gets excited, one loses all one's time — one loses one's time, loses one's energy, loses one's movements. To be very quiet, calm, peaceful, with the faith that what is true will take place, and that if one lets it happen, it will happen so much the quicker. Then, in that peace everything goes much better.

# 23 December 1953

*If the mind "is incapable of finding knowledge"[1] what part of the being finds knowledge?*

One must enter the knowledge which belongs to the supramental region.

*But in order to bring it down?*

Every time something attracts this knowledge (something which is evidently ready to receive it), it comes.

*It does not come down into the mind, Sweet Mother?*

Yes, it descends into the mind. Into a higher part of the mind or rather into the psychic. One may have knowledge from the psychic — though it is of another kind and is not formulated as in the mind. It is a sort of inner certitude which makes you do the right thing at the right moment and in the right way, without necessarily passing through the reason or mental formation.

For instance, one may act with a perfect knowledge of what should be done, and without intervention — the least intervention — of the reasoning mind. The mind is silent: it simply looks on and listens in order to register things, it does not act.

*Here you have said: "Knowledge belongs to a region much higher than that of the human mind, even beyond the region of pure ideas."*
"The Science of Living", On Education

*Sweet Mother, what do you mean by "pure ideas"?*

[1] "The Science of Living", On Education.

We have already spoken about this once, and not so long ago. Pure ideas are those which are translated into numerous thoughts. One idea may give birth to many thoughts, and can be expressed in many different ways; and yet it remains what it is.

*Sometimes we look fixedly at a point; one forgets everything at that moment and if there is a noise one is disturbed. What is this state?*

Concentration! It is exactly the very principle of concentration. Can you do it spontaneously?

*Yes, many times.*

Indeed, that's very good!

*Yes, Sweet Mother, but what I thought at that moment I cannot capture.*

Ah!... If you are suddenly pulled out from it, thought vanishes?

*Yes.*

That's because you enter a state of consciousness which is different from your ordinary state of consciousness and probably the link between the two is not established very well. That takes time. It is as though one had to build a bridge. Otherwise one takes a sudden jump to one side or the other, and then in jumping one forgets what was there. One leaves behind the experience one had. But if the thing is done methodically, that is, if every day one keeps a particular time for this, and meditates for ten or fifteen minutes in order to establish a contact between that and the outer life, well, after some time one succeeds and then one remembers, and this becomes very useful. It is very useful. And

## 23 December 1953

if your power of concentration is complete, then there is not a problem you cannot solve — I don't mean arithmetic problems (*laughter*), I mean problems about leading one's life, about decisions to be taken, psychological problems which need solving. There is not one that can resist this power of concentration.

And in fact it is very convenient to take a point: one looks steadily at the point, and so steadily that at a certain moment one becomes the point. One is no longer somebody looking at the point; one is the point. And then, if you continue with sufficient strength and quietness, without anything disturbing you, you may suddenly find yourself before a door which opens and you pass to the other side. And then you have the revelation.

Since when have you been doing this? This has always happened? Or is it recent?

*I don't know.*

You don't know? Perhaps you were doing it and were not aware of it!

*I didn't know.*

But you don't do it deliberately? It just comes upon you, takes hold of you?

*Yes.*

Ah! this is perhaps also one of the reasons why you don't remember.

(*Another child*) *Sweet Mother, when one passes into the region of knowledge, is it necessary to pass through the intermediary regions?*

Intermediary? But you see, if one does it by a methodical discipline, generally one is obliged to pass from one plane to another:

399

one wakes up in a particular plane, and then there one enters a sort of sleep and wakes up in another plane, and so on. And if one does it this way, then one remembers, for one does it with one's conscious will and witnesses the working — these movements for quietening the being, precisely, in order to enter somewhere and see what is happening there, and the movement of taking notes of what is happening and preparing oneself for another higher opening, all this establishes conscious contact between the different parts of the being, and then one can have experiences without forgetting anything, and even at will.

But there are some rather uneducated people, for instance, who suddenly develop a faculty and have a direct experience somewhere in the higher mind or the psychic being or in some other part of the being. There are many reasons for this: it may be the result of former lives, it may be a phenomenon of consciousness of this life, it could be many things. In any case, for it to be fully useful, it should be done with the will to use it for one's progress and become conscious of the different parts of the being in order to be able to do what one ought to do to the best of one's ability. For instance, I have known people who were absolutely ignorant and uneducated but had a gift of vision, and a remarkable gift: they were put into trance and saw marvellously and described things — they knew how to see and describe all they saw whilst they were seeing it. But when they came out of that condition, they were absolutely ordinary beings without any education and intelligence. Yet that was a marvellous gift. That means there are beings who can make the greatest progress from the spiritual point of view, and even the intellectual, and who yet are apparently and in their outer life quite ordinary. There are others — I have known some who had an absolutely marvellous spiritual realisation, who lived constantly in the divine Presence and yet never had a vision in all their life! And they used to complain about it.... It is a question of temperament, destiny, and probably of the work one has to do, for evidently one can't do everything — physically

23 December 1953

it is impossible. Consequently one must choose.

*When the body falls ill, do the mind and vital also fall ill?*

Not necessarily. Illness (I have explained this to you) comes usually from a dislocation between the different parts of the being, from a sort of disharmony. Well, it can very well happen that the body has not followed a certain movement of progress, for instance, that it has remained behind, and that, on the other hand, the other parts of the being have progressed, and so that disequilibrium, that rupture of harmony creates the illness, and the mind may be in a very fine state and the vital also. There are people who have been ill for years — with terrible, incurable diseases — and who have kept their mental capacity marvellously clear and progressed mentally. There is a French poet (a very good poet) called Sully Prudhomme; he was mortally ill; and it was then that he wrote his most beautiful poems. He remained charming, amiable, smiling — amiable with everyone, and yet his body was going to pieces. That depends on people. There are others still — as soon as they feel the least bit ill, everything is upset from top to bottom — they are then good for nothing. For each one the combination is different.

*It is said there is a relation between the body and the mind. If the mind is not quite all right, then what?*

But certainly there is a relation between the body and the mind! There is even more than a relation: it is a very close tie, for most of the time it is the mind which makes the body ill. In any case, it is the principal factor.

*And if the body is not well?*

That depends on people, I told you. There are people — as soon as the least thing happens to their body, their mind is completely upset. There are others still who may be very ill and yet keep their mind clear. It is rarer and more difficult to see a mind that's upset and the body remaining healthy — it is not impossible but it is much rarer, for the body depends a great deal on the state of the mind. The mind (I have written it there in the book) is the master of the physical being. And I have said the latter was a very docile and obedient servant. Only one doesn't know how to use one's mind, rather the opposite. Not only does one not know how to use it, but one uses it ill — as badly as possible. The mind has a considerable power of formation and a direct action on the body, and usually one uses this power to make oneself ill. For as soon as the least thing goes wrong, the mind begins to shape and build all the catastrophes possible, to ask itself whether it could be this, whether it could be that, if it is going to be like that, and how it will all end. Well, if instead of letting the mind do this disastrous work, one used the same capacity to make favourable formations — simply, for example, to give confidence to the body, to tell it that it is just a passing disturbance and that it is nothing, and if it enters a real state of receptivity, the disorder will disappear as easily as it has come, and one can cure oneself in a few seconds — if one knows how to do that, one gets wonderful results.

There is a moment for choice, even in an accident. For instance, one slips and falls. Just between the moment one has slipped and the moment one falls there is a fraction of a second. At that moment one has the choice: it may be nothing much, it may be very serious. Only, the consciousness must naturally be wide awake and one must be in contact with one's psychic being constantly — there is no time to make the contact, one must *be* in contact. Between the moment one slips and the moment one is on the ground, if the mental and psychic formation is sufficiently strong, then there is nothing, nothing will happen — nothing happens. But if at that moment, the mind according to its habit becomes a pessimist and tells itself: "Oh! I have

## 23 December 1953

slipped...." That lasts the fraction of a second; that doesn't take even a minute, it is a fraction of a second; during a fraction of a second one has the choice. But one must be so awake, every minute of one's life! For a fraction of a second one has the choice, there is a fraction of a second in which one can prevent the accident from being serious, can prevent the illness from entering in. One always has the choice. But it is for a fraction of a second and one must not miss it. If one misses it, it is finished.

*One can make it afterwards?* (laughter)

No. Afterwards there is yet another moment.... One has fallen, one is already hurt; but there is still a moment when one can change things for the better or worse, so that it may be something very fugitive the bad effects of which will quickly disappear or something which becomes as serious, as grave as it can be. I don't know if you have noticed that there are people who never miss the opportunity of an accident! Every time there is the possibility of an accident, they have it. And never is their accident ordinary. Every time the accident can be serious, it is serious. Well, usually in life one says: "Oh! he is unlucky, he is unfortunate, indeed he has no luck." But all that is ignorance. It depends absolutely on the working of his consciousness. I could give you examples — only I would have to speak about certain people and I don't want to. But I could give you striking examples! And this — this is the sort of thing one sees all the time, all the time here! There are people who could have been killed and who come out of it unscathed; there are others for whom it was not serious, and it becomes serious.

But that does not depend on thought, on the working of the ordinary thought. They may apparently have thoughts as good as the others — it is not that. It is the second of the choice — people knowing how to react just in the right way at the right time. I could give you hundreds of examples. It is quite interesting.

This depends absolutely on character. Some have such an awakened consciousness, so alert, that they are not asleep, they are awake within. Just at the second it is required they call the help. Or they invoke the divine Force. But just at the second it is needed. So the danger is averted, nothing happens. They could have been killed: they come out of it absolutely unhurt. Others, on the contrary, as soon as they have the least little scratch, something gets dislocated in their being: a sort of fright or pessimism or defeatism in their consciousness which automatically comes up — it was nothing, they had just twisted their leg and the next minute they break it. There is no reason for it. They could very well have not broken their leg.

There are others who climb up to a first floor on a ladder which gives way under them. They could have collapsed — they come out of that without the least hurt. How did they manage it? Apparently this seems wonderful, and still this is how things happen to them. They find themselves lying on the ground in an altogether fine state; nothing has happened to them. I could give you the names, I am telling you exact facts.

So, on what does this depend? It depends on whether one is sufficiently awake for the second of the choice to... And note that this is not at all mental, it is not that: it is an attitude of the being, it is the consciousness reacting in the right way. It goes quite far, very far, it is formidable, the power of this attitude. But as it is just a fraction of a second, it implies an altogether awakened consciousness which never sleeps, never enters the inconscient. For one does not know when these things are going to happen, isn't that so? Hence, one does not have the time to wake up. One must be awake.

I knew someone who, indeed, should have died and did not die because of this. For his consciousness reacted very fast. He had taken poison by mistake: instead of taking one dose of a certain medicine, he had taken twelve and it was a poison; he should have died, the heart should have stopped (it was many years ago) and he is still quite alive! He reacted in the right way.

23 December 1953

If these things were narrated they would be called miracles. They are not miracles: it is an awakened consciousness.

*How were we saved the other day when working down there with the crane?* [2]

I suppose you ought to know!

*We know partly.*

Very partially, vaguely, a sort of impression "like that" — an impression, almost an attitude, but not knowledge. How that works, one would not be able to say!

*It was by Grace.*

But if you can explain to me how that works, it would be interesting for everybody. It would be very interesting to know who exactly had that wakeful consciousness, had faith and a sort of... something that answered automatically, and perhaps not consciously.

There are degrees, many degrees. Human intelligence is such that unless there is a contrast it does not understand. You know, I have received hundreds of letters from people thanking me because they had been saved; but it is very, very rarely that someone writes to thank me because nothing has happened, you understand! Let us take an accident, it is already the beginning of a disorder. Naturally when it is a public or collective accident, the atmosphere of each person has its part in the thing, and that depends on the proportion of defeatists and those who,

---

[2] A team of young Ashram disciples was trying to lift a tree-trunk into a truck with the help of a crane, when the crane broke apart, flying into pieces on all sides, but without hurting anyone. Then the tree-trunk half lifted in began rolling slowly, causing the truck to lean on one side threatening to crush several boys, when, without any apparent reason or any physical object to hold it back, the trunk suddenly stopped in its course.

on the contrary, are on the right side. I don't know if I have written this — it is written somewhere — but it is a very interesting thing. I am going to tell you.... People are not aware of the workings of Grace except when there has been some danger, that is, when there has been the beginning of an accident or the accident has taken place and they have escaped it. Then they become aware. But never are they aware that if, for instance, a journey or anything whatever, passes without any accident, it is an infinitely higher Grace. That is, the harmony is established in such a way that nothing can happen. But that seems to them quite natural. When people are ill and get well quickly, they are full of gratitude; but never do they think of being grateful when they are well; and yet that is a much greater miracle! In collective accidents, what is interesting is exactly the proportion, the sort of balance or disequilibrium, the combination made by the different atmospheres of people.

There was an aviator, one of the great "aces" as they are called of the First [World] War, and a marvellous aviator. He had gained numerous victories, nothing had ever happened to him. But something occurred in his life and suddenly he felt that something was going to happen to him, an accident, that it was now all over. What they call their "good luck" had gone. This man left the military to enter civil aviation and he piloted one of these lines — no, not civil aviation: he came out of the war but remained with the military planes. And then he wanted to make a trip to South Africa: from France to South Africa. Evidently, something must have been upset in his consciousness (I did not know him personally, so I don't know what happened). He started from a certain city in France to go to Madagascar, I believe (I am not sure, I think it was Madagascar). And from there he wanted to come back to France. My brother was at that time governor of the Congo, and he wanted to get back quickly to his post. He asked to be allowed as a passenger on the plane (it was one of those planes for professional tours, to show what these planes could do). Many people wanted to dissuade my

## 23 December 1953

brother from going by it; they told him, "No, these trips are always dangerous, you must not go on them." But finally he went all the same. They had a breakdown and stopped in the middle of the Sahara, a situation not very pleasant. Yet everything was arranged as by a miracle, the plane started again and put down my brother in the Congo, exactly where he wanted to go, then it went farther south. And soon after, half-way the plane crashed — and the other man was killed.... It was obvious that this had to happen. But my brother had an absolute faith in his destiny, a certitude that nothing would happen. And it was translated in this way: the mixture of the two atmospheres made the dislocation unavoidable, for there was a breakdown in the Sahara and the plane was obliged to land, but finally everything was in order and there was no real accident. But once he was no longer there, the other man had all the force of his "ill- luck" (if you like), and the accident was complete and he was killed.

A similar incident happened to a boat. There were two persons (they were well-known people but I cannot remember their names now), who had gone to Indo-China by plane. There was an accident, they were the only ones to have been saved, all the others were killed, indeed it was quite a dramatic affair. But these two (husband and wife) must have been what may be called bringers of bad-luck — it is a sort of atmosphere they carry. Well, these two wanted to go back to France (for, in fact, the accident occurred on their way back to France), they wanted to return to France, they took a boat. And quite unexpectedly, unusually, right in the midst of the Red Sea the boat ran into a reef (a thing that doesn't happen even once in a million voyages) and sank; and the others were drowned, and these two were saved. And I could do nothing, you know, I wanted to say: "Take care, never travel with these people!"... There are people of this sort, wherever they are, they come out of the thing very well, but the catastrophes are for the others.

If one sees things from the ordinary viewpoint, one does not notice this. But the associations of atmosphere — one must take care of that. That is why when one travels in groups, one must know with whom one travels. One should have an inner knowledge, should have a vision. And then, if one sees somebody who has a kind of small black cloud around him, one must take care not to travel with him, for, surely an accident will occur — though perhaps not to him. Hence, it is quite useful to know things a little more deeply than in the altogether superficial way.

(*Looking at the child*) He looks as if he found life becoming very difficult in this way!

## 30 December 1953

*What do you mean by the instinct of destruction in children?*

It is not there in all children. I have known many who, on the contrary, were very careful.

Children are not as "concretised", materialised in their physical consciousness as older people — as one grows up, it is as though one is coagulated and becomes more and more gross in one's consciousness unless through a willed action one develops otherwise. For instance, the majority of children find it very difficult to distinguish their imagination, their dreams, what they see inside themselves from outer things. The world is not as limited as when one is older and more precise. And they are extremely sensitive within; they are much closer to their psychic being than when they are grown up, and much more sensitive to the forces which, later, will become invisible to them — but at this moment are not. It is not unusual for children to have some sort of fits of fear or even of joy in their sleep, from dreams. Children are afraid of all sorts of things which for older people don't exist any more. Their vision is not solely material. They have a kind of perception, more or less exact and precise, of the play of the forces behind. So, being in that state they are influenced by forces which otherwise have no hold over people who are shut up in themselves and more gross. And these forces — the forces of destruction, for example, or forces of cruelty, forces of wickedness, of ill-will — all, all these things are in the atmosphere. When one is more conscious and more well-formed within, one can see them as outside oneself and deny them any expression. But when one is very young and lives in a half-dream, these things can exercise much influence and make children do things which in their normal state they would not do. I believe it is due to that above all.

There is also the phenomenon of unconsciousness. Very often a child does harm without even being aware that it is doing harm; they are unconscious, they are shut up in their movement, and they are not aware of the effect of what they do. That happens very often.

That means that if a child is rightly educated, and if one appeals to his best feelings and explains to him that to do things in such and such a way is harmful to others (and one can make this very tangible for them with a little demonstration), they stop doing harm, very often.

It is above all a question of education. These half-conscious movements of cruelty — it is very rare for parents not to have them; well, that is enough to set its impression upon a child's consciousness. There are some — but that is a very small number — who have an adverse formation inside them. These are irretrievably wicked children. But they are very rare. There are none here, happily.

*"For it is certain that the nature of the child about to be born will depend very much upon the mother who forms it, upon her aspiration and will as much as upon the material surroundings in which she lives. The part of education which the mother has to go through is to see that her thoughts are always beautiful and pure, her feelings always noble and fine, her material surroundings as harmonious as possible and full of a great simplicity. And if in addition she has a conscious and definite will to form the child according to the highest ideal she can conceive, then the very best conditions are provided for the child to come into the world with the maximum of possibilities."*

*"Education", On Education*

**When great souls want to be born upon earth, do they choose their parents?**

*30 December 1953*

Ah! that depends on their state of consciousness, it depends on the state of their psychic formation. If the psychic being is completely formed, if it has reached the perfection of its being and is free to reincarnate or not, it has also the capacity of choosing. But I believe I have explained that to you already. They don't have a physical sight like ours so long as they are not in a body. So, evidently, they look for a body which is adapted and fit to express them, but they must give its share to the material inconscience, if it may be put thus, and to the necessity to adapt themselves to the most material laws of the body. So, from the point of view of the psychic, the choice of the place where one is born is important, it is more than an insignificant detail. But there are so many things that can't be foreseen. For instance, one chooses an environment, a country, a certain type of family, one tries to see the nature of the probable parents, one asks for certain already well-developed qualities in them and a sufficient self-mastery. But all this is not enough if one does not carry in oneself a sufficient dynamism to overcome the obstacles. So, all things considered, this is not enormously important. Anyhow, even at the best, even if the parents have collaborated consciously, there is an enormous mass of the subconscient and the yet lower inconscient which from time to time rises again to the surface, gets stirred up, damages the work, makes calmness and silence indispensable. Always, always a preparation is needed, even if one has chosen — a long preparation. Not to speak of the phenomenon of being half-stunned at the moment of birth, the descent into the body, which often lasts for a very long time before one can escape from it completely.

*Some children are wicked. Is it because their parents did not aspire for them?*

It is perhaps a subconscious wickedness in the parents. It is said that people throw out their wickedness from themselves by giving it birth in their children. One has always a shadow in oneself. There are people who project this outside — that does not always free them from it, but still perhaps it comforts them! But it is the child who "profits" by it, don't you see? It is quite evident that the state of consciousness in which the parents are at that moment is of capital importance. If they have very low and vulgar ideas, the children will reflect them quite certainly. And all these children who are ill-formed, ill-bred, incomplete (specially from the point of view of intelligence: with holes, things missing), children who are only half-conscious and half-formed — this is always due to the fault of the state of consciousness in which the parents were when they conceived the child. Even as the state of consciousness of the last moments of life is of capital importance for the future of the one who is departing, so too the state of consciousness in which the parents are at the moment of conception gives a sort of stamp to the child, which it will reflect throughout its life. So, these are apparently such little things — the mood of the moment, the moment's aspiration or degradation, anything whatsoever, everything that takes place at a particular moment — it seems to be so small a thing, and it has so great a consequence: it brings into the world a child who is incomplete or wicked or finally a failure. And people are not aware of that.

Later, when the child behaves nastily, they scold it. But they should begin by scolding themselves, telling themselves: "In what a horrible state of consciousness must I have been when I brought that child into the world." For it is truly that.

*Sometimes it so happens that a mother educates her child well, but the people around spoil it. Then what can the mother do?*

Yes, that's perfectly true. The worst of all (which men usually do) is to leave their children with servants. It is a crime. For these people have an altogether vulgar consciousness, altogether low, altogether obscure; and quite spontaneously, without wanting

30 December 1953

to do so, they let it enter the children. Naturally, there is also the age when children are put to school and there they begin to come in contact with a host of children who are not always very much to be recommended. It is very difficult to escape these relations. But all the same, if one has started life with a little consciousness and much goodwill, when one meets people who are not desirable company, one feels it. And if one is goodwilled, immediately one tries not to see them or not to be with them.

*But if the power of ill-will is greater than the other person's goodwill?*

Yes, that's true, that may happen. Fundamentally, this is why we always come back to the same thing: one must do all one can, as well as possible, and do it as an offering to the Divine, and then, once all this is settled and organised, well, if there is really an aspiration in the being, and a being that is a being of light, it can counteract all bad influences. But once one puts one's foot into this world, one can't hope very much to be quite pure and free from bad influences. Every time one eats, one absorbs them; every time one breathes, one absorbs them. Then, essentially, what is necessary is to do the work of cleansing, progressively, as much as one can do it.

*Why do some children take interest in things only when there is some excitement?*

They are tamasic. It is due to the large proportion of tamas in the nature. The more tamasic one is, the more does one need violent events, exciting circumstances. When the physical is tamasic, unless one eats spices and highly flavoured food, one does not feel nourished. And yet these are poisons. They act exactly like poison on the nerves. They do not nourish. But it is because people are tamasic, because they do not have a sufficient consciousness in their body. Well, mentally it is the same thing, vitally the same

413

thing. If they are tamasic, they always need new excitements, dramas, murders, suicides, etc. to get the impression of something, otherwise.... And there is nothing, nothing that makes one more wicked and cruel than tamas. For it is this need of excitement which shakes you up a little, makes you come out of yourself. And one must also learn, there, to discern between those who are exclusively tamasic and those who are mixed, and those who are struggling within themselves with their different parts. One can, one *must* know in what proportion one's nature is constituted, so as to be able to insist at need on one thing or another. Some people constantly need a whipping from life in order to move, otherwise they would spend their time sleeping. Others, on the contrary, need calming things, silence, a retirement in the country-side — all these things that do a lot of good but which must disappear as soon as one needs to make an effort for progress or to realise something or struggle against a defect, conquer an obstacle.... It is complicated, don't you think so?

The proportion is very important, this proportion of the three "gunas" (you know the three gunas?)[1] the proportion of the three gunas in the nature. And one must know the exact proportion in oneself and how to use one guna to fight the other, and so on. But there is a moment when one should attain a certain equilibrium, and then be capable of establishing it in oneself a little steadily and facing life without having to fall into holes or struggle against terrible things. From that moment on everything goes well.

*It had been proposed that education in our school and our university centre would be given in accordance with the ideals of Sri Aurobindo. But so far the education is given as outside; one follows the same programme.*

---

[1] The three principles of Indian psychology: *tamas*, *rajas* and *sattwa*. Tamas is the principle of inertia and obscurity; rajas the principle of passion, desire and dynamism; sattwa the principle of light and equilibrium.

*30 December 1953*

Yes, my child. And for years I have been fighting for it to be otherwise. When you — you children, here — when you are old enough and ready to become professors, then you will be entrusted with teaching the newcomers the right thing, in the right way. Essentially, for the time being, it is much more a school of professors than a school of students! What is wanted is that you prepare yourselves by learning what everybody knows — for there is an indispensable basis: it is not anything very much, it is not a very detailed or very deeply established basis, but still there is a basis of general human knowledge that's necessary — but once you have that basis and have at the same time benefited by the influence that is here, and when you have read and understood sufficiently well to be able to see from that angle — the angle of the true life — well, when you know all that, it will be you who will teach the children from outside what you have learnt. That is part of the work.

It is true that apart from a few rare exceptions, the teaching is given on the most ordinary principles. I know it. But, for instance, in order that it be otherwise, the books which are used should be prepared here, with the extracts chosen here, even with the method of teaching worked out here. I have asked several persons to do it. But this is one of those interminable tasks which make you always put off for the next year the possibility of taking a class which does not follow the grooves of the past. That preparation of the material, for instance, for the true understanding of things, that takes time. One has to face very concrete problems. It is difficult to teach children without their having books to be able to study. But these books, finally, are perforce ordered from the stock available. There is not much choice. One tries to find the best that is available, but the best that is there is yet not very good. There also, I need people to prepare them, these books. But I believe that it is just someone who has grown up here from childhood and felt things quite subconsciously when very young — in spite of everything that leaves a trace, it cannot go without any effect; and when one sees children brought up here beside those who come from outside, there is truly a great difference (perhaps not outwardly in the mechanical part of training, but in the understanding, the intelligence, in the inner awakening), there is a considerable difference, and the new ones need some time to come up to the same level. It is something beyond books, don't you see? It is like the difference between living in a pure atmosphere, filling the lungs with pure air every time one breathes and living in an infected atmosphere and poisoning oneself every time one breathes. From the point of view of consciousness it is the same phenomenon, and it is essentially the most important thing. And it is this which completely escapes the superficial consciousness. You are plunged in a sea of consciousness full of light, aspiration, true understanding, essential purity, and whether you want it or not it enters. Even for those who are shut up in their outer consciousness, well, they cannot sleep in vain. There is an action here during sleep which is quite considerable, considerable. So that has an effect, it is visible. I have seen people who had come altogether from outside, who knew nothing (only they had spent their life taking interest in children), well, the impression of these people — visitors, people just passing by — they are all quite bewildered: "But you have children here as I have never seen elsewhere!" For us, we are used to it, aren't we? They are spontaneously like that, quite naturally. But there is an awakening in the consciousness, there is a kind of inner response and a feeling of blossoming, of inner freedom which is not found elsewhere. Some of the children who come here are terribly well brought up — so polite, so well-bred, who answer you so... and one gets the impression of little puppets, just half alive, who have been well polished, well brushed, well groomed outside, but within there is no response. Here, I cannot say that we give an example of unusual politeness (!), one is rather a little... a little what people call "ill-bred". But in that too one is so alive! One feels a consciousness vibrating here. And that is the most important part of all. And of this one does not speak, for these

30 December 1953

are things one does but does not tell — an occasion like today's has to be there for me to speak to you about it. Indeed, it is many years that you have been here, and this is the first time I have had it. *Voilà*.

You have exhausted all your questions?

*It is outside the subject. Mother, every year you give a message on the first of January. What does it exactly indicate?*

Yes, every year.... During the war it was wonderful, it was like a prophecy of what was going to come. Now there is no longer any war and no more need of prophecy! But it is always an indication of the progress which has to be made. You will receive it tomorrow morning, the prayer.[2] But I advise you to reflect deeply on it. For truly it was spoken and considered as of great importance. Now we are becoming almost a thing of public interest, in the sense that there are lots of visitors coming and lots of people concerned about what we are doing here, and then they are taken round and told what we have supposedly done and what we are going to do and all that. And there was truly a great need to say: "I beg of you, don't speak so much about what we are doing: do it." That is all.

It is always better to do than to speak, and in the least details also.

There is another meaning too, much deeper. But about that I shall speak to you another time.

*Voilà, au revoir* my children.

---

[2] New Year Prayer of 1954:
"My Lord, here is Thy advice to all, for this year:
'Never boast about anything, let your acts speak for you.' "